AF262779

THE STORY OF PRINTMAKING

THE STORY OF PRINTMAKING

A Global History of Art

HOLLY EJ BLACK

YALE UNIVERSITY PRESS
NEW HAVEN AND LONDON

For information about this and other Yale University Press publications, please contact:
U.S. Office: sales.press@yale.edu yalebooks.com
Europe Office: sales@yaleup.co.uk yalebooks.co.uk

Set in Sabon and Trajan Pro by IDSUK (DataConnection) Ltd

Printed and bound in China

Library of Congress Control Number: 2025945529
A catalogue record for this book is available from the British Library.
Authorized Representative in the EU: Easy Access System Europe, Mustamäe tee 50, 10621 Tallinn, Estonia, gpsr.requests@easproject.com

ISBN 978-0-300-27408-0

10 9 8 7 6 5 4 3 2 1

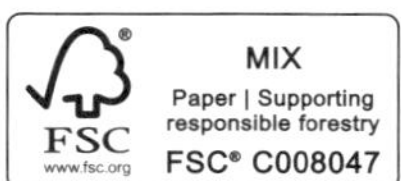

Contents

ACKNOWLEDGEMENTS

I have a great many people to thank for their support and expertise, and without whom I could never have written this book. I would like to thank Charlotte Mullins, whose mentoring and recommendation first led me to embark on the proposal, and Claire Wrathall, whose continued encouragement got me through what seemed like insurmountable challenges. Thank you to the team at PEW Literary, including my agent Cora MacGregor, and to my Yale editor Sophie Neve, for trusting me with such an important project. I am also indebted to The Society of Authors and the Authors' Foundation, for awarding me a grant from the K Blundell Trust, which allowed me to pursue my printmaking training.

The variety of voices present within these pages is echoed in the many incredibly generous people who gave their time and consideration, while I grappled with both the academic and tangible history of printmaking. Thank you to my print tutors: Adrian Holmes, Michelle Avison, Ali Yanya, Maggie Jennings and Graham Black (straddling the role of teacher and supportive parent) who nurtured my rudimentary skills, and also to Jake Garfield and Phil Sanders, both experts who make my text all the better for their suggestions. For offering further unprecedented insight, thank you to Larissa and Bill Goldston at Universal Limited Artist Editions; Essye Klempner and Deborah Cullen-Morales at the EFA Robert Blackburn Printmaking Workshop; Heather Hughes at the Philadelphia Museum of Art; Kim Berman at The Artist Proof Studio; and Mark Attwood at The Artists' Press. Thank you, also, to the late Norman Ackroyd, for sharing stories both in and beyond the studio.

To all the other family and friends who lent both kind ears and words of wisdom, I am forever grateful to you. To Milly, my discerning little sister who always serves as the perfect cultural litmus test, and to Kim, a mother whose patience has often been tested but never broken, and who always knows just what to say. Thank you to Naoya Komatsu, for his Japanese language expertise; to Vicki Reeve for her keen eye; Kira Goodey, my modern-day Renaissance woman; Billie Muraben and Jack Soilleux Till, who have metaphorically and physically picked me up when I was down; and to my gang at Beulah Road Studios, who withstood my sighs and helped alleviate my writer's block with plentiful cups of tea. Lastly a thank you to Bokochan, my constant companion, who will never understand a word of what I have written.

     ACKNOWLEDGEMENTS

FIRST IMPRESSIONS

A few years ago, while visiting a college library, I encountered an unlikely votive picture taped to the wall in a small room reserved for printing and photocopying. This unremarkable piece of paper depicted St John the Evangelist, writing at his lectern. The apostle stands over an industrious scene, where a man in overalls toils over a printing press and another sets up blocks ready to be inked. The pair are surrounded by the instruments of their trade and the fruits of their labour, namely rollers, engraved plates and towering stacks of paper, which will soon be disseminated en masse. The entire scene is bathed in divine and fiery light, as the sky bursts open in an act of enlightenment and salvation. It is accompanied by the inscription 'Saint Jean Porte Latine: Patron des Imprimeurs' (St John before the Latin Gate: patron of printers) and cites the name of its creator, Jean Chièze, a twentieth-century French printmaker known for his book illustrations and dynamic visions of the saints.

I, of course, was not encountering one of the works that emerged sticky with ink and impressed with a design born from a freshly carved block of wood. It was not produced within Chièze's lifetime or treated with any expert hand. This was a pale comparison, a facsimile dragged from the internet and broadcast through a screen as pixels, before being reconstituted through electronic data via a humble inkjet machine and affixed onto a cheap sheet of A4.

That both versions of this devotional image could be described as 'printed' demonstrates the complex, manifold and often misunderstood definitions associated with the process. The term 'print' can be used to describe an almost baffling number of techniques. It can represent the immediacy of the etching needle, used as deftly as a pencil by the likes of Rembrandt and Parmigianino; or the painstaking accuracy of a highly coloured Japanese woodblock, brought into being not just through the design of a master artist such as Hokusai, but through the skilled labour of an entire workshop of cutters, inkers and printers. It can be used to describe the sheafs of a daily newspaper; the impression of a thumb used for identification; or the hastily manufactured copies of pre-existing images, produced with varying degrees of quality and care.

It was with trepidation, then, that I embarked on setting out the definitions and parameters that would shape this book. Establishing a basic premise with which to summarise so many possibilities was a crucial first step. As such, I have determined the following: a print is created through the action of impressing one surface onto another, to transfer a design by way of ink or another viscous substance. In essence, it is also something that can be produced in multiple.

One vital caveat is that this book's focus lies with works on paper. The history of printing on textiles actually predates paper-based techniques, evident in the patterned remnants traced to the Indus Valley Civilisation in around the fourth century BCE, as well as in the burial rituals of pre-Columbian Peru and Mexico, and Ancient Egypt. This storied past has been well-documented elsewhere, as a significant and impactful global subject that stands alone. There are undoubtedly innumerable links to be forged across impressions made on both forms of surface, but for the sake of clarity they are not explored here.

Another important distinction lies in the very particular wording of the chosen book title. In discussing the story of 'printmaking', I am using a specific expression, one that is invariably used to denote a form of *artistic intent* in the creation of an image. It suggests an element of intimacy concerning production, whereby an individual either works independently or in close and collaborative quarters with experts. Printmaking is often viewed as distinct within the broader field of 'printing', which is deemed to encompass mass-volume and highly mechanised outputs, including what may be considered of little creative value.

These definitions are somewhat arbitrary, as the actions and associations of both terms quite naturally dovetail and intersect at various points throughout the stories told here. The vibrant and ephemeral poster culture of the Belle Époque (see chapter 5), for example, would not have been possible without innovations in automated lithography. Likewise, the brilliantly acerbic metal cuts of José Guadalupe Posada (see chapter 7) influenced generations of Mexican artists and vernacular culture, despite being designed for cheaply manufactured broadsheets.

Just as St John's protection was chiefly concerned with the written word, so the long-standing association with printing as a textual force is also worth due consideration. The significance of typographic innovations can occasionally underplay the potency of printing's visual culture. The world of the printed *image* – the prevailing concern of this book – is inextricably tied to that of text, but it is far more than a mere companion. It is an inventive force all of its own.

These concessions immediately demonstrate how any fixed understanding of printmaking is intrinsically flawed. Categorising creativity is often a reductive and ungratifying task that strips a work of its plurality. To delineate any form of artistry through specific metrics is to embark on a dissection of sorts. It can feel somewhat clinical, robbing us of a much more rewarding reality. This is why I have sought to embed the stories of how prints are created within a much wider contextual and historical framework. Art is, and always will be, more than the sum of its parts.

Printmaking has been particularly susceptible to demarcations of not only individual process, but also country and culture. Eurocentric readings habitually place Gutenberg's moveable-type press as a lodestar, dismissing the innovations that occurred in East Asia centuries before (see chapter 1) and commencing the narrative in northern Europe, in the early stages of the Renaissance.

Such a perspective is just one piece in a far more vibrant and intricate puzzle. The accounts assembled here traverse continents and span centuries, infiltrating grand palaces, street corners, artist studios and private homes. There are objects of religious propaganda from ancient China and Japan; anonymous and collective expressions of social justice emanating from Germany, Mexico and South Africa; and intimate experiments from the Netherlands to the United States. Through their dissemination, many of these prints were able to effect creative exchange, inspire political dialogue, and establish artistic celebrity, in a manner that a standalone and static work of art might struggle to do.

The ten chapters that follow are designed to work as a constellation, revealing the global, interconnected nature of the printed image and its multiple histories, while illuminating the lesser-known players who have been deliberately or erroneously overlooked. I could never claim that this is a comprehensive chronicle – what one book could be? – but it does aim to promote a far greater understanding of the enormously rich and varied world of printmaking, in all its complex and at times contradictory glory.

To truly grapple with these intricacies, I went straight to the source, returning to the printmaking studio for the first time since completing my undergraduate degree at London College of Printing. Amid the acid baths and the silkscreens, the aquatint boxes, chisels and etching plates, I was able to rebuild my material understanding of how exceptional works of art came into being. I hope I have managed to relay that knowledge in this book, but a glossary of useful terms is included as an additional aid (see p. 232).

I owe a debt to the many brilliant teachers who have imparted their expertise and helped me labour over various experiments. Through these tactile encounters I have gained a far deeper appreciation of not only materials and method, but also the essential tenets of process and problem-solving, which are fundamental in the production of something truly extraordinary. Too often, in the field of art history at least, the tangible understanding of how something is actually made can become obscured, yet without it you are – almost literally, in this case – only seeing half the picture.

Spending time in these training workshops, in addition to visiting other professional studios, revealed to me anew the bountiful, reciprocal environments that have long developed behind closed doors. Here, true wonder is found in acts of facilitation, as much as creation. Beyond the myth of the silent and insular artist (who is content to produce every element of a work themselves) there is the far more common setting of dialogue and exchange, where close collaboration and advice from 'master' printers allows for the translation of an idea into something entirely new. Once again, it is worth noting that there are complex connotations related to the various roles one might encounter in the studio, particularly the titles of 'printer' and 'printmaker'. While the former might refer to a commercial profession, skilled tradesman or expert individual, the latter holds something of the creative imagination at its heart.

Among the figures explored in this book are those who are lauded within the field of printmaking, but remain less familiar within a broader art context. They include Stanley William Hayter (see chapter 6), who moulded the minds of both European Surrealists and the young Abstract Expressionists, and Robert Blackburn (see chapter 8), who helped establish the careers of so many creatives, while imparting his own influence on the language of the civil rights struggle and the Pop Art boom. Both Hayter and Blackburn were printers of unprecedented skill and authority, who easily wore the titles of 'artist', 'printmaker' and 'master printer'. In truth, these designations are never entirely fixed, proving once more that the lines drawn between various forms of visual culture remain utterly permeable.

This book also gives due consideration to those who had no great technical skill of their own but used their acumen to support and encourage the work of others. Volcxken Diericx (see chapter 3) went into business with her husband Hieronymus Cock, founding one of the most significant and revered publishing houses of the sixteenth century. She was a formidable force in her own right, commissioning some of the greatest artists and printers of the day long after she was widowed. Over three hundred years later, Siberian refugee Tatyana Grosman (see chapter 8) went to the United States and set up a lithography studio with no prior knowledge, confident only in her ability to identify and nurture the talent in other people, be they printer, artist or both.

Beyond these individuals, there are also the great scores of acutely trained craftsmen who have formed the printing workforce throughout history, and who remain largely anonymous. As was common in artisanal trades, a sixteenth-century apprentice might enter the workshop as a child, mastering the most basic functions such as dampening paper or cleaning rollers, before undertaking rigorous tuition that instilled a dogged sense of duty (this set-up is beautifully illustrated in Jan Collaert I's *The Invention of Copper Engraving*; see fig. 3.3). Among them were Cock and Diericx's beloved employee Sander Janssen, who received an unusually generous pension following decades of service. An even greater mark of gratitude is evident in the case of José Sánchez (see chapter 7), the lithography specialist and member of the Taller de Gráfica Popular, who lost his arm in an accident with a printing machine. Unfazed, he offered advice from his hospital bed before returning to work, with the aid of a prosthetic purchased by his compatriots.

Such vivid accounts are vital to bringing the stories of printmaking to life. There are often many hands involved in bringing a piece of work into being, and it is my hope that individual inspiration, close collaboration and collective labour all receive due recognition here. Ultimately, the ambition of this book is to celebrate the long, multifaceted history of printmaking on a suitably global scale, and to prove that prints and their makers have done far more than simply replicate our world – they have shaped it.

CHAPTER 1

GODS, EMPRESSES AND ANCIENT SCROLLS

PRINT'S ORIGINS IN ASIA

Whoever wishes to gain power from the charms must write 77 copies and place them in a pagoda

— *Diamond Sutra*, 868 CE

THE GOBI DESERT is a magnificent wilderness. This sparsely populated expanse stretches from the depths of Mongolia to the borders of the Tibetan Plateau, in an epic arc that encompasses rocky plains, shifting sand dunes and frozen mountain peaks. It is also a land of ancient commerce, where traders undertook treacherous yet vital transit along the Silk Roads from as early as 130 BCE. They traversed the western edges of the desert on the backs of camels, laden with spices, textiles, porcelain and jade, trading in places as far flung as India, Turkey and Spain.

These itinerant merchants would no doubt have passed through the city of Dunhuang. This vibrant oasis stood at a strategic crossroads, serving as the gateway to China from the west. It was a cultural melting pot, dubbed the 'Blazing Beacon' by weary travellers, where both goods and knowledge were exchanged. It is here, in a waterside enclave close to the bustling frontier, that our story begins.

The Mogao Grottos, otherwise known as the 'Caves of a Thousand Buddhas', are extraordinary in their artistry, age and scale. In 366 CE, a Buddhist monk named Yuezun began chiselling openings into the cliffs that border the Mingsha dunes, to realise his vision of a colossal site of worship. Other monks soon followed, puncturing the rock face in distinct rows to build hundreds of lavishly decorated temples. These were funded by the wealthy ruling elite, who filled them with extravagantly carved clay figures, enormous golden statues, filigree shrines and an astonishing number of elaborate murals, which are said to cover almost half-a-million square metres of wall space.

For hundreds of years, thousands of people made pilgrimages to this sacred site, which continued to grow and expand well into the fourteenth century. However, as technology advanced, conflicts arose and traditional trade routes dwindled, these great caves slowly faded from memory. By the nineteenth century, they had been swallowed up by the sands.

It was a chance encounter that brought an itinerant Daoist monk named Wang Yuanlu (1849–1931) to this forgotten land in 1900. Although accounts of the ruins occasionally appeared in the preceding decades, there was little appetite for any kind of organised excursion. Wang, on the other hand, was awestruck by what he found. He became the unofficial custodian of the caves, camping out on site and raising money for restorations. The further he excavated, the more treasures he found, yet it was his penchant for cigarettes that led him to an almighty haul that would change how we understand the origins of print, forever.

While carrying out repairs on Cave 16 (as it is now known), Wang noticed that his tobacco smoke had drifted through a wall demarcating the entrance passage. After some investigation he dis-covered a secret door, which he pried open. It revealed a small chamber honouring the monk Hong Bian, who had died over a thousand years prior, in 862. He had presided over a considerable period of the caves' construction and was renowned for translating Buddhist scriptures from their original Indian Sanskrit. Could this be why his shrine was piled high with mountains of manuscripts, which numbered into the tens of thousands? These myriad pieces of paper spanned at least 17 languages and 24 scripts, from Tibetan prayers and Turkic divination guides to Khotanese silk paintings and Sanskrit aphorisms known as *sutras*.

Wang could not read most of these texts, not least because many of the tongues were practically extinct, but he inherently knew that they were documents of considerable value. Unfortunately, his attempts to stoke scholarly interest among local officials were met with indifference. He was waved away and instructed to leave his findings untouched. Frustrated, yet nevertheless compliant, he went about his restoration work.

It took the arrival of Aurel Stein (1862–1943) in 1907 to unlock the many mysteries of the so-called 'Library Cave' (fig. 1.1). This Hungarian-born, British explorer was a linguist and Indologist known for his expeditions across western Asia.[1] He travelled with a team of assistants that included surveyors, a handy-man, a cook and a fox terrier known as 'Dash the Great'. After months of negotiations mediated by his translator Jiang Xiaowan, Stein managed to convince Wang to let him view some of the precious documents.

It was among these densely packed bundles that Stein made a phenomenal discovery. A five-metre-wide scroll, cracked and stiffened by the centuries, contained the Chinese translation of a Buddhist sermon known as the *Diamond Sutra*. With its delicate characters and exquisitely illustrated frontispiece (fig. 1.2), it depicted Buddha delivering wisdom to Subhuti, his elderly disciple. This document

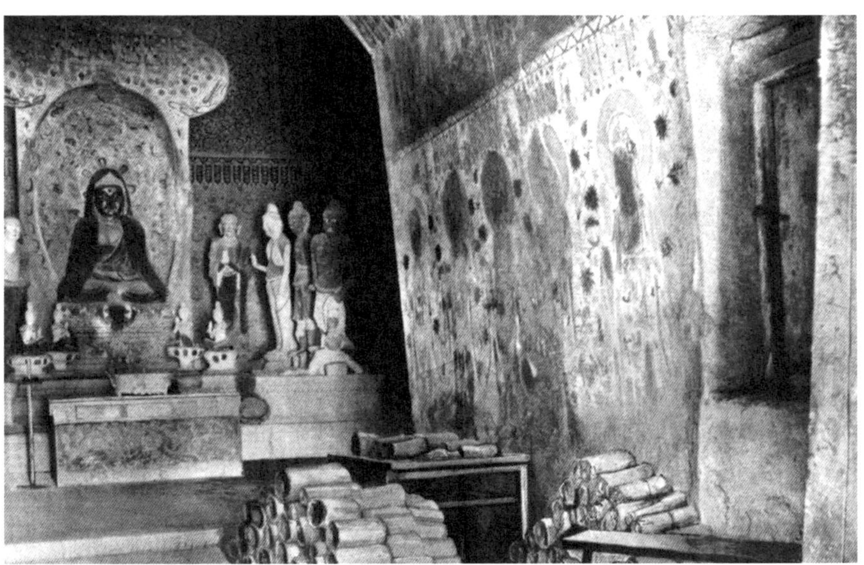

Fig. 1.1 A composite photograph taken in 1907, featuring documents gathered by Aurel Stein from the Library Cave at the Mogao Grottos. Its small entrance is visible on the right.

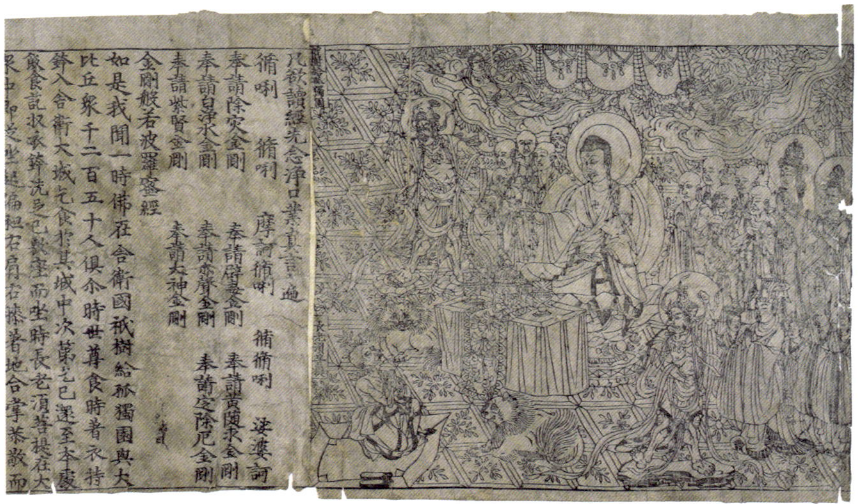

Fig. 1.2 The frontispiece of the *Diamond Sutra*,
printed on 11 May 868 CE. Woodcut.

also had unusually detailed provenance, with a dedication that read: 'Reverently made for universal free distribution by Wang Jie on behalf of two parents on the fifteenth day of the fourth month of the Xiantong reign', translating to 11 May 868.

On closer inspection, Stein discovered something even more wondrous. Each and every inked line was not the work of a painter's brush, but the printed impression of a carefully carved block of wood. This sophisticated marriage of text and image was not the only example found among the scrolls (other pieces include a multilingual mystic manuscript depicting a sacred medallion),[2] but it clearly predates them by at least a century. Stein had uncovered, quite by chance, the oldest printed and dated book ever discovered.

The woodblock is, in turn, one of the earliest forms of printing in existence. The process itself is simple, but demands inordinate skill and considerable strength. Traditionally, a design is sketched on paper by hand, before being pasted or otherwise transferred onto a piece of hardwood such as cherry or pear. To obtain the 'relief', with the composition standing proud from the wooden surface, every inch of negative space must be carved away. This requires specialist tools, which vary from enormous gouges to blades of surgical

                                        THE STORY OF PRINTMAKING

precision – as well as an extremely steady hand. After only a short session of carving, any amateur will begin to detect an ache in their shoulders, as the pressure needed to incise these marks reverberates through the body, down to the tip of the chisel. A master carver, however, will command all the strength they need from exemplary posture, dexterous fingers and the careful angle of each cut.

Once the block is carved, printing can begin. For each impression, a mild dispersing agent such as rice paste is applied, before a layer of ink is rubbed onto the surface with a stiff brush. While the pigment is still wet, a piece of paper is pressed on top of the block, with the reverse side then burnished with a brush or pad. Finally, the paper is carefully peeled away to reveal the desired image, and the entire cycle can begin again. It is not unusual, while pulling those early tests known as 'trial proofs', to experience a moment of tense expectation. This is the juncture at which any number of errors can reveal themselves, from fuzzy outlines (over-inking) and patchy areas (lack of pressure) to unexpected smudges caused by careless movement. When multiple blocks are used to create layers of colour (a technological advance that is explored in chapter 5; see pp. 106–8), aligning, or 'registering', each element is an intensive task all of its own.

The exceptional precision of the copy of the *Diamond Sutra* found at the Mogao Grottos is proof of a highly advanced printing industry that flourished long before the document's creation. Wang Jie's reference to 'free distribution' also confirms that mass dissemination, which printing could so readily facilitate, was already a familiar concept. In fact, the act of repetition holds a special significance within Buddhism. Repeatedly chanting a *sutra* is an act of devotion, and this particular sermon declares that: 'Whoever wishes to gain power from the *dharani* [charms and mantras] must write 77 copies and place them in a pagoda'. In other words, reproducing such a text could bring a Buddhist closer to enlightenment.

Stein's hurried efforts to gather this scroll among his considerable hoard was partly due to the approach of his rival, a French explorer by the name of Paul Pelliot, who had a far greater understanding of ancient Chinese texts. Although Stein paid Wang Yuanlu a nominal fee to remove over 28 cases filled with manuscripts, paintings and relics, and technically received permission from a low-level official, it is clear that he was keeping their cultural and historical value under wraps. Why else would he surreptitiously cart off his parcels in a wheelbarrow under the cover of night?

Although a growing number of Chinese scholars had already begun to plead with their government to stop exporting these treasures, it would be several years before they came under official protection. Ye Changchi, a minister who eventually presided over the Dunhuang area in the years after Pelliot had taken his own haul, wrote of his distress: 'A Frenchman had taken all the bundles using two hundred *yuan*. This is a pity. The local official and the people on the borders do not know how to appreciate ancient objects. . . .'[3]

Stein's collection is now held at the British Library, as part of the International Dunhuang Project. This research group brings together scholarly minds from institutions across the world, to better understand the cultural significance of the grottos. A section of the *Diamond Sutra* remains on display in the library's Treasures Gallery. Inscribed on what would once have been vivid, yellow-dyed paper, these printed letterforms faithfully replicate every delicate calligraphic stroke. The lines remain surprisingly crisp, as if the ink has only just dried.

Gazing at this ancient scripture, the mystery surrounding the origins of printing in East Asia is perplexing. How did this formative technology develop and prosper without any definitive record? This is particularly confounding when considering China's well-chronicled invention of paper, without which printmaking would not be possible. The development of this revolutionary material, which greatly amplified the production of literature, art and architecture, is credited to a man named Cai Lun, in around 105 BCE. As the director of the Imperial Workshops at Luoyang (the capital city at the time), he began soaking and pressing plant fibres, probably as the result of experiments with textile waste, thus creating a cheap and resilient alternative to the silk scrolls and bamboo strips that had long been used in calligraphy and painting. Without this innovation, printing might not have flourished for centuries. This was certainly the case in Europe, where parchment prepared from dried animal skins remained the primary writing surface until at least the twelfth century.

The true origins of printmaking have yet to be uncovered, but there are clues to be found amid the relics of East Asia's ancient dynastic rule. In order to piece them together, we must travel back another two hundred years, to encounter the iron grip of two formidable female rulers.

* * *

Wu Zetian's life (624–705) did not have particularly auspicious beginnings. She entered the harem of Taizong (598–649), the second emperor of China's Tang dynasty, in around 635. As the middle daughter of a minor aristocrat, she held the fairly low position of a fifth-rank concubine, with duties comparable to that of a senior servant. Yet this was a woman of great wit and ambition. She used her considerable intelligence to achieve promotions and eventually became personal secretary to the emperor, thus gaining valuable knowledge of state affairs, as well as his favour. Upon Taizong's death, Wu was expected to join her fellow courtesans to live out her final days in a nunnery. She escaped this fate by becoming romantically involved with Gaozong (628–683), the heir to the throne, who reinstated her. After competing with other members of the new harem, using tactics that included blackmail, executions and possibly infanticide, she successfully dispatched her rivals and was installed as empress.

While embattled attempts to become the supreme royal consort were nothing new, Wu's quest for power was unprecedented. She ruled as an equal to her husband, becoming his proxy during ill health and regent once she installed two successive sons as puppet monarchs following his death. Finally, in 690, she broke three thousand years of tradition by conferring upon herself the title of 'Holy and Divine Emperor', using the masculine form to assert absolute dominance. She ruled in her own right for the next 15 years.

There is legitimate reason to claim that Wu was an important patron of print, even if the evidence is not entirely concrete.[4] The Tang dynasty period (618–907) was one of great economic prosperity, when multiculturalism, art and literature flourished. Wu was hugely well read, devouring everything from political treatises to agricultural manuals in her pursuit of governing knowledge and progressive policies. She also enjoyed painting and writing poetry, and is credited with commissioning great religious structures, not least a 35-metre-tall golden Buddha at the Mogao Grottos. Indeed, it was during her reign that Buddhism was consolidated as the dominant religion in China, outstripping the indigenous philosophies of Confucianism and Daoism, at least for a time.

The all-powerful ruler would have been aware of a form of replication that predates traditional printing techniques. The act of carving text into a stone tablet, so that ink rubbings might be taken from it, had been established to ensure faithful copying of the Confucian Classics as early as 175 BCE. In Wu's own lifetime, rubbings of essays by the revered calligrapher Ouyang Xun (557–641) were highly sought after (fig. 1.3).[5]

The use of imperial seals was also vital for the effective running of China's sprawling bureaucracy. These special insignia stamps were carved from wood and were almost certainly a precursor to the woodblock print. More significantly, Wu references the technology in a letter from 691, informing one of her subjects that they may enter the palace under her protection, by showing the guards a piece of paper printed with her official emblem.

Other references during this period are found in the public record. Trade officials mention the use of prints as a form of mercantile certification along the Silk Roads, while an instructional text by the influential monk Fazang (who counselled his sovereign on religious matters) goes so far as to use the printing process as an analogy for Buddhist thought. For this idea to resonate, the practice must have been widely known and well understood.

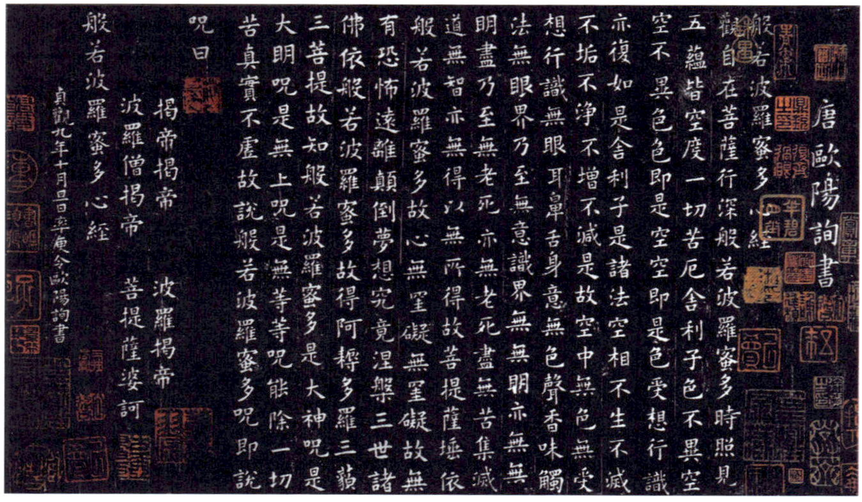

Fig. 1.3 *Heart Sutra* text, by scholar and calligrapher Ouyang Xun, 635 CE. Ink rubbing.

The existence of these accounts, without the physical evidence to match, is deeply frustrating. Never is this truer than in the case of an ambitious royal decree that Wu dispensed in the latter years of her reign, in an attempt to thwart her impending deposal. She announced the production and dissemination of 100,000 copies of *The Great Spell of Unsullied Pure Light*, a spiritual text that just happened to foretell the arrival of a divine female ruler.

Unfortunately, not a single copy has ever been found, and the question of whether these texts were handwritten or printed remains unanswered. One can only posit that, with such technology seemingly available, it would certainly have been swifter and more accurate than employing thousands of hand-copyists. It is also worth noting that the lack of evidence relating to this spiritual quest is hardly surprising, given that future governments sought to eradicate Wu's legacy. A damning indictment of attitudes towards the only official female ruler in Chinese history is found at her tomb in the Qianling Mausoleum. Upon her death, she left instructions to omit an epitaph, so that subsequent generations might inscribe their own accounts of her accomplishments. To this day, the monument remains conspicuously blank.

Despite efforts to scrub Wu's reign from the record, her influence endures in the tangible printed histories of neighbouring Korea and Japan. Most notably, a scroll containing a version of her scripture was discovered hidden in the stonework of Bulguksa Temple in Gyeongju, Korea, in 1966. It is believed to date back to around 751, making it an even older artefact of printing than the *Diamond Sutra* – though without the exceptional illustrated artistry. What is more, there is evidence of several 'forbidden characters' introduced by Wu, which were discontinued after her forced abdication. Such a find clearly points to the success of her religious propaganda campaign, which flourished in countries where Chinese script was once the official written language of the day.

It might be assumed that the presence of a powerful female monarch, who utilised nascent printing technology to assert her dominance, would be an absolute anomaly in ancient East Asia. However, a mere 13 years after Wu's death, another formidable woman entered the picture – one who ruled Japan not once, but twice.

* * *

In 718, Emperor Shōmu (701–756) and Empress Kōmyō (701–760) welcomed a baby daughter into the world. Princess Abe (718–770) was born at the dawn of a new age in Japanese history, when influences from China and Korea led to the introduction of a single-ruler state and a permanent capital. Only a few years prior, tradition dictated that every royal succession meant an entirely new seat of government, complete with a freshly built palace. However, the city of Nara now operated as the official centre of political and religious supremacy, while consolidating Buddhism as the state-sponsored faith. Much like Tang dynasty China, this involved a campaign of propaganda and shrine construction, in this case to displace native Shinto practices. The emperor was devout, dedicating his life (not to mention the royal coffers) to honouring his religion. His magnum opus was the enormous Tōdai-ji Temple in central Nara, which houses a 15-metre-high bronze statue of Buddha. Even now this gigantic figure invokes awe, welcoming any human presence with a soft gaze and enormous upturned hands.

When the princess inherited the throne in 749, assuming the name Kōken, she found herself at the mercy of her mother and cousin. The dowager empress had exerted considerable political influence during her time as consort and had no intention of relinquishing control. She collaborated with her nephew Fujiwara no Nakamaro (706–764) to sideline her daughter, turning the ruler's initial decade-long tenure into nothing more than a façade. The pair eventually supplanted her with a more favoured heir, leaving this former sovereign to retire into a life of quiet religious devotion.[6]

Kōken's position might have remained static, were it not for her mother's death in 760. The shock sent her into a deep depression, alarming imperial doctors to such a degree that they called upon a 'master of healing' by the name of Dōkyō (700–772), to offer treatment and solace. On meeting this charismatic monk, Kōken experienced a near-miraculous recovery and became irrevocably tied to her healer as she began to strategise a second reign. Dōkyō no doubt counselled her on how to seize power and was soon reaping rewards for his loyalty, in the form of lofty new titles and ever-increasing influence. Court gossip speculated that the couple must be romantically involved, such was the ferocity of their attachment, yet the scandal was not enough to stop Kōken from gaining enough

   THE STORY OF PRINTMAKING

support to overthrow her successor and execute her cousin. She returned to the throne as Shōtoku in 764.

What was a newly triumphant female ruler, whose bloody ascent was at odds with her spiritual devotion, to do in order to secure her reputation? Although there is no clear evidence that Shōtoku paid heed to the endeavours of her Chinese forerunner, the parallels are uncanny. Soon after her enthronement, she ordered the production of 'one million miniature pagodas', each of which was to be filled with *dharani* drawn from another translation of *The Great Spell of Unsullied Pure Light*. While a 'million' was probably a notional figure, thousands of these relics, which are collectively known as the *Hyakumantō Dharani* (million charms), were indeed distributed to temples across the country. They were housed in specially constructed halls called *shōtōin*, or 'miniature pagoda halls' (fig. 1.4).

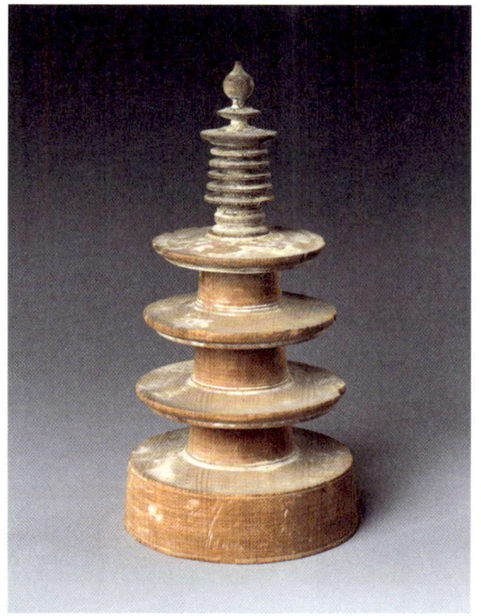

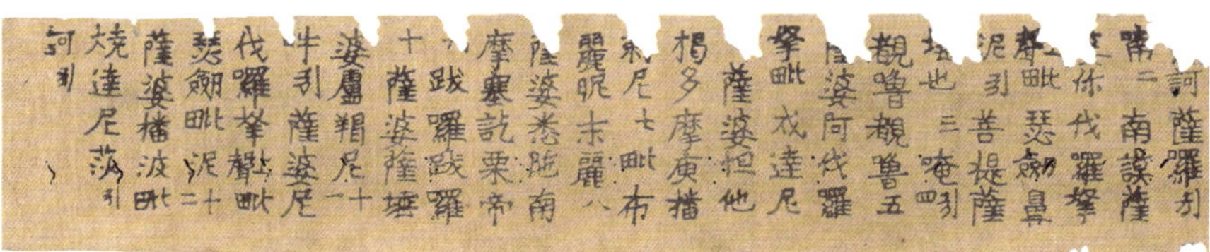

Fig. 1.4 One of the 'One Million Pagodas' (*Hyakumantō*) and Invocations containing a printed scroll, *c*.764–70.

Unlike Wu's edict, where any evident use of printing remains out of reach, these tiny scrolls bear the indelible mark of relief techniques. What is more, thanks to inscriptions on many of the surviving pagodas, they can be accurately dated to between 764 and 770. Each tiered wooden tower stands at approximately 21 cm tall, complete with a finial that was used as a stopper, to safely secure each tightly rolled piece of paper within a small cavity. The charms hidden within each mini-edifice were not designed to be opened and read, but rather gained their potency through the physical act of copying and dissemination.[7]

For Shōtoku, this enormous commission was not only a show of political strength, but also a spiritual necessity that upheld the legacy of her father's ambitious building projects. Sadly, her aspirations for a long and prosperous rule were cut short. She died only a few months after her mandate was completed, leaving her favoured advisor to be exiled in disgrace.

As with Wu, history has not been overly kind to this unorthodox Japanese ruler. She was ridiculed for her alleged indiscretions and the perceived failings of her gender, while the fate of her *Hyakumantō Dharani* became increasingly precarious. Over the ensuing centuries these sacred objects were lost, destroyed or sold off, with only a handful remaining at a single temple: the great Hōryū-ji in Nara. Others can be found scattered across museum and private collections throughout the world, either as lone examples or in extremely diminished numbers.

Despite this unfortunate and fractured ending, the significance of Shōtoku's project within the history of print cannot be overlooked – although it often has been. Along with the *Diamond Sutra* and the extant Korean copy of *The Great Spell of Unsullied Pure Light*, the sheer scale and artistry of this undertaking establishes the existence of a vibrant and masterful early printing industry within East Asia, which stretches back further than any known object. In fact, while it is clear that the minute letterforms in Shōtoku's collection of *dharani* are the result of mass print production, exactly how they were formed remains up for debate. Some experts claim that woodblocks would have been used, in keeping with comparable ancient printed items. Others insist that a metal mould must have been cast, such was the enormity of the task and the visual clarity of the resulting characters.

 THE STORY OF PRINTMAKING

While evidence certainly points to woodcut's dominance within the field, another major innovation within print's nascent history emerged back in China in around 1041, over two hundred years after Shōtoku's last tiny pagoda was placed in its grand hall. Bi Sheng (990–1051) was an artisan and engineer hailing from the city of Yingshan, who developed a form of moveable type whereby individually crafted characters could be repositioned and reused. Rather than carving wood, he moulded clay and baked it to create resilient, hard blocks that represented individual letterforms. These components could be arranged within an iron frame and inked, leading to a much swifter and adaptable form of text production.

This invention led to a surge in printed literature and civic activity throughout China's Northern and Southern Song dynasties (960–1279). While the availability of new text-based information certainly improved literacy levels, reading was still a relatively elite affair. For the working classes, pictures remained the dominant form of communication. It is unsurprising, then, that the woodblock print took hold among everyday people, not to produce complex impressions of lengthy script, but graphic images that promised protection, good luck and long-lasting prosperity.

* * *

Protective door guardians also have a long history in ancient China. Their painted likenesses have adorned the entrances of all kinds of residences, from palaces to modest homes, since the second century BCE. While their roots lie in a variety of religious allegories that span multiple faiths, their unifying trait is to defend households from evil spirits with a violent tenacity. Among the most popular figures are a pair of warriors called Shen Shu and Yu Lei. They always appear as a set, heavily armoured and often using a rope to catch their wicked prey. The great demon slayer Zhong Kui is another fine example. He frequently wears a special hat featuring magical tassels designed to detect trouble.

The woodblock presented the opportunity to produce endless iterations of these door gods, which proved ideal for the abundant festivities of the Lunar New Year. Holiday preparations took weeks: houses were cleaned and courtyards swept, while images of the guardians were either wiped away or torn from the walls and doors, ready to be replaced as part of a literal and figurative process of renewal.[8] This latter ritual gave rise to the term *nien hua*, or 'New Year's pictures', which soon came to describe a whole host of popular prints that represented not only ancient deities (fig. 1.5), but also family ancestors, folk tales and auspicious symbols – plump babies were a firm favourite.

These vibrant mass-produced depictions were sold as single sheets in the grand markets of sprawling cities like Bianliang (modern-day Kaifeng) and Chengdu, appearing in private homes, tea houses, theatres and bars, or else rolled up and strapped to the backs of peddlers who traipsed from village to village, touting their wares and cashing in on the festive season. The industry comprised both well-staffed workshops and less refined home enterprises, where an individual might buy a block or carve their own, before running off a handful of impressions, in the hope of supplementing a meagre income. As the writer Meng Yuanlao (active 1126–47) recalled in his memoir of cosmopolitan life, *The Eastern Capital: A Dream of Splendour* (1147): 'When the New Year nears, street markets all print and sell pictures of door guardians, Zhong Kui, lions and tigers, as well as cut paper designs using gold and coloured papers to hang or paste on the door. This market is very large and thriving.'[9]

Despite this definitive record, most of the prints still in existence date no earlier than the Ming period (1368–1644). However, it is believed many might stem from re-carved copies of older blocks. This is largely due to the fact that prints were usually discarded after use, or else burned in rituals, thus allowing for the depicted spirit to return to the celestial plane in a plume of smoke. This was certainly the case for the 'stove god', a beloved deity who represented the heart of the home. He witnessed the actions of a family and reported his findings to the governor of heaven: the Jade Emperor. The venerated informant is often seen accompanied by his wife, along with a pair of jars representing the 'good' and 'bad' deeds collected throughout the year. The head of the household would smear the stove god's mouth with some form of confectionery such as honey, to either sweeten his words or stick his jaw shut (fig. 1.6).[10]

                                    THE STORY OF PRINTMAKING

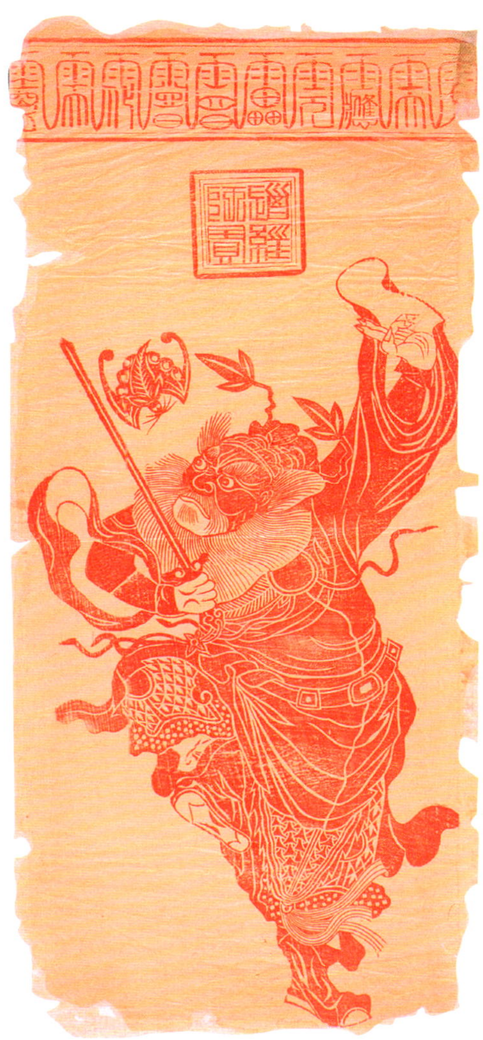

Fig. 1.5 A *nien hua* print
of Zhong Kui, 1930–9.
Woodcut.

While a considerable number of these early prints were lost
(examples have been found balled up in wall cavities as insulation),
there is still remarkable diversity found in those that survive. Some
feature dense, expressive lines that evoke a sense of dynamism,
particularly in visions of the door gods. Others have a delicate,
geometric precision that promotes order and hierarchy, in keeping
with the veneration of senior deities and ancestors. Symbolism also

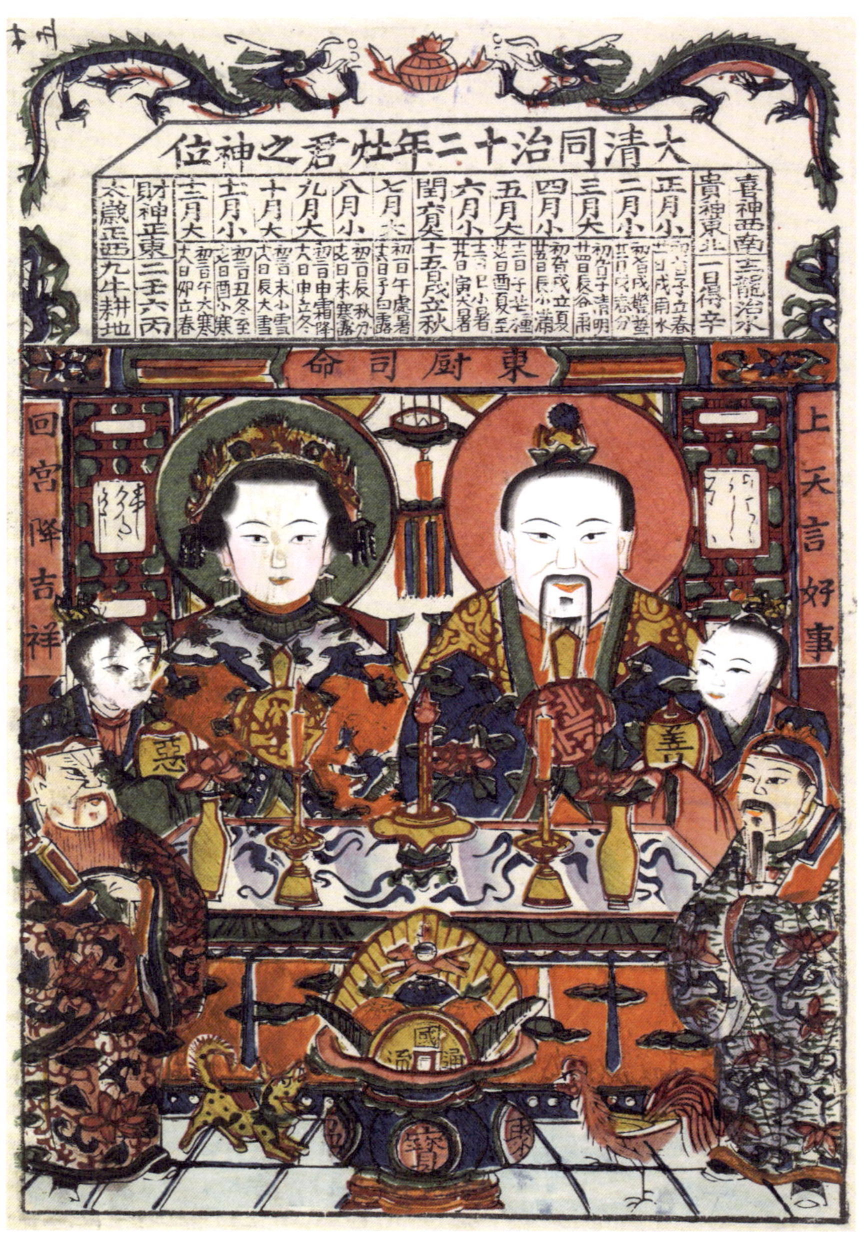

Fig. 1.6 A hand-coloured *nien hua* print featuring the stove god Zaou Jun and his wife, 1873. Woodcut.

     THE STORY OF PRINTMAKING

varies widely, depending on a design's origins. For example, the stove god might be surrounded by icons of wealth such as pearls and jade, or rural signifiers including dogs, horses and roosters. Door guardians, meanwhile, are often accompanied by a bat, as the word is a homophone for 'blessing'. Other recurring motifs include pomegranates, lotus flowers and magpies, all of which represent good fortune.

These popular prints have never gone out of style. They have continued to evolve, becoming ever more intricate and highly coloured as technologies have developed and adapted. To this day, various imprints of door gods and auspicious emblems can be found decorating homes in China (as well as other East Asian nations, including Japan and Korea). Just like the Buddhist scriptures discussed throughout this chapter, the longevity of the *nien hua* makes it clear that a print can be much more than a facsimile. Oftentimes, it can hold a transcendental power.

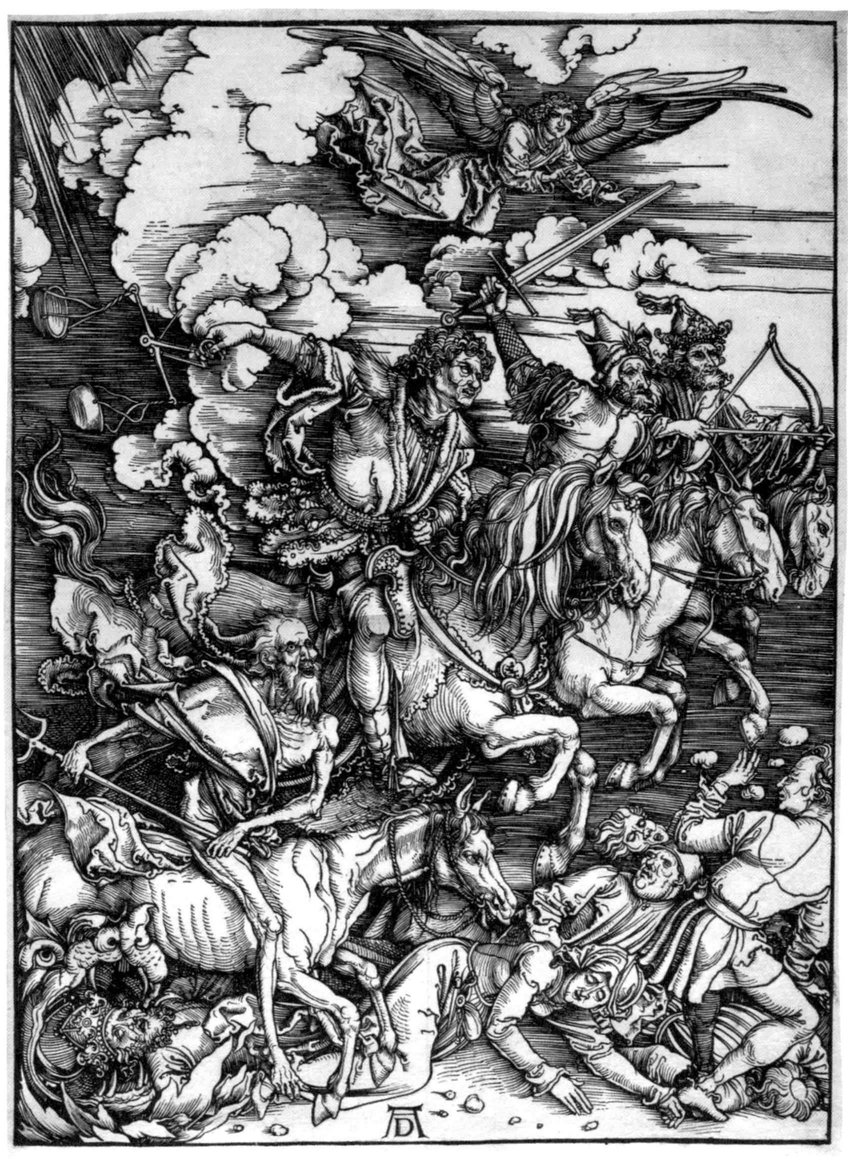

Fig. 2.1 Albrecht Dürer, *The Four Horsemen*, from the series
'The Apocalypse', *c*.1498. Woodcut.

RENAISSANCE REVELATIONS
THE ADVENT OF ENGRAVING AND ARTISTIC CELEBRITY

Beware, you envious thieves of the work and invention of others,
keep your thoughtless hands from these works of ours
— Albrecht Dürer, 1511

IN THE CURRENT climate, the impending apocalypse is most likely defined by visions of melting ice caps, rising sea levels and burning rainforests. The medieval mind, however, would have conjured something quite different. Wrathful angels, divine transcendence and the extinction of non-believers are what define a biblical reckoning. These scenes were preached from the pulpit and coded in lines of Latin scripture, but everyday people, who were widely illiterate and had little opportunity to travel, would rarely encounter pictures of the calamities.

One can only imagine, then, the force with which Albrecht Dürer's (1471–1528) printed spectacle hit fifteenth-century Europe. In around 1498, the authoritative German artist produced an astonishing portfolio containing 15 woodcuts, known as 'The Apocalypse', which features a vivid depiction of the Four Horsemen (fig. 2.1). These harbingers of destruction gallop across the page, pressing against its borders in a striking diagonal that vibrates with cinematic motion. Swirling lines articulate everything from rolling clouds to a skeletal hand with a distinct assuredness, evoking terror and awe in equal measure.

Dürer impacted the visual language of the Renaissance like no other artist. He revolutionised the printed image and its application across Europe, through his unparalleled command of the medium and exceptional commercial nous. His insatiable hunger for knowledge stretched across science, philosophy and the natural world, and he possessed a keen understanding of how to exploit religious and secular iconography in a time of widespread sectarian turmoil. His most outstanding achievement, however, was completely redefining what artistic celebrity could be, through his pioneering use of a closely guarded trademark.

The artist was born into a craftsman's pedigree in the cosmopolitan city of Nuremberg, the third of 18 children. His mother was Barbara Holper, the daughter of a goldsmith with whom her husband, a Hungarian known as Albrecht Dürer the Elder, apprenticed. The younger Dürer came of age amid a new wave of artistic production made possible in no small part by the revelatory invention of the 'moveable type' printing press. This groundbreaking machine utilised individual metal letterforms, perfected by another European goldsmith named Johannes Gutenberg (d. *c*.1468) in around 1450, at least two centuries after a similar conception in Korea. The earliest surviving book printed in this manner is the *Jikji*, a Buddhist text printed in Cheongju in 1377.[1]

A key reason for the comparative delay was Europe's scarcity of paper. Knowledge of the versatile, fibrous pulp spread from China, along the Silk Roads and through the Islamic world where it supplanted parchment and Egyptian papyrus. Baghdad established its first water-powered paper mill in 794, and the city soon became a hub of paper-selling and bookshops, not least at the sprawling Al-Mutanabbi street market.[2] By contrast, paper did not become a commercially viable entity across most western nations until the thirteenth century.

With the eventual development of European paper mills came refined, pliant sheets that allowed for the mass expansion in book production, yet hand-copying (and rudimentary forms of woodblock cutting, in which entire texts had to be fastidiously carved one letter at a time) was still slow-going and took considerable manpower. Gutenberg's invention revolutionised the trade. By 1440 he had perfected a mechanised form of text-based printing, whereby individual

  THE STORY OF PRINTMAKING

metal characters are carved in reverse and assembled to form large blocks of lettering, before being inked and passed through a press. Impressions on multiple pieces of paper could be collated as sheets or in books, and amended or adapted with relative ease. To this day, the influence of 'letterpress' is felt in the language we use to describe type. 'Upper case' denotes the capital letters that the printer stored in a high cabinet, while the more diminutive 'lower case' was stored in another below. The job of sorting through the less familiar 'hell box', where used pieces of type were discarded, was the job of apprentices. The arduous tasks of the workshop afforded them the epithet 'printer's devil'.

The press itself works on the premise of an enormous screw that exerts extreme pressure. Once metal type pieces have been selected and bound together with string, they are placed on the printing bed (a flat, wooden platform) and held tightly within a frame. The text is covered in oil-based ink, using large leather pads called beaters, before a damp piece of paper is laid on top using a hinged mount.

In theory, a light impression could be made by simply rubbing the back of the sheet, just like the earliest Asian prints discussed in the previous chapter (see p. 11). However, Gutenberg wanted crisp lines and jet-black letters produced rapidly and with an exceptional degree of continuity. His machine made it possible, by placing both text block and paper under another platform known as the 'platen'. When this is screwed downwards by pulling a large wooden handle, the paper is pressed onto the inked letterforms with enormous force. Once released, it is peeled off the block, making a sticky, sucking sound often called a 'press kiss'.[3] While the machine undoubtedly does most of the work, there is no lack of human effort. On very old devices there are clear indentations visible on the handle, where thousands of pairs of printers' hands have grasped hold in exactly the same position, and pulled with all their might.

Gutenberg used his press to create a 42-line Latin Bible, which became the best-seller of its day. Of the original run of approximately 180 books, only around 35 were printed on vellum (made from treated calfskin), which is evidence of the nascent acceptance of paper as the preferred material in Europe during this period. Despite failing to include images in his own magnum opus, Gutenberg set the blueprint for the mass dissemination of pictures, particularly those that could be printed alongside text, as both woodblocks and letterpress are produced in relief.

Other presses inspired by his design soon became commonplace, and printed pages swiftly proliferated in huge numbers across the continent. William Caxton (*c.*1422–*c.*1492) introduced the press to England in the 1470s after living in Flanders and Cologne, and went on to print over one hundred books, including the first English-language edition of *The Canterbury Tales* (1476),[4] with a second woodcut-illustrated version published in 1483. His innovation is immortalised in a stained-glass window at Westminster Abbey, which depicts him giving a print demonstration to King Edward IV. Back on the continent, Maximilian I had his own portable press by the time he was crowned Holy Roman Emperor in 1486, so that he could readily disseminate his pronouncements throughout his realm, which then stretched from Burgundy to the Low Countries and tranches of northern Italy. Both words and pictures could now travel directly to the people with unprecedented speed and in considerable volume. It is no wonder that the German word for these printed materials – *Flugblätter* – means 'flying leaves of paper'.[5]

It was against this backdrop that a young Dürer first saw the untapped potential of the medium. In the 1480s, printed pictures still tended to be illustrative, or else rudimentary copies of paintings. The artist's career began through learning his father's goldsmith trade while he was barely a teenager, but he certainly yearned to paint. His next apprenticeship – with the artist Michael Wolgemut (1434–1519) – proved eye-opening. His master was renowned for both works on canvas and his skills as a woodcut designer, and on joining the workshop Dürer came to understand the possibilities of print as a new form of easily disseminated high art. While people had to travel to see a celebrated painting or sculpture, a print could come to them.

Scholars have debated whether the young apprentice was involved, or even present, when Wolgemut embarked on his greatest collaboration: the production of the *Weltchronik* (also known as the *Nuremberg Chronicle*; fig. 2.2). This groundbreaking, extensively illustrated encyclopedia was published in Latin and vernacular German by Dürer's godfather, Anton Koberger (*c.*1440–1513), who was Europe's most successful book publisher. It was intended as a universal narrative

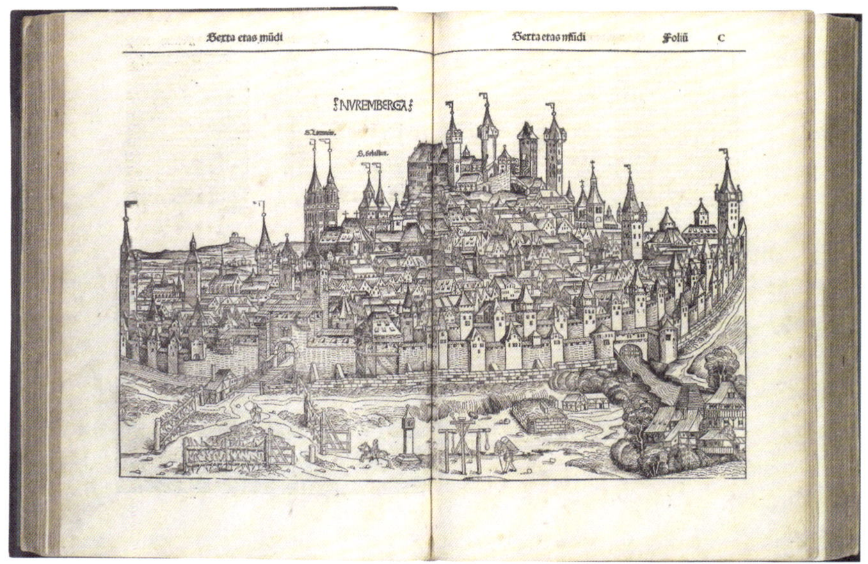

Fig. 2.2 *Weltchronik* or *Nuremberg Chronicle*, with text by Hartmann Schedel and woodcuts by Michael Wolgemut and Wilhelm Pleydenwurff. Published by Anton Koberger, 1493.

of the western world that combined religion, humanist thought and mythology, with text by the doctor and bibliophile Hartmann Schedel (1440–1514). It features approximately 1,800 illustrations printed from over 600 woodblocks designed by Wolgemut and fellow draftsman Wilhelm Pleydenwurff (1460–1494). It is both technically and aesthetically outstanding, consisting of maps, divine images, monsters, portraits and topographical views, all while utilising white space and narrative pacing in a nascent form of graphic design. Through a vast network of agents, distributors, investors and fellow printers, these works were exported across the continent, bringing acclaim and further business to the Koberger enterprise.

Through this rigorous training in both artistry and commerce, coupled with his own thirst for innovation, Dürer conceived utterly original compositions that were specifically designed as prints. He married the formal lines of the Gothic aesthetic with the classical sensibilities of the Italian Renaissance, inspired by his travels through northern Italy and the creative mecca of Venice, towards the end of the fifteenth century. During these formative years, he mastered not only the graphic power of the woodblock, but also that of another printmaking technique, which evolved naturally from the decorative work of the goldsmiths that had long surrounded him: it is known as engraving.

* * *

Nuremberg was already renowned for its fine metalwork by the time Dürer was born, and it became one of the most significant cities in the history of Renaissance printmaking. The powerful city-state's ceaseless trade included musical instruments, clocks, compasses, crockery, jewellery, sandglasses and astrolabes (a kind of spherical astrological chart), but elaborately decorated armour was one of its greatest exports.[6] Not content with the most technically proficient designs, customers wanted flair, leading craftsmen to develop stylish flourishes and figurative scenes that were scored into the metal suits with sharp tools. This paved the way for engraving prints, a process which is defined not by cutting away material to create a relief, but by incising lines into a metal plate.

Engraving is the earliest of the intaglio processes – an umbrella term used to describe a number of techniques explored in this book. The word stems from the Italian *intagliare*, meaning 'to engrave', but it has come to represent any form of printmaking that involves inscribing lines into the surface of a plate. The engraver's greatest friend is the burin, a steel cutting stylus that takes its name from the French for a 'cold chisel' (i.e., a chisel used to work with metals that are not being heated). It features a wedge-shaped point and a round pommel not unlike a toadstool, which allows the artist to exert considerable pressure while gouging V-shaped grooves into a sheet of carefully polished metal. Copper is the traditional choice, due to its strength and durability, but Renaissance printmakers also favoured its reddish tone for theoretical reasons. The hue was associated with the powerful planet Venus, as well as the 'hot' and 'dry' bodily humours, which were believed to dominate masculinity.[7]

Once a design is complete, ink is warmed and applied across the plate's surface, with the aid of a cylindrical 'dabber', or a bundle of gauze known as 'scrim' or 'tarlatan', so that the pigment enters every crevice. Next, a single piece of scrim is used to polish the plate, so that the inked lines are clearly defined and the surface shimmers.

It might seem logical to use freshly laundered gauze for this task, but ink-covered specimens actually adhere better when removing unwanted excess. The natural oils in the palm of a clean hand follow the same principle, and are often used for a final, gentle swipe to remove any remaining residue.

Relief presses rely on Gutenberg's stamping motion, but intaglio presses are more akin to a mangle. The completed plate is placed in the middle of the printing bed, with a piece of damp paper carefully positioned on top. Both elements are then covered in several felt blankets to create an even pressure, before a large wheel is used to squeeze the bed through two rollers, exerting hundreds of pounds of force. Finding the right balance is a fine art, with printmakers spending a lifetime learning the exact specifications for their machine. Incorrect set-ups can be disastrous, causing uneven prints, broken plates and damaged rollers. Once the squeezing is complete, the paper is lifted. The resulting print should feature well-defined marks and a strong indentation that outlines the shape of the plate, caused by the extreme pressure. This obvious recess is the easiest way to recognise any intaglio print.

* * *

The earliest printed engravings date to the 1430s, and are attributed to semi-anonymous German goldsmiths-cum-printmakers, such as the Master of the Playing Cards (active *c.*1430–50) and Master E.S. (active 1450–67). Their diminutive designs often depicted religious subjects, or – as the former's moniker would suggest – they took the form of decks of cards, featuring wildlife and mythological scenes. Surviving examples, with light and occasionally blurred outlines that are evidence of 'slipping', suggest that they were printed by hand. Dürer was familiar with both printmakers, but he was most enamoured by the work of Martin Schongauer (*c.*1445–1491), an Alsatian artist who was famed for his deft rendering of texture, light and dynamic compositions. The young devotee travelled to the French town of Colmar in 1492, hoping to meet the influential engraver. Unfortunately, he had died the previous year, most likely of the plague.

While Dürer was unable to meet his hero, he made great study of his work and perfected his command of both woodcut and engraving. Although there is no definitive record, it is most likely that he would have created detailed designs on thin sheets of paper, known as 'cartoons', before passing them to a master cutter. These would then be either pasted or 'pounced' onto the block or plate. The latter technique was originally used to produce frescos, and it involves creating pin pricks along a drawing's outline, before dabbing a fine powder such as charcoal across the surface. Once the paper is removed, the marks remain on the surface below, creating what is in effect an elaborate dot-to-dot. Some historians attest that Dürer produced his own blocks, which can be verified if his statement about the wonders of printing are to be taken at face value: 'Thus it comes that a man may draw something with his pen on a half-sheet of paper in one day, or dig something in a little piece of wood with his tool, that will be finer and better than a big thing by another who industriously worked a whole year at it.'[8]

The questions surrounding Dürer's level of involvement are symptomatic of the complexities surrounding printmaking and its production during the early Renaissance. Whereas the medieval attitude towards artistic creation had followed a craft model largely defined by materials, this newly enlightened era was more expansive, often bridging the gap between areas of artisanal expertise, such as goldsmithing and highly skilled woodwork, and the so-called 'fine' arts, which included painting and sculpture. However, the continued prevalence of guilds – associations of craftsmen and merchants that strictly controlled who could operate, and how they traded – had a profound effect on how print was categorised and disseminated. These structures were often unique to individual cities or regions throughout northern Europe and the Italian provinces, and a lack of consensus on how woodblock and engraving should be defined meant that they could often be practised outside of meticulous restrictions, or else they fell under multiple groups. Antwerp, Amsterdam and Haarlem categorised paintings, sculptures, prints, books and maps together, while Venice and Mantua placed prints under the jurisdiction of painters' guilds. Such intermixing also allowed for diverse forms of training, which could duly be conducted in a painter's studio or in a metal workshop. This relative freedom meant that artists, craftsmen and jobbing technicians had the opportunity to try their hand at printmaking, without fear of repercussions or unexpected trade fees.[9]

THE STORY OF PRINTMAKING

It was Nuremberg's complete lack of guilds that made it the perfect place for print to thrive, as the central government allowed for free trade across different disciplines. In the case of Koberger (along with other book publishers), this meant that he was able to commission talent from across various workshops within and beyond the city – something that guilds would not have permitted. During this period, a number of different models arose, including book publishers with large, permanent workforces consisting of carvers, engravers and printers. In addition, specialist workshops emerged, and even individual tradesmen, who might carry out commissions. In the fields of woodblock and card-making, in particular, small household businesses prospered.

Generally speaking, production was defined by the activities of a designer, a cutter and a printer, with costs usually assumed by the commissioning publisher. This role might be fulfilled by a printer who ran their own shop, or a powerful professional publishing house. As printmaking developed, so too did the market for works that helped to forge associations with leading painters and sculptors who were considered to be masters of both 'invention' (the creative idea) and 'design' (its execution) – two concepts that were of real significance to Renaissance theory. While the latter could be executed through the labour of a dedicated craftsman, the former could only be accomplished by a true artist.

Among those who fitted such categorisation, and who were in Dürer's orbit, were the Bavarian Albrecht Altdorfer (1480–1538) and the child prodigy Lucas van Leyden (1494–1533; fig. 2.3), as well as the celebrated portraitist Hans Holbein the Younger (*c.*1497–1543) and the strident Reformationist Lucas Cranach the Elder (1472–1553).[10] However, Dürer remained a dominant and highly influential figure, thanks to his command of both woodblock and engraving, and an aesthetic prowess that possessed a distinct blend of the familiar and the fantastical. *St Jerome in his Study* (1514) is a key example. This astonishing engraving transplants the scholar to an ordinary domestic setting. His docile lion sleeps contentedly alongside a small dog, while symbols usually associated with the saint – a skull, crucifix and hourglass – are installed among household clutter. Light pours in through windows comprised of glass roundels, which were a common fixture in sixteenth-century Nuremberg homes. Such a

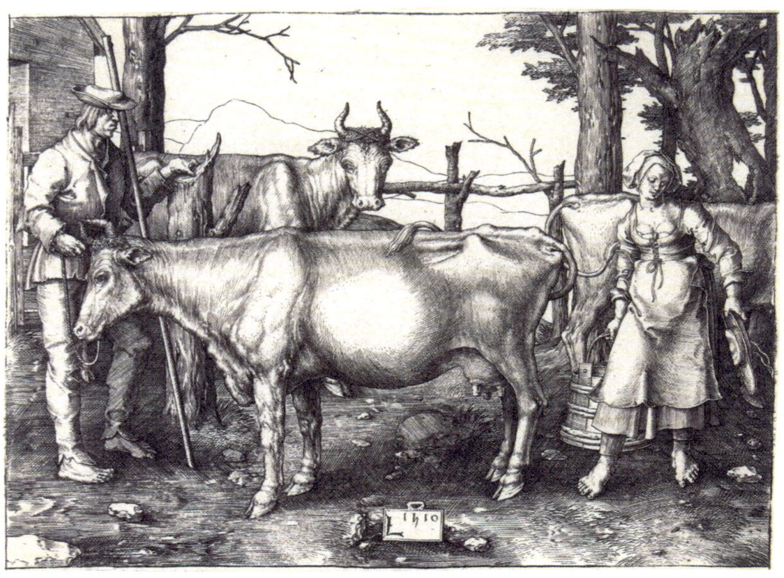

Fig. 2.3 Lucas van Leyden, *The Milkmaid*, 1510. Engraving.

scene would have been surprisingly relatable for an audience well versed in the traditional motifs of religious instruction.

In the more cryptic vision of *The Sea Monster* (fig. 2.4), a fevered eroticism runs throughout a scene of mythological abduction, which is believed to be inspired by both classical myth and the Germanic folk tale of the kidnapped Queen Theudelinde. The hybrid male is a fusion of aquatic and woodland creatures harking from some unknown land, but his captive wears an elaborate headdress in keeping with Milanese fashions of the period, which is at odds with her nudity. The artist further roots this bizarre premise in reality, thanks to a familiar backdrop depicting Nuremberg Castle.

Dürer was at the cutting edge of Renaissance thought, filling his works with new inventions and philosophical concepts that mirrored this age of enlightenment. He fastidiously studied the latest innovations, and even purchased a house that had belonged to the mathematician and astronomer Bernhard Walther (1430–1504). It came complete with an astronomical observatory and a scientific library amassed by the great scholar Johannes Regiomontanus

   THE STORY OF PRINTMAKING

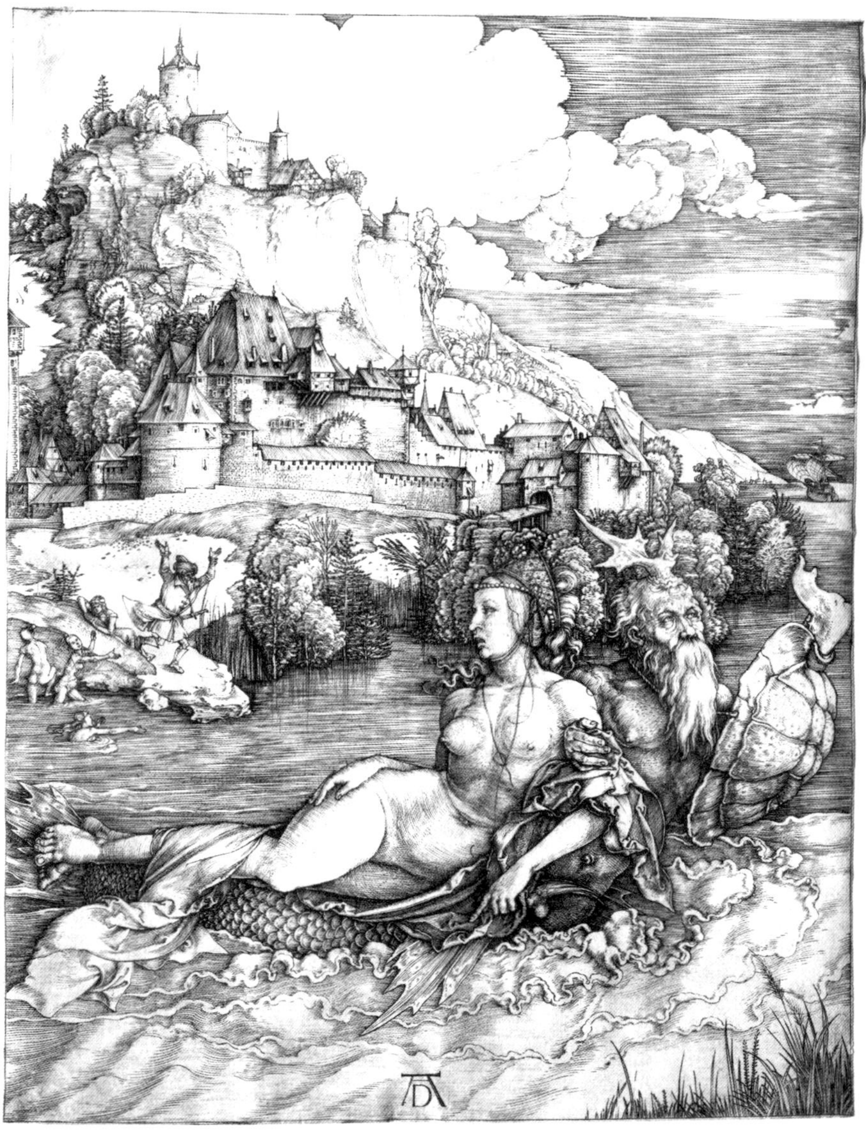

Fig. 2.4 Albrecht Dürer, *The Sea Monster*, *c*.1501. Engraving.

(1436–1476), who set up the first scientific printing press (the property is now the Dürer House museum). To this day, the full extent of the symbolism in *Melencolia I* (1514), which was usually coupled with *St Jerome*, has confounded experts. Elements including a sullen angel, an ailing canine, an hourglass and an inexplicable polyhedron continue to be assessed mathematically, astrologically and psychoanalytically.

Beyond Dürer's supreme artistic skill, it was his business acumen that truly set him apart. By 1497 he had acquired his own press; indeed, he was probably the first artist to do so, which enabled him to control the production and dissemination of his work with the aid of a fully staffed workshop. He enlisted the assistance of both his mother and his wife, Agnes Dürer (1475–1539), to manage the household and business while he travelled. He also contracted a number of sales agents who sold his work further afield across mainland Europe and England, complete with pricing structures so that the cost could be increased if a certain print became particularly popular. By prioritising printing – for he was certainly a renowned painter, too – he effectively freed himself from traditional patronage and forged his own path, finding entirely new audiences in the merchant and professional classes, who could never dream of commissioning an original work from a master artist.

Dürer's fastidious use of a monogram cemented his fame. The distinct 'AD' appears everywhere, embedded into his prints as physical objects, including hanging signs and inscribed tablets, or else placed on prominent display elsewhere in the work. This signature bears a striking resemblance to the hallmarks used by Nuremberg metalworkers, which were protected against counterfeiting by robust civil legislation.

Unlike these craftsmen, Dürer used his trademark to construct an idea of solitary genius, which was in keeping with the burgeoning individualism that characterised Renaissance humanist thought. This philosophy was heavily influenced by classical Greco-Roman teachings, and championed the pursuit of all forms of knowledge, from literature to science and the arts. This intellectual rigour, coupled with the exercise of free will and moral judgement, was seen as integral to achieving a spiritually fulfilling and virtuous life. Although copying masterworks was considered a crucial part of artistic education, with mimicry being both a commonplace and celebrated activity, Dürer objected strongly to unsanctioned copying of his work. This signified a considerable break from tradition, and was further complicated by the fact that he sought to regulate an art form that is, by its very definition, one of multiples.

Dürer's standpoint was tied directly to the novel form of mass production and dissemination. Reproducing a painting in the same medium was a long and arduous task, but a print could be duplicated with relative ease, even if quality was lacking, and the sale of counterfeits was effectively taking money straight from the artist's pocket. While on his second trip to Italy, Dürer bemoaned the situation in letters to his friend, the humanist Willibald Pirckheimer (1470–1530): 'I have many good friends among the Italians who warn me not to eat and drink with their painters, for many of them are my enemies and copy my work . . . wherever they can find it.' He also commented on his international acclaim, which surpassed his recognition back home: 'Here I am a gentleman, at home a parasite.'[11]

Eventually, the artist decided to take matters into his own hands, mounting lawsuits in Nuremberg (accusing an unknown 'foreigner') and in Venice, against the remarkably talented Italian engraver Marcantonio Raimondi (c.1470–c.1534), effectively launching the earliest artist copyright claims in history.[12] The Venetian dispute is the more famous of the two cases, due to its retelling by the famous artist biographer Giorgio Vasari (1511–1574), in his second edition of *The Lives of the Artists* (1568). He speaks of Marcantonio's first encounter with Dürer's woodcuts in the markets of San Marco. The former was apparently so taken with Dürer's genius that he bought as many sheets as he could carry, and set about reinterpreting the compositions in engraved metal. He sold the prints on, under the pretence that they had been produced by his German peer.

Dürer was furious with this infringement and demanded that Marcantonio cease production altogether. The courts settled on a different outcome, which demonstrates the Renaissance attitude towards imitation. Marcantonio could continue producing his facsimile compositions, but he was banned from using the prized monogram. While it is impossible to know whether this ruling met the artist's satisfaction, his subsequent work would suggest otherwise. In the publication of his 1511 woodcut series, *The Life of the Virgin*, he included a virulent warning against would-be copyists:

Beware, you envious thieves of the work and invention of others, keep your thoughtless hands from these works of ours. We have received a privilege from the famous Emperor of Rome, Maximilian, that no one shall dare to print these works in spurious forms, nor sell such prints within the boundaries of the empire.[13]

***

If Dürer had hoped to quash Marcantonio's printmaking career through the Venetian dispute, he would have been sorely disappointed. The engraver continued his work (omitting the trademark from existing designs) and travelled to Rome, where his talents caught the eye of Raphael (1483–1520). The Italian master had seen the power of Dürer's celebrity, and sought to achieve the same via printed replicas of his paintings. Rather than this being a case of a didactic master issuing instructions, the two worked in partnership, with Raphael deferring to his designer's greater expertise in the medium. These new interpretations involved a complete re-rendering of drawn or painted marks for overall effect, as opposed to fastidiously replicating every stroke, in an artistic and technical transliteration that only the greatest engravers could attain. Too often, the term 'reproductive' is used to suggest that these prints were nothing more than copies of great paintings and drawings. In reality, they were entirely new inventions.

The success of Raphael and Marcantonio's relationship is evident in works such as *The Judgement of Paris* (fig. 2.5), an epic depiction of the Trojan prince surrounded by the goddesses Juno, Minerva and Venus, as well as naiads, nymphs and river gods. A keen eye might spot a similarity in the right-hand grouping with that of Édouard Manet's renowned modern masterwork, *Le Déjeuner sur l'herbe*,[14] which demonstrates the lasting influence of this engraving. It is signed by both artists, thus elevating Marcantonio's position from that of mere copyist – of which there were many – to one of active collaboration.

Marcantonio was by no means the only sought-after talent for artists hoping to reimagine their work in print. Other notable names included Ugo da Carpi (*c.*1480–*c.*1532), who worked with both Titian (d. 1576) and the early Mannerist master Parmigianino (1503–1540). This self-described cutter and printer travelled around Venice, Rome and Bologna, and was renowned for his chiaroscuro woodcuts, which utilised multiple blocks in a variety of colours to create exceptional painterly tone (the term 'chiaroscuro' – given to a technique that uses dramatic contrasts between light and shadow – comes from

　　　　THE STORY OF PRINTMAKING

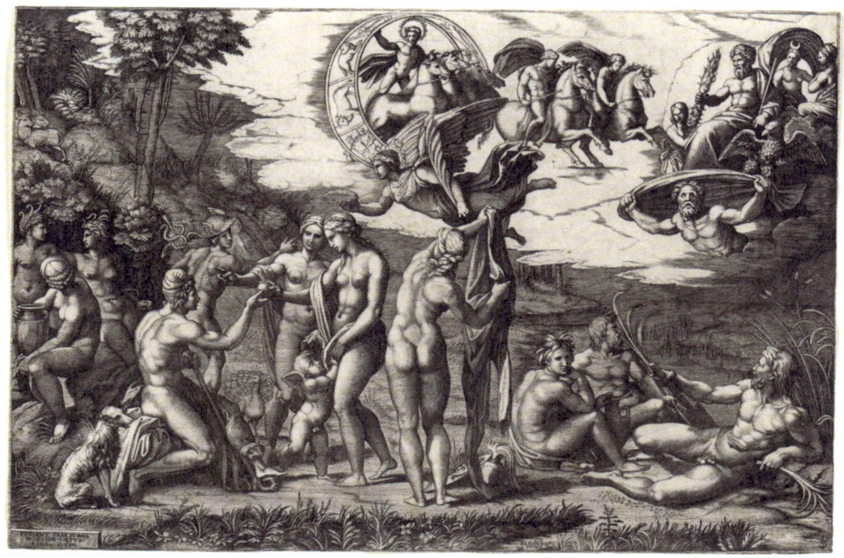

Fig. 2.5 Marcantonio Raimondi and Raphael,
The Judgement of Paris, *c*.1510–20. Engraving.

the Italian, literally meaning 'light–dark'). Until this point, prints
were almost exclusively monochrome and usually black, such were
the capabilities of a single inscribed surface. Ugo's masterpiece is
undoubtedly a four-colour woodblock depicting the Greek philosopher Diogenes (d. *c*.320 BCE), who dedicated his life to meditating
from within the confines of a wooden barrel (fig. 2.6). The print's
subtle amalgam of light and shadow is so refined that it could easily
be mistaken for a painting. The classical composition is undercut by
the presence of a rather surreal plucked chicken, which is a reference
to Plato's definition of man as a 'featherless biped'.

Ugo set about claiming his own patent for this particular method
of printing, despite its simultaneous development in Germany by
Hans Burgkmair (1473–*c*.1531), who was Schongauer's pupil. He
had some success with a papal privilege granted by Pope Leo X,
but his own fastidious copying of other artists' work, including
several designs by Marcantonio, rendered the idea of copyrighting
individual designs impossible.

The competitive nature of this newly commercial art form meant
that clashes were not only reserved for litigation. One notorious story

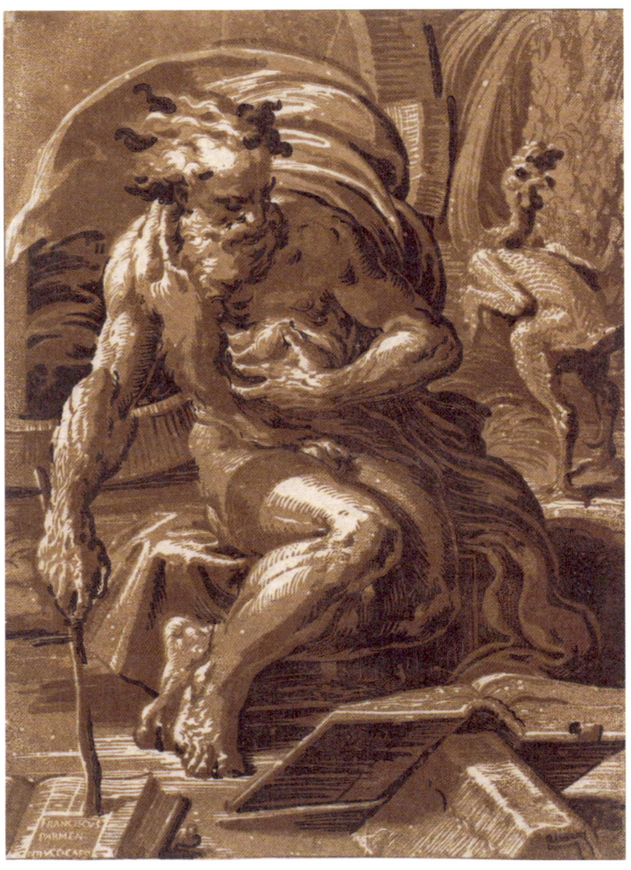

Fig. 2.6 Ugo da Carpi, after Parmigianino, *Diogenes*,
1502–32. Woodcut.

centres on Andrea Mantegna (1431–1506), a master of perspective
when it came to painting, and rare in his hands-on approach to
engraving.[15] He often used both sides of the copper plate for expressive
experimentation, deploying metal like a sketchpad, as demonstrated
in the fluid lines of his *Virgin and Child* (fig. 2.7). Once he began
working with other engravers to expand his repertoire, he proved
meticulous and overbearing, issuing considerable fines to anyone
who dared show his designs to those beyond the workshop. His
paranoia led him to order the murder of fellow artists Zoan Andrea
and Simone da Reggio,[16] whom he claimed had emulated several of
his prints. The attempt, though unsuccessful, shows just how far an
artist would go to protect their work.

                              THE STORY OF PRINTMAKING

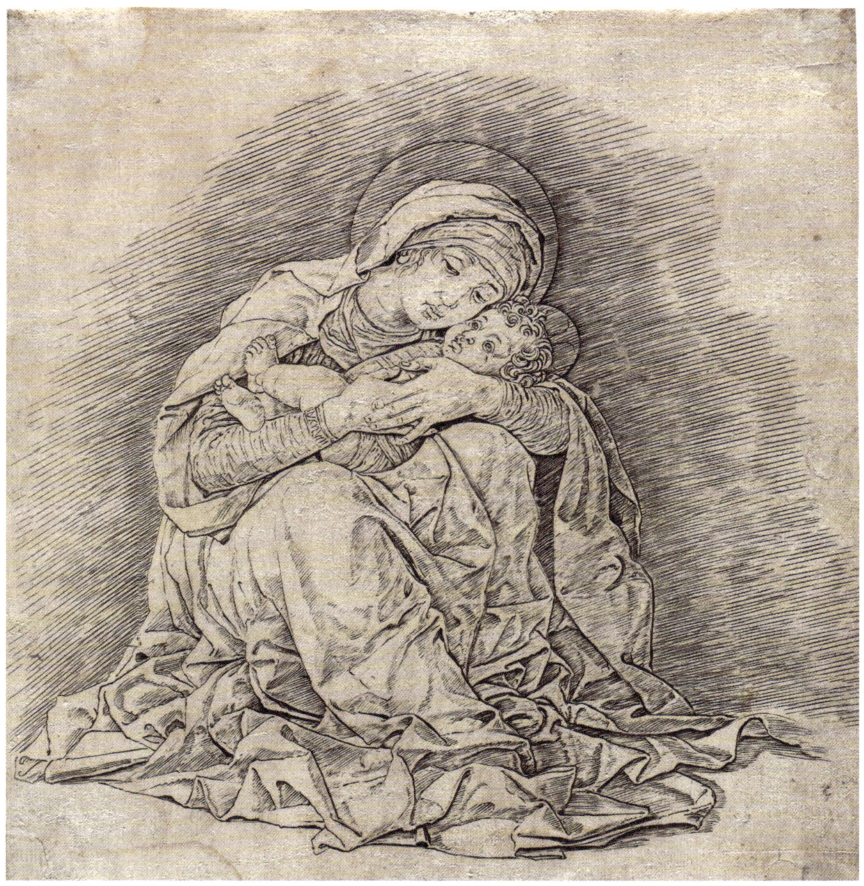

Fig. 2.7 Andrea Mantegna, *Virgin and Child*, 1485–91. Engraving.

The value placed on these precious plates and blocks is also clear in the case of Antonio da Trento (*c.*1508–1550), another celebrated woodcut printer who collaborated with Parmigianino. He sought refuge at the artist's home in Bologna following the Sack of Rome in 1527, yet following a period of fruitful work he abandoned his friend, making off in the middle of the night and stealing all of the prints, plates and drawings he could carry. Parmigianino never heard from him again.

These rather extreme accounts speak to the increasing value that was being placed on printmaking, not just in monetary terms, but also in regard to its sizeable artistic influence. Artists and dedicated

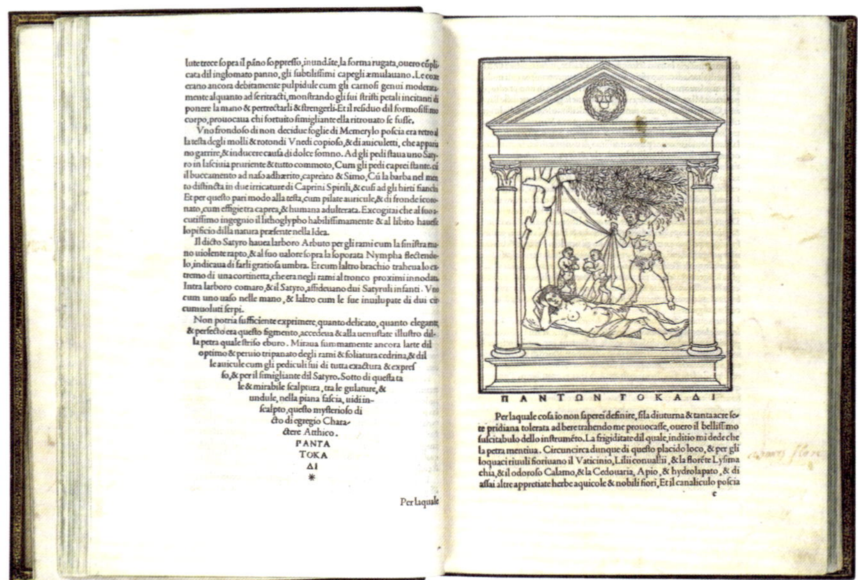

Fig. 2.8 The *Hypnerotomachia Poliphili*, with text by Francesco Colonna, featuring the woodcut *Satyr Sleeping with Nymph*. Published by Aldus Manutius, 1499.

printmakers sought to protect the integrity of both their invention and design, which was locked within the plate or block, whether this was created by a single pair of hands or many. As the gestation of imagery continued to grow, so too did innovation and reach. Rather than being dismissed as simple copies of paintings or sculptures, soon printed images were shaping visual culture itself.

A striking example is the *Hypnerotomachia Poliphili* (fig. 2.8), a labyrinthine, antiquated text that was republished by Aldus Manutius (*c.*1449–1515) in Venice, in a fashionable pocket-sized edition. While the story itself was somewhat dense, the addition of sensual and at times overtly erotic woodcut illustrations made the book hugely popular (although officially anonymous, the designs have been associated with both Mantegna and Raphael). In fact, these images proved so groundbreaking that they informed an entirely new motif within Renaissance art, known as the 'sleeping Venus'.

Illustrated editions of Ovid's *Metamorphoses* (written *c.*8 CE) were equally influential – so much so that the epic narrative poem

   THE STORY OF PRINTMAKING

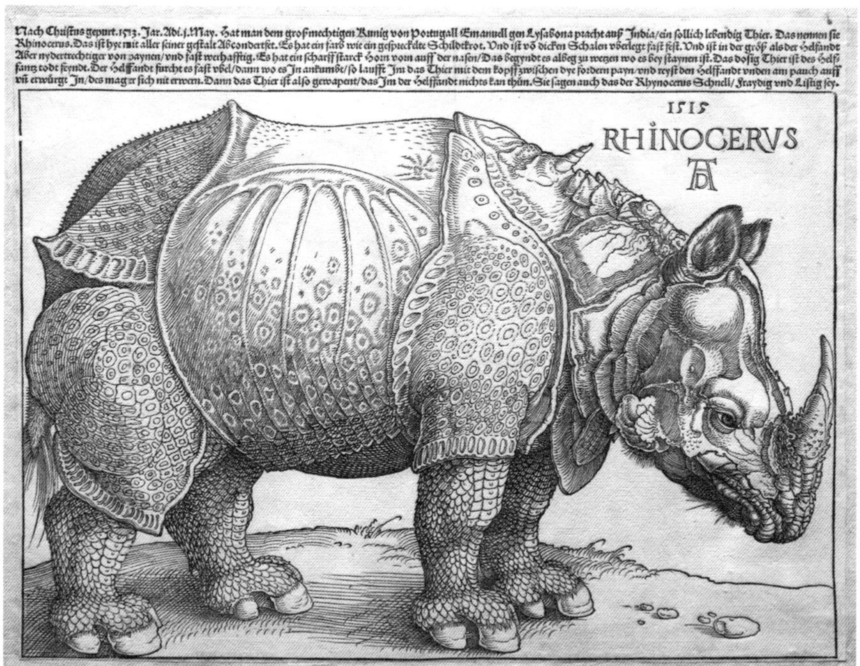

Fig. 2.9 Albrecht Dürer, *The Rhinoceros*, 1515. Woodcut.

has become known as the 'painter's bible'. It was first printed in
Bruges in 1484, complete with a selection of woodcuts depicting its
ancient mythological motifs, and it is believed that over a hundred
versions were in circulation over the ensuing century.

Another testament to print's far-reaching influence comes, once
again, from Dürer. His most enduring image is not a biblical vision,
nor a densely packed allegorical scene, but an animal. *The Rhinoceros*
(fig. 2.9) is a portrait of a beast that would have seemed impossibly
exotic to the average sixteenth-century European. This woodcut was
based on a real rhino, given by Sultan Muzaffar Shah II of Cambay
(present-day Gujarat) to King Manuel I of Portugal as a diplomatic
gift. Dürer never saw the creature, but relied on a description from a
friend, which accompanies his picture: 'It has the colour of a speckled tortoise, and is covered with thick scales. It is like an elephant
in size but lower in its legs and almost invulnerable. It is also said
that it is fast, lively and cunning.'[17]

This account is far from accurate, yet Dürer's image was so indelible that it surpassed more precise renditions, and remains sought after to this day. The rhino's armour-like exterior alludes to the metalworkers of Nuremberg, while its whiskered chin and ears are not unlike a dog's or cat's (the artist often studied and sketched both). It is said that up to 15,000 prints were taken from the original block, such was the hunger for this uniquely stylised image.

The magnetism of Dürer's rhino has continually appeared in other works of art. It has been replicated in prints, tapestries, paintings, and even a metre-wide edition of Meissen porcelain.[18] That this image should command such a hold for over two centuries – and, one might argue, still prevails – is a testament to the enduring allure of an artistic fantasy. Salvador Dalí, for one, kept a copy of the print in his home.

While this picture seems impervious to the passage of time, the creature that inspired it was far less fortunate. After it had spent a year in Lisbon, King Manuel decided to gift his prize to Pope Leo X and organised transportation across the Mediterranean. Disaster struck when a sudden, deadly storm took hold. The animal that inspired so many, as an enduring icon of the Renaissance, drowned while shackled to the deck of a sinking ship.

CHAPTER 3

ETCHING THE ARTIST'S LINE

CREATIVITY, COMMERCE AND CHIAROSCURO

You bravely undertook a business that transcends your sex . . .
Ensuring always that what may fascinate the lover of art
Is engraved in copper and published
          – Dominicus Lampsonius to Volcxken Diericx, 1573

IT WAS ONCE again the armourers who spearheaded innovations in intaglio. As the demand for increasingly elaborate sheathing and weaponry intensified throughout sixteenth-century Europe, metalworkers looked for more efficient ways to transpose their designs onto breastplates, helmets and gauntlets, which could supersede labour-intensive engraving. The answer lay in the corrosive properties of acid, which could be manipulated to eat away at metals such as iron and copper to articulate complex designs.

The development of 'vitriols' can be traced back to alchemists practising in the Islamic world from the eighth century onwards, but recipes for corrosive mordants only appeared in Byzantium and medieval Europe several hundred years later. Their nascent use in printmaking first appeared in the early 1500s, and it should come as no surprise that the first proponents were armourers and craftsmen working in many of the same commercial hubs mentioned in the preceding chapter.[1]

Among them were Daniel Hopfer (1471–1536), an outstanding armour etcher from Augsburg, who developed a dot-shading drawing technique still known as the 'Hopfer style'. Surrounded by the technical expertise and constant innovation of the city's artisans, he experimented with etching metal plates that could hold and transfer ink to paper. Along with his sons, Lambrecht (active *c.*1525–50) and Hieronymus (*c.*1500–1563), he established a workshop that began by capitalising on an appetite for devotional prints bought as pilgrimage souvenirs, before branching out into all manner of imagery, including famous portraits, ornamental architecture and copies of pre-existing pieces (particularly works by Dürer). By 1520, the technique had gained traction in Nuremberg and Antwerp, as well as Bologna, Venice and Fontainebleau. This occurred against the backdrop of the Reformation, when religious conflicts and reforms stoked a proliferation of printed materials that espoused the teachings of both Protestant and Catholic doctrines.

The popularity of etching lines (as opposed to tonal processes developed later, which are discussed in subsequent chapters) was down to much more than its comparative speed. Engraving and woodblock are specialist crafts, demanding considerable strength and skill to cut lines that appear free-flowing. By contrast, etching is more akin to the expressive and fluid act of drawing on paper, with ample scope for experimentation. For anyone hoping to try their hand at printmaking, this familiarity is extremely attractive, provided one has access to the correct materials and the privilege of expert advice.

To begin the process, a metal plate is covered in an acid-resistant layer known as a 'ground', which is traditionally formed from bitumen (distilled from crude oil) and wax. It is then left to dry and harden, before a design is drawn across the surface with an etching needle. When first picking up this tool, the temptation is to score into the plate with considerable force. This is unnecessary, as the lightest touch will disturb the ground's surface and reveal the metal underneath. Once the plate is dipped in the acid bath, the solution will 'bite' any exposed area and corrode the material, leaving sharp indentations wherever the needle has made contact.

The longer a plate is exposed, the deeper the marks, and the darker they will appear when printed. Determining the appropriate timings and mordant recipe is an art in and of itself, as is deciding whether a plate requires further submersion to increase the depth of line. Etching studios usually feature several basins filled with corrosive solutions

  THE STORY OF PRINTMAKING

that are designed to react with different materials such as copper, steel and zinc. They will also be littered with diagrams, calculations, magnifying glasses and test strips, putting one in mind of a laboratory.

Thanks to its caustic processes, etching can certainly feel like a melting point of magic and science, which is often tinged with peril. There are many possibilities for error, from 'foul bite' where pock marks appear due to a badly prepared ground, to overly corroded lines caused by overzealous biting. Even summoning the confidence to declare a design complete – before the acid commits it to a state of permanence – can be daunting. When the decision is made, the plate can be cleaned and prepped for printing. Just like engraving, ink must be pushed into every crevice using a dabber or bundle of gauze, before the surface of the metal plate is wiped down. Once it is placed on the printing bed, a sheet of damp paper is laid delicately on top, before both are run through the press. The paper is then peeled off, to reveal its final mirror image.

The ample experimental possibilities of this process were brilliantly exploited by Daniel Hopfer, who was not only an early etcher, but also a truly innovative one. He introduced variation into crisp, graphic lines by using an array of different-sized needles, and developed dramatic shadowing by applying acid directly to the plate with a brush.

These techniques are more than evident in *Death and the Devil Surprising Two Women* (fig. 3.1), a menacing memento mori that decries the sin of vanity. It features a noblewoman and her attendant, who are articulated in deft contours that perfectly define their delicate features and the folds of their elaborate costumes. The pair seem unaware that they are being followed by a withered harbinger of death, whose corporeal being is articulated in the same sketched style as their own. The shadowy hollow of his torso is outdone by the utterly macabre devil that skulks behind him, attended by several other diminutive demons. Unlike the rest of the print, which follows the conventional etching style of black marks on white paper, the devil's supernatural pelt appears as a black mass, as if he has just clawed his way out of the depths of Hell.

Hopfer achieved this remarkable effect by using a technique known as 'stopping out'. Put simply, an acid-resistant varnish is used to stop further corrosion and protect areas of the plate. When the metal is

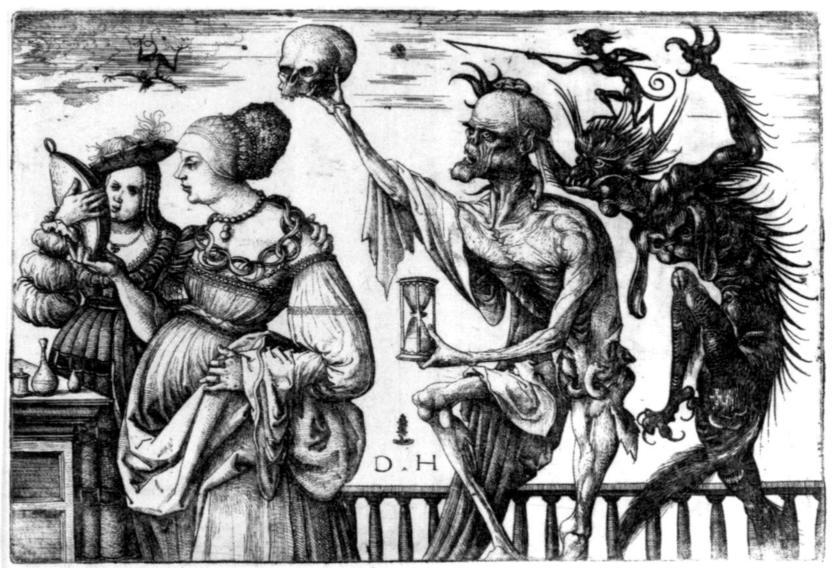

Fig. 3.1 Daniel Hopfer, *Death and the Devil Surprising Two Women*,
*c.*1515. Etching.

dipped again, the acid only affects the exposed areas. In this case, the original etching would have been nothing but line work. After stopping out most of the image so that it remained intact, the devil and his fiendish friends were left uncovered. The resulting, deeply bitten areas produced a much denser tone than cross-hatching could achieve, perfect for creating the demon's dramatic, shadowy visage. Hopfer incorporated one final flourish in this image. Using a quill, he drew in the devil's teeth and hairy texture using the same impenetrable stop-out varnish, thus creating dynamic, white highlights.

Hopfer's innovations are a testament to the experimental attitude many artists and printmakers brought to this new medium. However, etching certainly did not surpass the popularity of engraving and woodblock during this period. For many, including Dürer and Lucas van Leyden, who both produced just a handful of etched works before returning to their preferred techniques, it was nothing more than a brief foray into unknown territory.

Others, such as Parmigianino, relished the opportunity for intimate and spontaneous expression. During his time in Bologna,

                    THE STORY OF PRINTMAKING

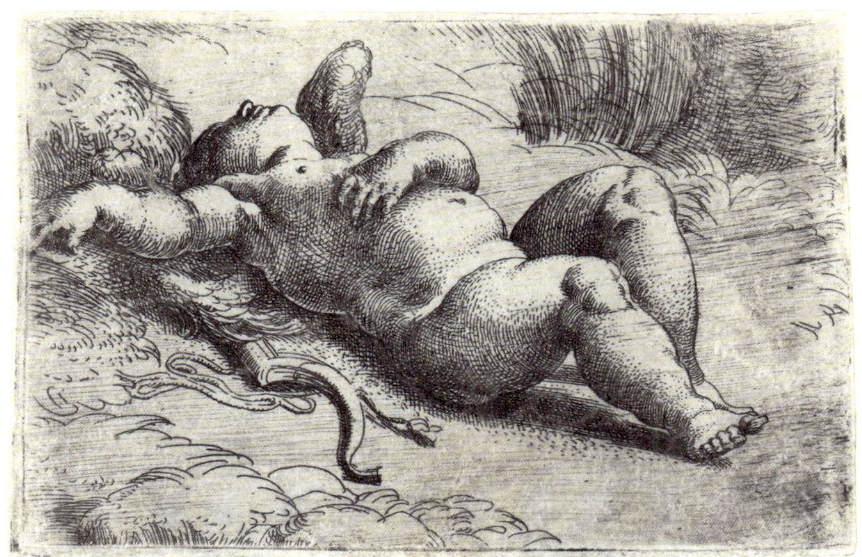

Fig. 3.2 Parmigianino, *Sleeping Cupid*, 1513–40. Etching.

the artist executed at least 18 etchings, including *Judith with the Head of Holofernes* (1520–40) and the utterly charming *Sleeping Cupid* (fig. 3.2). However, despite this evident propensity for the vitality of the etching needle, he continued to collaborate with master engravers and woodblock designers to reimagine his drawings and paintings (as discussed in chapter 2; see p. 38, p. 41).

The real shift in etching's prevalence came not from individual artists, but from publishing houses. This nascent industry, pioneered by the likes of Anton Koberger, grew out of the books trade and flourished during the mid-sixteenth century as the market for both bound and single-sheet prints steadily increased across Europe. The appetite for prints was also aided by a burgeoning fashion for collecting among the merchant class, as a symbol of both wealth and intellectual acuity. The prevailing style shifted, too, from classical order and harmony to the exaggerated artifice of Mannerism.

With this new form of enterprise came a move towards entire workshops of craftsmen, with publishers often designing and cutting plates themselves. These houses became truly centralised, controlling

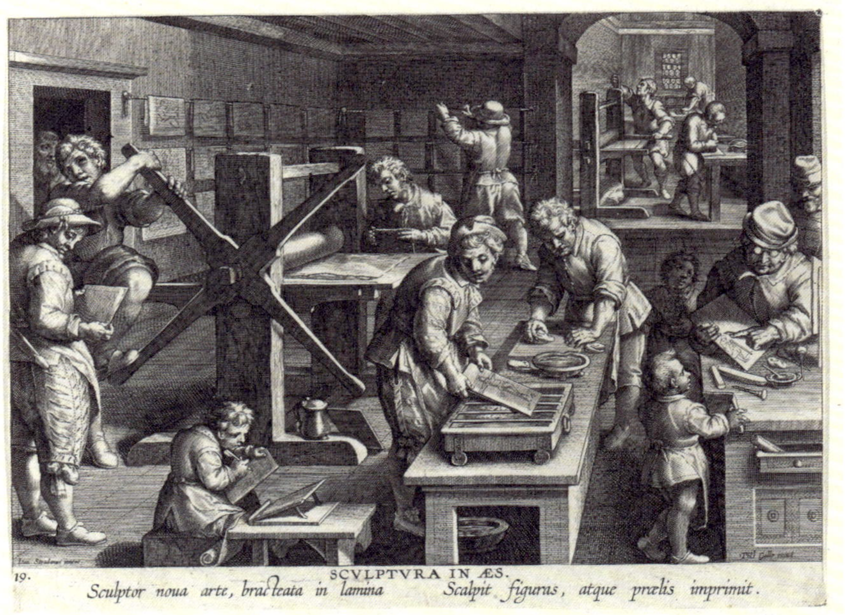

Fig. 3.3 Jan Collaert I, after a design by Jan Stradanus, *The Invention of Copper Engraving*, from 'New Inventions of Modern Times'. Published by Philips Galle, *c*.1600. Engraving.

design, production and publication, all from a single site. Such an industrious working environment is depicted in an engraving by Jan Collaert I (*c*.1525–1580), after a design by Jan Stradanus (1523–1605), which was issued by the prolific Dutch publisher Philips Galle (1537–1612), in a series known as 'Nova Reperta' or 'New Inventions of Modern Times'. In something of a portrait of his own enterprise, workers are seen grinding ink, wiping plates, rotating the enormous handle of the press and hanging completed prints to dry (fig. 3.3). In the foreground, juvenile apprentices (startlingly young to contemporary eyes) are educated in the art of drawing and cutting. This formal delineation of duties marked an evolution in print production, and in its increased commercialisation.

This scene focuses solely on the engraving workshop, yet Galle would have been familiar with the fashion for etching, particularly in the Low Countries. Its popularity was thanks in no small part to his former employers, a husband-and-wife duo whose groundbreaking business pioneered the professionalisation of etching, controlling a veritable printmaking monopoly from their enviable position in the heart of Antwerp.

* * *

In 1548, Hieronymus Cock (1518–1570) and Volcxken Diericx (*c.*1525–1600) received government permission to establish a printing and publishing house in the Flemish port city they called home. They were not long married and Cock had recently joined the Guild of St Luke as a master painter, thanks to his father's influential standing.

Despite this privilege, the commercial promise of printmaking proved extremely attractive, particularly as a plethora of businesses had blossomed in and around the famed Lieve-Vrouwpand (Our Lady's Market). This enormous centre of art retail, which was one of the largest in Europe at the time, was filled with luxurious items including sculptures, silverware, textiles, paintings and prints, and served as an emblem of Antwerp's ceaseless trade.

The city had flourished since the early sixteenth century due to its strategic position as the Habsburg Empire's centre of colonial commerce. In fact, as early as 1425, the Castilian historian Pedro Tafur had identified its cosmopolitan nature and considerable wealth: 'Who wants to see the world, or a large part of it, he can find it. Here, you can see the most beautiful things of the world and the greatest riches. . . .'[2] With a population of over 100,000 inhabitants, including approximately 2,000 merchants and artisans, it was nothing short of a metropolis.

Cock and Diericx decided against settling in the immediate orbit of the famed market. Instead, they bought up a corner plot on the newly established Exchange, perhaps pointing to the couple's grand hopes for the business. They named their workshop Aux Quatre Vents, or 'At the Four Winds', alluding to the international reach of their venture.[3] A rather creative vision of their storefront is depicted in *Imaginary View of a Street with the House 'Aux Quatre Vents'* (fig. 3.4), which shows Cock standing in the doorway with an outstretched arm, ready to welcome customers. Diericx can be glimpsed inside at the counter, in front of stacks of prints waiting to be sold.[4]

This work is coded with a wealth of information pertaining to the publishing house's success. The very fact that both man and wife are featured is testament to their equal partnership, which is further cemented by an inscription that reads: 'Laet de Cock coken om tvolckx Wille'. This can be translated as either 'Let the cook

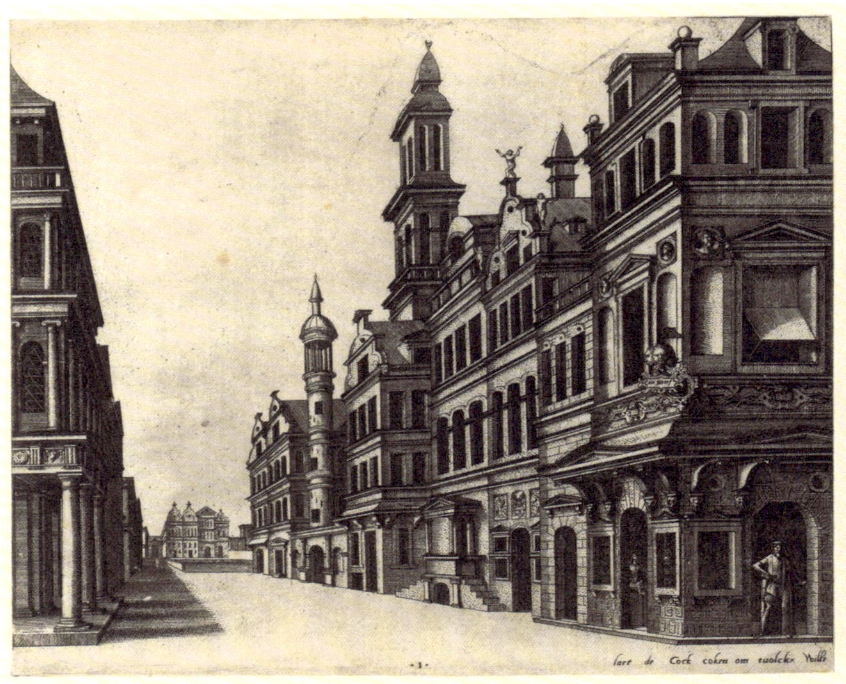

Fig. 3.4 Johannes and Lucas van Doetecum, after a design by Hans Vredeman de Vries, *Imaginary View of a Street with the House 'Aux Quatre Vents'*. Published by Cock and Diericx, 1560. Etching.

[Cock] do the cooking for the sake of the people', thus alluding to the pair's diverse customer base, or else 'for the sake of Volcxken', in a more explicit reference to obeying the woman of the house.

The print's composition was conceived by Hans Vredeman de Vries (1527–*c*.1606), a Dutch architect and engineer renowned for his designs of ornamental architecture and perspective. These were popular subject matter, along with scenes of Ancient Roman ruins, which were in step with a fashion for antiquarianism. De Vries's elaborate vision, complete with elegantly carved stonework and a sign featuring four *putti* facing in each cardinal direction, was a work of at least partial fantasy.

Cock and Diericx fully embraced these trends and many others, to feed an insatiable market for printed images across the Low Countries and beyond. They developed large-scale cartography, serialised allegorical scenes and embraced a vogue for vernacular Netherlandish

　　　　　　　THE STORY OF PRINTMAKING

landscapes. Cock even produced his own etchings of the latter, most of which served as motifs that painters might use as backdrops for their own compositions. The pair also utilised the services of sales agents, operating in other cities such as Paris and London, to increase their reach. In only a few short years, Aux Quatre Vents had become one of the most influential publishing enterprises in Europe.

The success of the business lay not only in a robust trading network and an inherent ability to predict aesthetic trends, but also in an acute understanding of the importance of diverse expertise in the workshop. Cock and Diericx courted the greatest draftsmen, engravers and etchers of their day – including established masters such as Giorgio Ghisi (1520–1582), who created major compositions after Bronzino and Raphael – as well as seeking out promising new talent.

For example, the much-admired Cornelis Cort (1533–1578) was most likely an apprentice before he went on to produce the spectacular series 'The Labours of Hercules' (1563). The success of this enterprise, which was inspired by long-lost paintings by Frans Floris (1516–1570), certainly contributed to Cort's renown, and he later moved to Italy to work with Titian.

Pieter Bruegel the Elder (*c.*1525–1569), who was considered the stylistic heir to Hieronymus Bosch (*c.*1450–1516), was also nurtured by the printing house. In fact, the implicit association between the two artists was exploited in popular prints such as *Big Fish Eat Little Fish* (1557). This visualisation of the age-old adage was wholly the work of Bruegel, despite a misleading attribution claiming the design lay with Bosch. Such pretence was surely an attempt to boost sales, with little chance of recourse as the elder artist had died some four decades previously.

Other exceptional talent included Hieronymus Wierix (1553–1619) and Johannes Wierix (1549–1615), who could cut technically perfect copies of Dürer's engravings by the ages of 12 and 16, respectively, but rarely made their own designs. *Imaginary View of a Street with the House 'Aux Quatre Vents'* was also cut by a pair of acclaimed siblings, Johannes (active 1551–1605) and Lucas van Doetecum (active 1554–1572), who perfected a subtle amalgam of engraving and intricate cross-hatched etching, for which they were well known.

One of the most vital, yet thoroughly overlooked, employees was Sander Janssen (active *c.*1563–*c.*1581), who held the title of 'master printer' due to his technical authority in the workshop (the term is still bestowed on experts within the field to this day). The significance of his contribution is evident in the generous pension of 50 florins that he received from Aux Quatre Vents following his retirement, yet his lack of authorship in surviving prints speaks to the perception of his position as a facilitator – a role that is rarely given ample due.

Despite this inequity, there is no doubt that Cock and Diericx greatly valued expert technique. They were entirely committed to intaglio, something that separated them from other influential Antwerp publishers such as Hans Liefrinck (*c.*1518–1573).[5] By forgoing woodblock completely, they pioneered new possibilities in copperplate which quickly took hold elsewhere. Such focus also bore exceptional output, with thousands of plates cut between 1548 and 1600, when Diericx died.

* * *

Diericx has been widely cast as nothing more than Cock's widow, despite her instrumental position as an equal partner in Aux Quatre Vents. Most texts suggest that she merely acted as a caretaker for the publishing house in the thirty years following her husband's death, if she is mentioned at all. Although this can be partially attributed to the fact that her name never appeared on prints (Cock's did), it is primarily an issue that affects historical records the world over – one in which a woman's achievements are either ignored or else remembered only through her association with men.[6]

In Diericx's own lifetime, she was well-regarded – even famed – within the industry. She commissioned ambitious projects and continued to unearth new talent, alongside running the company finances. In an engraved portrait by Johannes Wiericx, which would have been marketed to collectors of famous faces, her understated yet luxurious outfit reveals her sizeable wealth and status. She was also praised by the poet and painter Dominicus Lampsonius in his introduction to *Effigies of Some Celebrated Painters from the Low Countries* (1573), in which he declares:

> You bravely undertook a business that transcends your sex
> And now follow in the path your husband once trod:
> Ensuring always that what may fascinate the lover of art
> Is engraved in copper and published[7]

This accolade was penned as Diericx guided Aux Quatre Vents through the rampant political and religious turmoil of the Eighty Years' War, which culminated in the defeat of the Spanish Habsburgs and the formation of the Dutch Republic in 1648. Ever the astute business owner, she invested abroad to protect her assets and bought several properties. Even another marriage – which so often ended female entrepreneurship during this period – failed to deter her trade.

Diericx was in a rather unique position as a commercial publisher, but that is not to say she was the only woman to engage in printmaking around this time. In fact, after a printing press was founded in 1476 at the Convent of San Jacopo di Ripoli in Florence, it relied entirely on the labour of its nuns to produce both religious and secular books, including typesetting and pulling the press.

Beyond ruling women's valuable art patronage (Mary, Queen of Hungary, and Catherine, Queen of Portugal, were both collectors of note), personally inscribing plates was an acceptable practice for noblewomen. Marie de' Medici, Queen of France (1575–1642), produced and signed her own woodcuts alongside her considerable sponsorship. The aristocratic Sofonisba Anguissola (1532–1625), who was one of the first female painters to establish an international reputation, also dabbled in the discipline.[8]

For everyday women, opportunities to develop a printmaking craft were constrained by the social order, but some still managed to carve their own niche through associations with male relatives, much like Diericx. They include Roman sisters Geronima Cagnaccia Parasole (*c.*1564–1622) and Isabella, also known as Elisabetta, Parasole (*c.*1575–*c.*1625).

The pair were involved in family businesses, where they could pursue their vocation in a relatively private setting with varying degrees of autonomy. Geronima, for one, was highly regarded for her skills in woodcut, as seen in a piece conceived with Antonio Tempesta (1555–1630), titled *Battle of Lapiths and Centaurs* (*c.*1600). This furious scene includes two scrolls featuring the names of its inventors, embedded among the carnage of soldiers and mythical semi-equine warriors. It is telling that the mark of the printmaker sits centre stage and clearly legible, while her collaborator's appears crumpled and obscured by a shield.

Isabella, meanwhile, eventually broke away from the family workshop to pursue collaborative projects with her husband Leonardo. These included an array of lace and needlework pattern books that she designed herself, capitalising on an ever-growing market of female consumers. Undoubtedly, her inventions would have travelled far and wide, not just on the printed page but stitched into the fabric of countless garments.

Ripples of influence also travelled through Magdalena van de Passe (1600–1638), who was arguably a more accomplished printmaker than either her father or her brothers, whom she worked alongside in Cologne. She specialised in the landscape genre, producing pieces for a series depicting that ever-popular subject of Ovid's *Metamorphoses*. Her greatest legacy, however, was training Anna Maria van Schurman (1607–1678). This Dutch polymath was a classical scholar, philosopher, linguist and artist, who was also the first female university student in Europe. Her groundbreaking feminist text *The Learned Maid; or, Whether a Maid may be a Scholar?* (fig. 3.5) features a commanding engraved self-portrait, along with a rather grand epigraph: 'Written In Latine by that incomparable Virgin Anna Maria à Schurman of Utrecht'.[9]

Producing a likeness of one's self was a radical act of self-determination for women who forged their own artistic careers, particularly in the wake of the Protestant iconoclasm that dominated the Low Countries and other parts of Europe. Moreover, despite the enlightened attitudes of Renaissance philosophy and the realities of female labour, the idea of a woman representing herself independently remained somewhat scandalous.

Van Schurman's decision to include her engraving as a frontispiece asserts her own agency, while promoting a necessary image of piety and refinement. It is no coincidence that female painters working in the same period, including Anguissola, Lavinia Fontana (1552–1614) and Artemisia Gentileschi (1593–1654), all made pictures of themselves bearing the tools of their trade.

The delicate line that so many of these professionals were forced to walk is exemplified by Diana Mantuana (1536–1588), an Italian engraver who is regarded as the most famous female printmaker of the era. Unfortunately, her legacy has been diluted by several cases of mistaken identity, which scholars are continuing to unpick. The confusion is thanks in no small part to Giorgio Vasari who, on

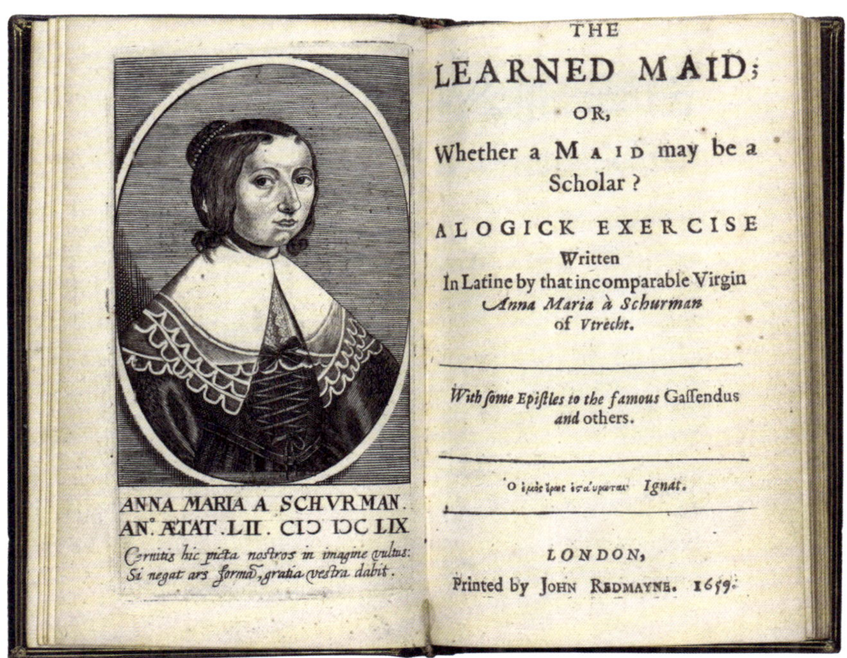

Fig. 3.5 Anna Maria van Schurman, frontispiece from *The Learned Maid; or, Whether a Maid may be a Scholar?*, 1659. Engraving.

meeting Mantuana in her father's workshop where she was training, mistakenly assumed she was the wife of another apprentice, Giorgio Ghisi (the same prolific artist who was later courted by Aux Quatre Vents). The misattribution persisted until the twentieth century, when she was retroactively afforded a new designation of 'Scultori', her father's surname. Given that she never used such a title, she is now referred to by one she inscribed herself: 'Mantuana' or 'Mantovana', meaning 'from Mantua'.

Vasari's recollections of their meeting in 1566 clearly present her as a rare exception, even a novelty, in the world of printmaking. In the same edition of *The Lives of the Artists* that praises Dürer (see p. 37), he declared:

[A] daughter named Diana also engraves so well that it is a wonderful thing: and when I saw her, a very well-bred and charming young lady, and her works, which are most beautiful, I was stunned.[10]

In this brief account, the biographer inextricably links Mantuana's aesthetic talents with her physical appearance and manners. Such an assertion is certainly problematic, but it was not out of step with society. Indeed, the young engraver clearly understood the value of cultivating a genteel image. Despite her middle-class status, she took part in life at the Gonzaga court, where artistic pursuits and expert craft were valued. She was noted for her excellent deportment and received noble patronage that furthered her legitimacy. She even managed to gain an unprecedented papal privilege once she moved to Rome with her husband, an architect named Francesco da Volterra, in 1575.

In terms of the historical record, some have been quick to pigeon-hole Mantuana as nothing more than a copyist who engraved to promote her husband's business. While she certainly produced astounding prints of finials, volutes and columns, to say that her work was merely supplementary to her spouse is erroneous. In fact, Mantuana was the more famous of the two, having cultivated her name long before her marriage. Her status is referenced in a letter written in 1583 by an agent working for Count Ferrante II Gonzaga, who was instructed to search for a court architect. He wrote:

> M. Francesco da Volterra, who years ago was in the service of Signor Don Cesare Gonzaga and is married to the famous Diana, daughter of the deceased M. Giovanni Battista Scultori, would also like to serve your Highness there, however his manner is rather sickening . . . .[11]

This scathing note confirms widespread knowledge of Mantuana's favoured position in society, even if any allusion to her work is absent. In reality, her oeuvre extended far beyond the architectural, encompassing religious imagery, historical scenes and mythology, in keeping with the market of the day. She favoured compositions after Giulio Romano (1492–1546), an extremely successful artist who had influenced her father's workshop, but she was not afraid of making her own alterations, like so many other expert printmakers.

In her sizeable, printed version of Romano's frescos at the Palazzo Te (a Mannerist villa in the Mantuan suburbs), she reimagines Cupid and Psyche's erotic encounters as a more jubilant celebration, renaming the scene *The Feast of the Gods* (1575). This delightful articulation

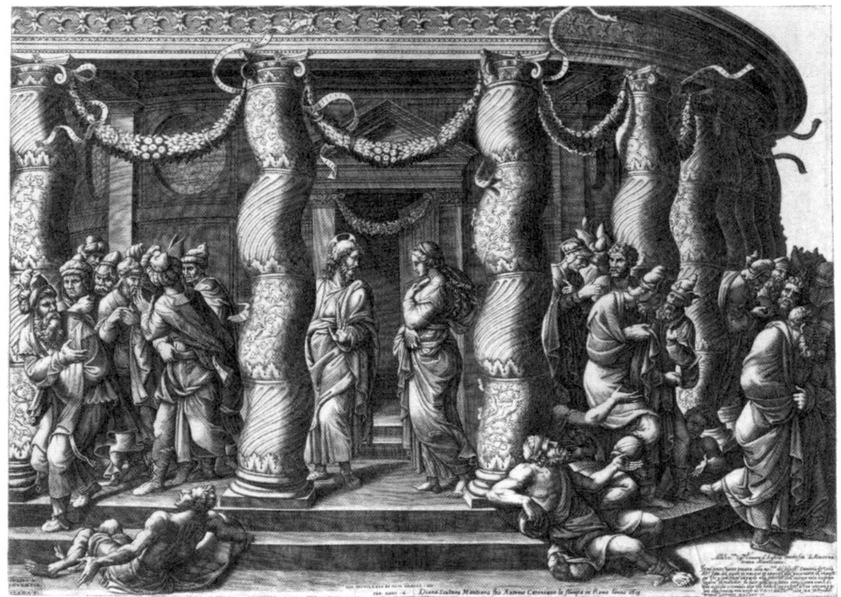

Fig. 3.6 Diana Mantuana, after Giulio Romano, *Christ and the Woman taken in Adultery*, published by Antonio Caranzano, 1575. Engraving.

of rolling flesh and florid garlands demonstrates her considerable skills regarding line and tone. The same can be said of *Christ and the Woman taken in Adultery* (fig. 3.6), which places the biblical subjects amid a fashionable architectural backdrop dominated by elaborate Solomonic columns.

There is much more work to be done in unearthing the oeuvres and biographies of these women, who capitalised on printmaking as a means of both creativity and commerce. Due to the complex nature of print signatures and attributions, it is no surprise that research concerning their practices is still in its nascency. What is indisputable, however, is that these individuals built careers that both enriched and shaped the vast ecosystem of printmaking that developed throughout Europe, whether it be through the content of their production or the relationships they fostered.

A sure-fire example of this influence (which has nevertheless been overlooked) was an astute partnership between Volcxken Diericx and the unrivalled Mannerist printmaker Hendrick Goltzius (1558–1617). When she was the sole proprietor of Aux Quatre Vents, Diericx called upon the talents of this gifted young engraver, thus setting him on a path to sizeable celebrity.

* * *

From an early age, Goltzius seemed destined for a life of art-making. He hailed from the German-Netherlandish border town of Mülbracht (now Brüggen), where he was born to a family of artisans and exhibited an insatiable appetite for drawing that often extended to the walls of the house. By the age of ten he had already apprenticed to his father, who fabricated and painted stained glass.[12] Despite a childhood accident involving burns that permanently damaged his right hand, Goltzius commanded the burin with exceptional skill. Following some self-study, he undertook a second apprenticeship in Haarlem, with the distinguished printmaker and exiled statesman Dirck Volckertszoon Coornhert (1522–1590), who greatly influenced his protégé's developing style.

Goltzius's self-assured technique consisted of astonishing, swelling grooves and arching cross-hatching that could effectually emulate the dimensionality of sculpture. By his early twenties, he was sought after by the great Antwerp publishers. He engraved a variety of epic religious scenes for Diericx and collaborated with Philips Galle, while catching the eye of elite clientele including William, Prince of Orange, and Charlotte de Bourbon, as well as the Holy Roman Emperor Rudolf II. He went on to establish his own workshop in Haarlem, effectively breaking up the monopoly previously held by the Belgian city.

During his lifetime, Goltzius's acclaim was such that he often had to travel in disguise. He revelled in this deception, often asking individuals what they thought of the great printmaker with the withered hand. When travelling in Munich, for instance, he was invited to the home of fellow engraver Johannes Sadeler (1550–1600). Goltzius's servant played the role of the virtuoso, while the artist claimed to be an ignorant Dutch cheese merchant, extolling the wonders of his dairy products with promises of gifts for the host's wife. The ruse caused great offence, yet ultimately did nothing but bolster the printmaker's fame.

Goltzius's flamboyant engravings depict scores of rippling bodies that seem to hail from another dimension. They hold a balance of mathematical precision and absurd anatomy that would not look out of place in a modern-day superhero franchise. They were informed by the classical statuary of Rome, which he saw in person during an excursion in around 1590, despite years of mysterious ill health that often left him vomiting blood. In *Farnese Hercules* (fig. 3.7), for example, a colossal three-metre-high statue of the great hero is viewed from behind, in an erotically charged scene that is almost comically undercut by the presence of two awestruck onlookers standing below.

This image, while exaggerated in its muscular tone, is nothing when compared to *The Great Hercules* (1589). The latter presents such a ludicrously hulking form that it has been afforded the affectionate nickname Knollenman or 'bulbous man'. This exemplar of Mannerist

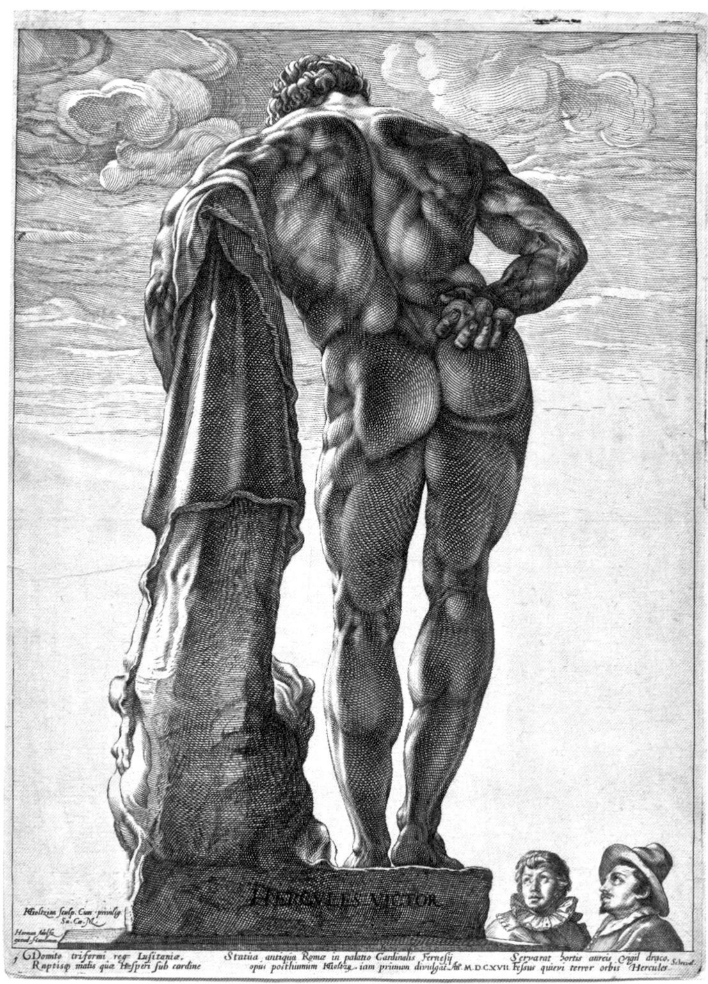

Fig. 3.7
Hendrick
Goltzius,
*Farnese
Hercules*,
1592.
Engraving.

style, which favoured symbolic artifice over realism, was made at the height of Goltzius's influence. In this iteration, his hero is designed to represent the might of the Dutch spirit against oppressive Spanish rule, as opposed to articulating any believable human form.

Goltzius masters the art of translation and exemplifies how a printmaker can surpass the accomplishments of their source material. One need only look upon the exceptional roundel series 'The Four Disgracers' (1588) to understand his superb articulation of dynamic perspective through nothing but line. These prints – in which the doomed protagonists appear to fall from above in perfectly implemented *figura serpentinata* (from the Italian for 'serpentine figure'; their limbs spiral dramatically around a central axis) – were based on designs by the painter Cornelis Corneliszoon van Haarlem (1562–1638), but the printmaker's execution undoubtedly brought them to life.

Goltzius's masterful skill is at its zenith in *The Dragon Devouring the Companions of Cadmus* (fig. 3.8), a gruesome print that once

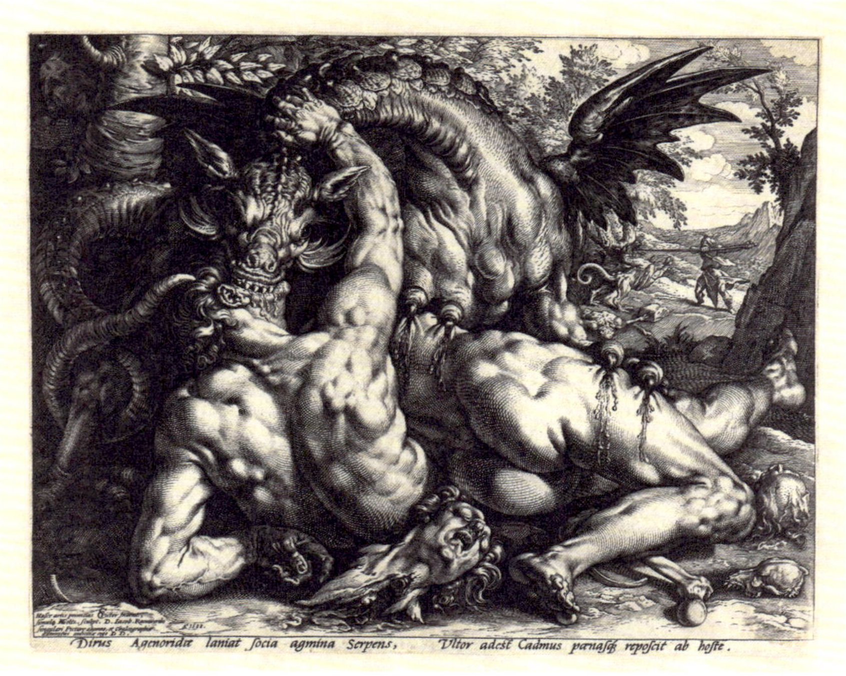

Fig. 3.8 Hendrick Goltzius, after Cornelis Corneliszoon van Haarlem, *The Dragon Devouring the Companions of Cadmus*, 1588. Engraving.

                                THE STORY OF PRINTMAKING

again translates a piece by Cornelis. The original painting appears pallid and hazy, almost dreamlike in its sense of remove. By comparison, Goltzius's graphic lines are charged with a visceral brutality that fully embodies the horror of its subject.

In 1600, when he was at the height of his fame, this sensational engraver stopped making prints altogether, focusing solely on painting for the rest of his career. This abrupt decision has puzzled historians for centuries, and remains a mystery to this day. Perhaps he had grown tired of the workshop and was content to leave it in the capable hands of his younger relatives, or else, contrary to the evidence of his own career, he succumbed to the dominant narrative: that, despite the ingenuity and innovation of the printmaker, one must paint or sculpt in order to be a truly great artist.

* * *

Although printmaking maintained a secondary position within the pantheon of art during this period, celebrated painters and sculptors continued to embrace it as both a creative and commercial tool. Anthony van Dyck (1599–1641), for one, was feted as a portraitist in the courts of King James I of England and Archduchess Isabella of the Spanish Netherlands. Though he was primarily known as a painter, his 'Iconography' etchings of famous figures (*c*.1632) proved enormously popular. His mentor, the prolific Peter Paul Rubens (1577–1640), is credited as the first Flemish artist to set up a printmaking business, which he populated with master engravers. They were tasked with transposing his paintings, drawings and tapestry designs – notable for their portrayal of voluptuous human flesh – at an exceptional rate.

The greatest printmaker of this period and surely the greatest artist, however, was Rembrandt Harmenszoon van Rijn (1606–1669). Although born in Leiden he is most closely associated with Amsterdam, where he made his home in his twenties and remained until his death. His adoptive city underwent a period of affluent transformation amid the turmoil of the Eighty Years' War, in which Netherlandish rebel forces claimed independence from the ruling Spanish Habsburgs and founded a new republic.

Commerce, philosophy, scientific discovery and artistic production all flourished in what was a relatively tolerant metropolis, dominated by a merchant class. It became the jewel in the Netherlandish crown during the Dutch Golden Age, a term that describes a period of exceptional abundance that stretched from the latter half of the sixteenth century to the war-riddled *Rampjaar* ('disaster year') of 1672.[13] This epoch, while historically celebrated as an exemplar of civilised prosperity, was rooted in colonial expansion, exploitation and enslavement.

Rembrandt was one of many artists who travelled to Amsterdam to reap newfound riches amid the fertile creative milieu. He occupied a number of residences across the city, but it is his home in the Jodenbreestraat (Jewish Broad Street) that is best known. It is now a museum, but one can still marvel at the hearth flanked by Delft Blue tiles, the curtained bed where his wife Saskia van Uylenburgh (1612–1642) once slept, and the vast collection of curiosities and antiques that informed his sizeable oeuvre. Rembrandt's penchant for collecting bordered on the pathological. Among his inventory were 24 bronze statues, 28 marble busts, 25 stuffed birds, 9 teapots, 92 carpets, a lion skin, and an incomplete whale skeleton.[14]

The thrill of everyday life inspired Rembrandt's work like no other. He brought the dynamism of human existence into every work, encoding both quotidian experience and classical allegory within his figures. He was ultimately a renegade, one who eschewed the convention of the period in favour of an innate, visceral sensibility. In *The Night Watch* (1642), he turns a stale civic guards commission into a colossal, frenetic action scene in which militia practically stride out of the canvas. In his prints, he often undercuts biblical allegory with commonplace – even lewd – activities, yet he also produced intimate and tender familial portraits that offer a precious glimpse into his own psyche.

This astonishing artist used the etching needle much like one would use a pencil. He eschewed the formality favoured by most printmakers (particularly those practising in the most prolific commercial workshops) and surpassed others who had employed the medium's natural fluidity merely to imagine cherubs and virgins, and to make brief anatomical studies. Instead, he employed this delightful line in a plethora of reflective self-portraits, where he appears both as industrious artist and ostentatiously costumed gentleman. Each image, built up through an array of shadowy hatching, feels as personal and private as a diary entry. For example, in his exceptional dual portrait with Saskia (fig. 3.9), he looks directly out at the viewer as if peering into a mirror. His reflected being is sketching, as if foretelling the image seen before us in a strange, concurrent collapsing

   THE STORY OF PRINTMAKING

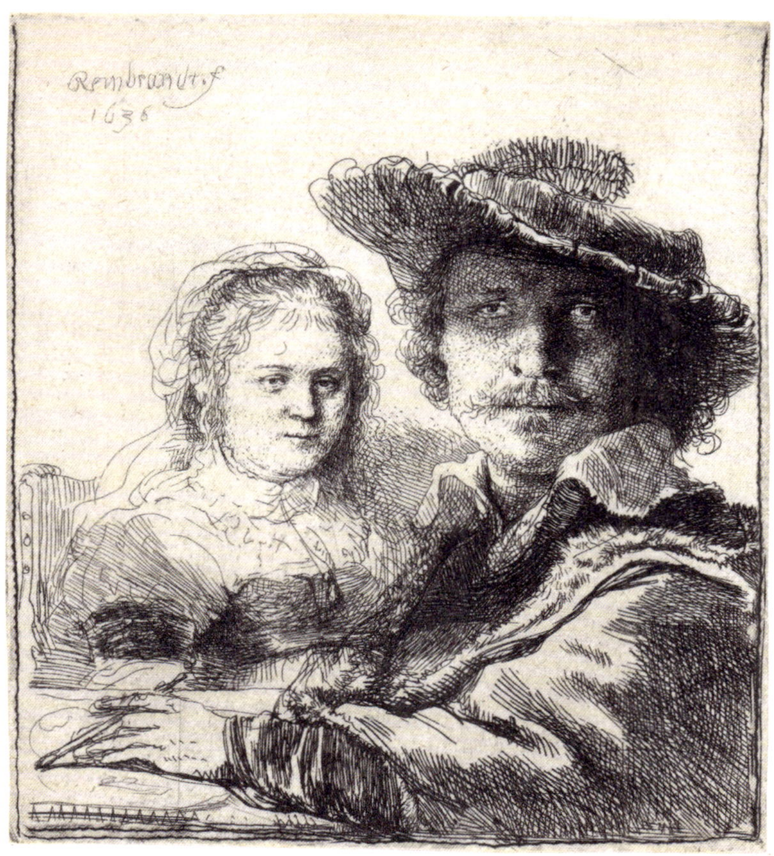

Fig. 3.9 Rembrandt van Rijn, *Self-portrait with Saskia*, 1636. Etching.

of time. Despite an innate sense of perspective, the couple's bodies also appear fused, in a visual interpretation of a popular motto of the period: 'Love gives birth to art'.[15]

This arresting realism carries through into grander religious motifs. Rembrandt's vision of *Adam and Eve* (fig. 3.10) injects one of the most recognisable scenes of the Christian canon with a carnal physicality that borders on the grotesque. The doomed pair appear hunched over their prized fruit, their figures covered in densely hatched lines that enhance, as opposed to disguise, their genitalia.[16] The dragon-like serpent that dominates the foreground is borrowed from Dürer's woodcut *Christ in Purgatory* (1512), once again demonstrating

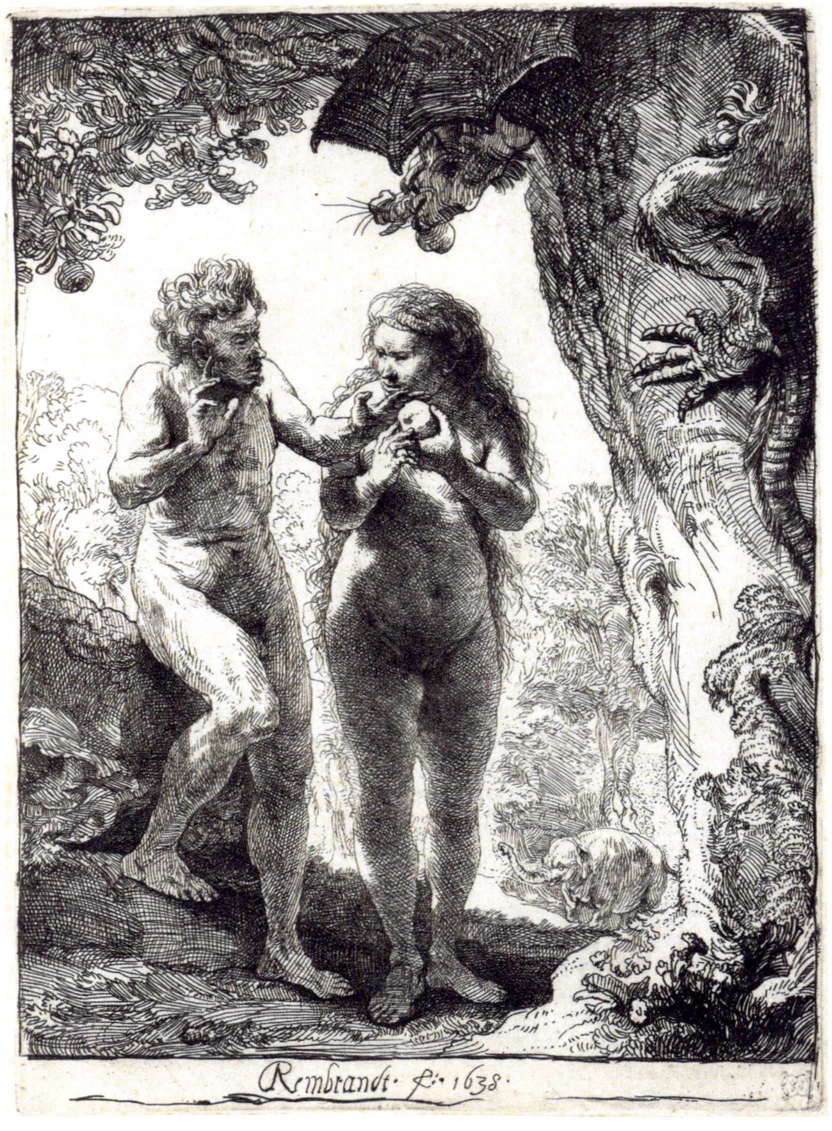

Fig. 3.10 Rembrandt van Rijn, *Adam and Eve*, 1638. Etching.

the far-reaching influence of his practice. Notably, Rembrandt held an impressive selection of prints by earlier masters, including Dürer, Van Leyden and Tempesta. The remnants of these influences can be found like ghostly impressions throughout Rembrandt's printed oeuvre.

 THE STORY OF PRINTMAKING

As a maestro of chiaroscuro, it is no wonder the artist was also struck by the appeal of drypoint. The technique sits somewhere between acid-reliant etching and the labour-intensive scoring used in engraving. It involves scratching directly into a copper plate with a needle, so that every line displaces small amounts of metal filings on either side of each groove. Unlike engraving, which would demand that these particles be removed, they are savoured in drypoint, creating a textured edge that holds greater amounts of ink. The resulting velvety soft line is known as a 'burr'. It creates a rich, feathered quality perfectly suited to shadowy scenes. The shallow scratches can wear down quickly, however, so print runs are shorter than those possible with engraving. Beyond its aesthetic appeal, drypoint can also be used to amend or retouch areas of an etched plate. Once printed, the different processes can be difficult to distinguish.

Rembrandt turned to drypoint to create more impassioned and sombre interpretations of the scriptures, made all the more transcendent by their combination of spiritual light and earthly darkness. In *The Hundred Guilder Print* (fig. 3.11), the nuanced tonality of a

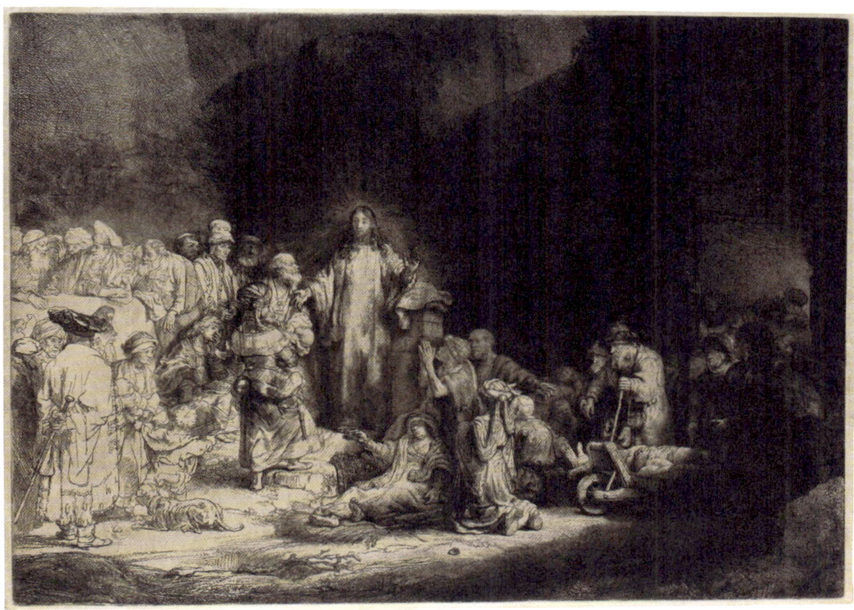

Fig. 3.11 Rembrandt van Rijn, *The Hundred Guilder Print*, *c*.1648. Etching, drypoint and engraving.

scene dominated by Christ's heavenly glow is achieved through both etching and drypoint, as demonstrated by the luxurious blackness of a gateway from which his followers emerge. The title derives from the supposed high price demanded during Rembrandt's lifetime, which was approximately a hundred times the value of an average print and equal to that of a painting on canvas.[17] Such a fee would amount to roughly a quarter of a skilled artisan's annual income.

The most outstanding example of drypoint as a standalone technique is evident in *Christ Crucified between the Two Thieves*, otherwise known as *The Three Crosses* (fig. 3.12). This epic composition is swallowed by violent, angular lines that convey the agony of the Messiah's crucifixion. The dynamic impact of the burr is at its apex in this instance, where indistinguishable lines nevertheless portray the congested depths of the crowd. Despite the relative fragility of the large-scale plate (it measures over 40 centimetres across), Rembrandt

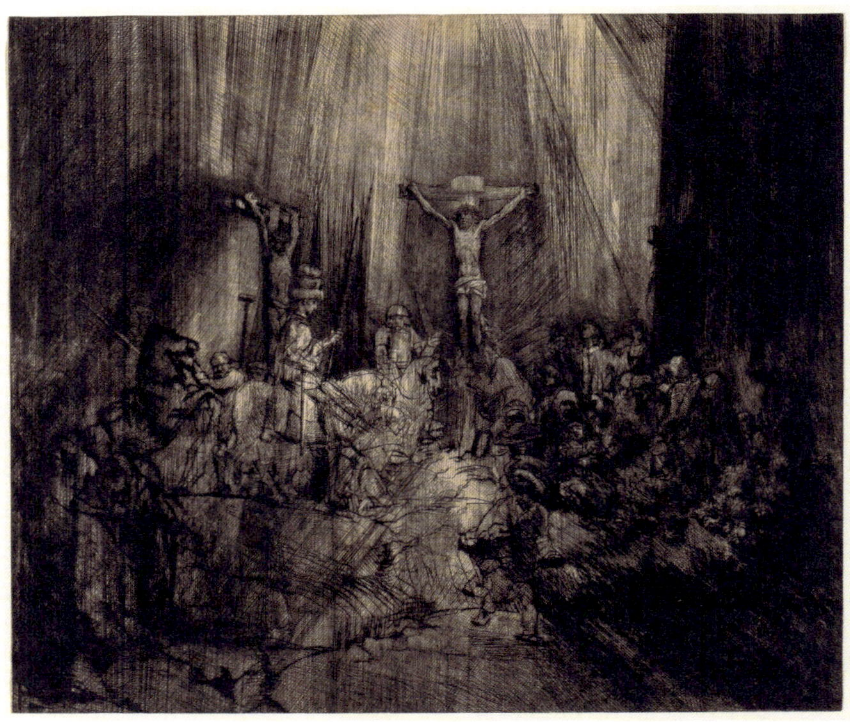

Fig. 3.12 Rembrandt van Rijn, *Christ Crucified between the Two Thieves* or *The Three Crosses*, 1653–c.1660. Drypoint.

   THE STORY OF PRINTMAKING

reworked it considerably, altering the headwear of the man on horseback and the appearance of various onlookers. In between these amendments he pulled prints, resulting in successive variations that are evidence of the building stages of a print, known as 'states'. He also experimented with inking, choosing to leave excessively wet areas to enhance the tenebrous drama of the plate's outer edges.

These dramatic distinctions exemplify Rembrandt's impact on the world of printmaking. He paved the way for a new kind of thinking, commanding the absolute creative authority of the artist, where discrepancies among a suite of impressions were viewed not as unfortunate errors but as vital experimentation. These assorted iterations populate museums, libraries and archives throughout the world, and are often filled with such distinct variations that it seems almost inconceivable that they originated from a single plate.

The volatility of Rembrandt's personal life goes some way to explaining how the majority of his copper plates ended up in the hands of French engravers. He was never particularly good with money and relied on his wife's inheritance and her considerably more astute financial acumen to manage their affairs, until her untimely death in 1642. Soon after, the artist became embroiled in various quarrels with his in-laws, concerning rightful ownership of property and funds bequeathed to his young son Titus. He also saw to it that his housekeeper Geertje Dircx (*c*.1610–*c*.1656) was imprisoned following their illicit relationship, her legal challenge on the grounds of an alleged marriage proposal, and her attempts to pawn his late wife's jewellery.

This tumultuous period has often been identified as a probable cause for Rembrandt's dramatic reduction in painterly output. However, given that some of his most remarkable prints were yet to be produced, one must consider that he simply shied away from the tribulations of demanding commissions in favour of more intimate, self-directed production. He was certainly still regarded as a giant of Dutch art, as proven by a visit from the Tuscan Prince Cosimo de' Medici – an art connoisseur – in 1667. What remains indisputable is that, by the time of his death in 1669, Rembrandt was practically destitute.

Evidence suggests that the artist's plates were spared repossession during his bankruptcy hearing in 1656, but they were most probably broken up after his passing, with at least 74 appearing in the estate of Clement de Jonghe, who was both his friend and a respected print dealer. By the eighteenth century, various plates were in the hands of French art dealers including Henri Louis Basan, who printed a limited series of new impressions, and later Alvin Beaumont, who followed suit. By this stage, the plates had endured considerable wear and the quality of the ensuing prints had diminished, thus the decision to continue to use them was met with some consternation. In a surprising resolution, and an ultimate testament to the beauty of these utilitarian objects, Beaumont submitted each plate to a final inking, before varnishing them. He then mounted each piece of copper on framed green leather and inscribed their titles in gold. In so doing, the history and tangible process of Rembrandt's print-making became quite literally etched in time.

CHAPTER 4

SATIRE AND SHADOWS

MEZZOTINT AND AQUATINT IN BRITAIN AND BEYOND

The whole operation, in the simplest manner, shows what lights and shades alone will do

– William Hogarth, 1753

AROUND THE MIDDLE of the seventeenth century, an artistically minded soldier stationed in the German countryside awoke one morning to find that droplets of dew had settled on his musket, rusting its barrel with an array of picturesque dots and patterns. He was so taken by this unusual phenomenon that he set about replicating the effect on copper, so it might be used to create atmospheric prints that were comprised entirely of gentle changes in tone.

This fanciful tale concerning the origins of mezzotint was contrived by Prince Rupert of the Rhine (1619–1682), son of the exiled king of Bohemia and an influential Royalist cavalry commander during the English Civil War. When not involved in military pursuits, he indulged his interest in the arts. He was a key proponent in bringing about the popularity of this innovation, despite keeping knowledge of its development among the gentry so that it might not be 'prostituted' on the open market. He regaled his story to the diarist John Evelyn, who in turn wrote that the prince had happily demonstrated the technique 'with his owne hands in the yeare 1661' and that it was 'the devise of a Comon Souldier in Germany'.[1]

There is some truth in this statement. Mezzotint's origins can be traced back to Ludwig von Siegen (*c*.1609–*c*.1680), an Utrecht-born soldier who enjoyed an aristocratic education, despite not being of noble birth. He pursued a successful military career alongside an amateur art practice in Amsterdam, and it is entirely possible – if not proven – that he met Prince Rupert while visiting the court of Emperor Ferdinand III in Vienna, in 1654.

What is indisputable is that the earliest known mezzotint is by Von Siegen's hand. It takes the form of a portrait of his patron, Amelia Elizabeth, the regent of the tiny German province of Hesse-Kassel (fig. 4.1). He sent the print to her son, William VI, with the following statement: 'There is not a single engraver, a single artist of any kind, who can account for, or guess how this work is done.'[2] Though rather stiff in execution, this print does indeed incorporate what was then an entirely novel form of printing. Every fold of fabric, every curl of hair, every facial crease is rendered from a delicate balance of light and shadow. The familiar line born from an engraved or etched incision is nowhere to be found.

Fittingly, the term mezzotint translates as 'half-tone' in Italian, alluding to this subtle gradation. Unlike other intaglio methods, this process is defined by drawing light out of darkness. The depth and texture are akin to the velvety black lines of drypoint, and the distinctive tonality makes it the natural bedfellow of painterly chiaroscuro, which it is often employed to replicate. It is no wonder that William Hogarth (1697–1764), in his authoritative treatise *The Analysis of Beauty* (1753), spoke of its alluring qualities a century after its invention:

> Could mezzo-tinto prints be wrought as accurately as those with the graver, they would come nearest to nature, because they are done without strokes or lines . . . as [the artist] proceeds in burnishing the lights, and clearing up the shades, he is obliged to take off frequent impressions to prove the progress of the work, so that each proof appears like the different times of a foggy morning, till one becomes so finished as to be distinct and clear enough to imitate a daylight piece. I have given this description, because I think the whole operation, in the simplest manner, shows what lights and shades alone will do.[3]

  THE STORY OF PRINTMAKING

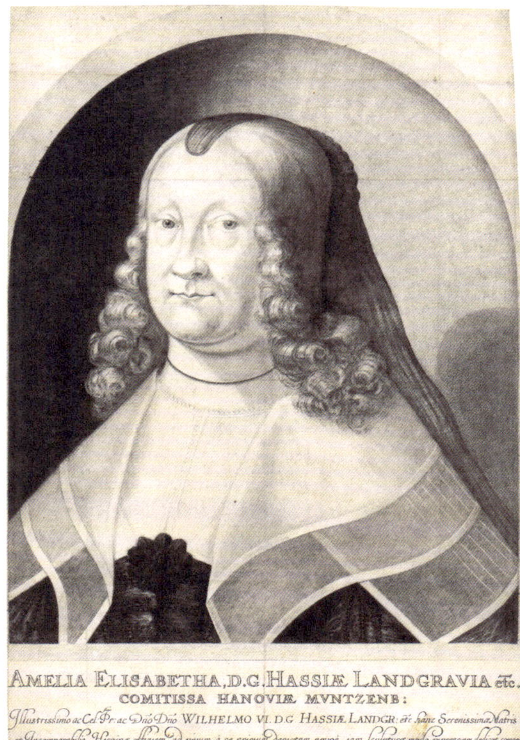

Fig. 4.1 Ludwig von Siegen, *Amelia Elizabeth, Landgravine of Hesse*, 1642. Mezzotint.

When embarking on a mezzotint, the preparation of the plate is the deciding factor. Engraving and etching demand a polished sheet of metal on which marks are incised, but mezzotint requires a textured surface. To begin, the plate is roughened by using a curved steel blade known as a 'rocker', so named because of the back-and-forth motion that is employed. Hundreds of delicate lines are cut into the surface at carefully calculated angles, until the plate has the quality of light-grade sandpaper. The work is laborious and repetitive, so it is no wonder that many contemporary artists choose to buy their plates mechanically pre-prepared.

The purpose of this intensive texturing is to create thousands of crevices, or 'teeth', that catch and hold on to the ink when it is transferred from plate to paper. If a print is pulled at this stage the result would be a rectangle of pitch black, akin to a starless sky. Coaxing an image out of this rough plate takes considerable patience. Using a series of specialist metal scrapers, including a textured cylinder known as a 'roulette', areas of mid-tones and light are gradually burnished away. The smoother the groove, the less ink it will hold, meaning that any area intended to be bright white must be polished completely flat. Reaching such a state can take weeks, as the teeth must be slowly and steadily worn down. Work too quickly, or with too much force, and the delicate textured surface could become damaged and produce unsightly smears when printed. Although a light touch is required, repetitive strain is still somewhat inevitable when administering thousands of individual scrapes.

Working in good light is also crucial, as the only way to perceive a design in progress is to find the perfect moment of refraction, thus revealing the subtleties of tone that are slowly being created. Unlike an engraving or etching, where the drawn design is visible on the plate, a mezzotint is nothing more than a ghost until it is printed.

In this technique, one need not worry about adulterating any chemical reactions with pigment. In fact, as Hogarth suggested, pulling a print midway through burnishing can be a valuable way to see how the tones are progressing, while the oiliness of residual

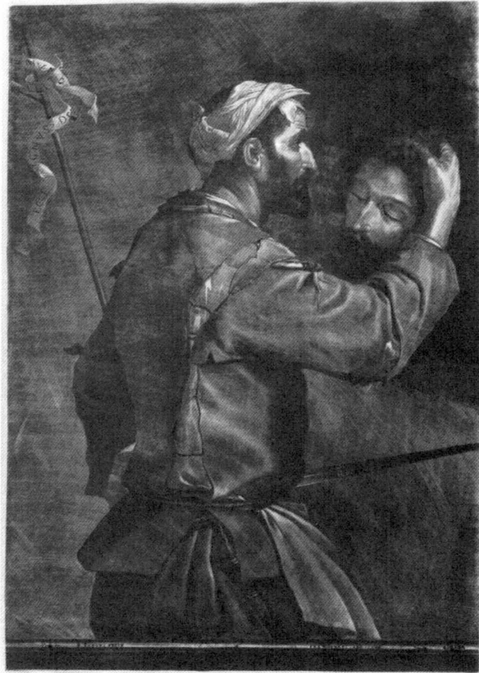

Fig. 4.2 Prince Rupert of the Rhine, *The Great Executioner with the Head of Saint John the Baptist*, 1658. Mezzotint with engraving.

THE STORY OF PRINTMAKING

ink can be useful when smoothing out particularly delicate areas. Just like any other intaglio process, the plate is passed through a roller press, leaving a deep indentation that frames the darkness.

* * *

As Von Siegen's invention became better known, technical innovations were swift. An early experiment by Prince Rupert, *The Great Executioner with the Head of Saint John the Baptist* (fig. 4.2), demonstrates the introduction of dynamic, sweeping marks drawn out of a heavily textured and methodically cut ground that he introduced and developed. However, his talents were arguably surpassed by his assistant Wallerant Vaillant (1623–1677), who commanded the atmospheric possibilities of the medium in domestic scenes such as *A Woman Peeling Pears* (*c.*1650) and the wonderfully eerie *Sculpture Bust of a Child, to the Right* (fig. 4.3).

The restoration of the monarchy in England in 1660 renewed a national obsession with portraiture, which was coupled with a print market that had thus far relied on imports from the continent. Certainly, the arrival of Dutch innovators such as Abraham

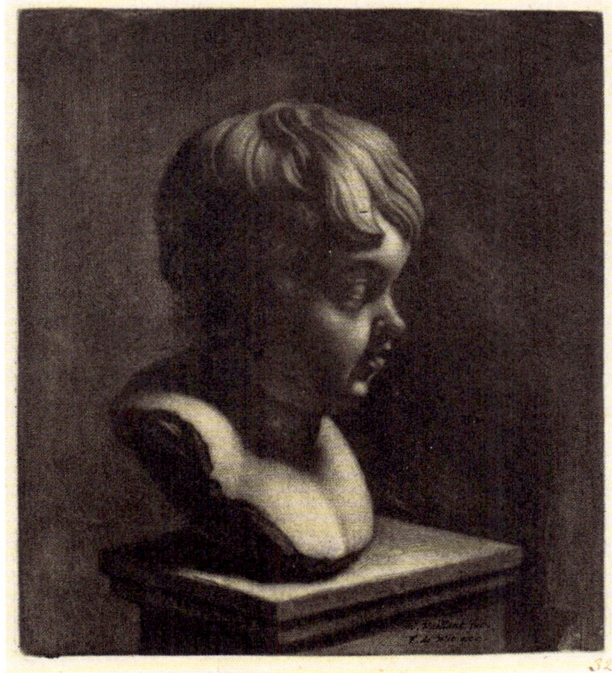

Fig. 4.3 Wallerant Vaillant, after François Du Quesnoy, *Sculpture Bust of a Child, to the Right, c.*1650. Mezzotint.

Blooteling (1640–1690) – who fled persecution once French troops invaded the Netherlands – was welcomed, while the most celebrated court painters of the period, including the Flemish expat Peter Lely (1618–1680) and his successor Gottfried Kniller (1646–1723), whose name was later anglicised from the German to Godfrey Kneller, saw mezzotint as a way of replicating the textural refinement of their works on canvas and furthering their public recognition. With the aid of master mezzo engravers such as Isaac Beckett (1653–1688) and his pupil John Smith (1652–1743), their images were disseminated both at home and abroad. The medium became synonymous with England – so much so that it was known by the moniker *la manière anglaise* (the English style).

Beyond its abilities to replicate oils, mezzotint's inherent darkness can be employed as a narrative device in and of itself. For example, in a depiction of a London fireworks celebration produced by Bernard Lens II (1659–1725), one can almost hear the violent crackle of the enormous bonfire casting light on the surrounding revellers, while rockets explode in bright, narrow arcs across the night sky. Subsequent artists commanded this nocturnal sensibility to equally astonishing effect. William Pether (*c.*1738–1821) and Valentine Green (1739–1813) both interpreted 'candlelight' paintings by Joseph Wright of Derby (1734–1797), as seen in *An Academy by Lamplight* (fig. 4.4) and *A Philosopher Shewing an Experiment on the Air Pump* (1769), which reconceive the original works in striking yet subtly executed monochrome.

* * *

Hogarth never used mezzotint, despite his aforementioned praise. The master of moral satire preferred the exacting line of engraving, which remained hugely popular in Georgian England. His 'Modern Moral Subjects' decried the frivolities of high society and were born out of an ever-increasing appetite for prints that reflected every element of contemporary life. The rise of a literate, affluent, urban middle class stoked a hunger for all kinds of printed media, including standalone images, pamphlets and newspapers. In fact, it is estimated that in 1750 annual newspaper circulations stood at some 7.3 million.[4]

Hogarth was informed by his own relatively impoverished childhood, which was largely the result of his father's all-consuming debts. The latter made an ill-fated investment in the form of a coffee

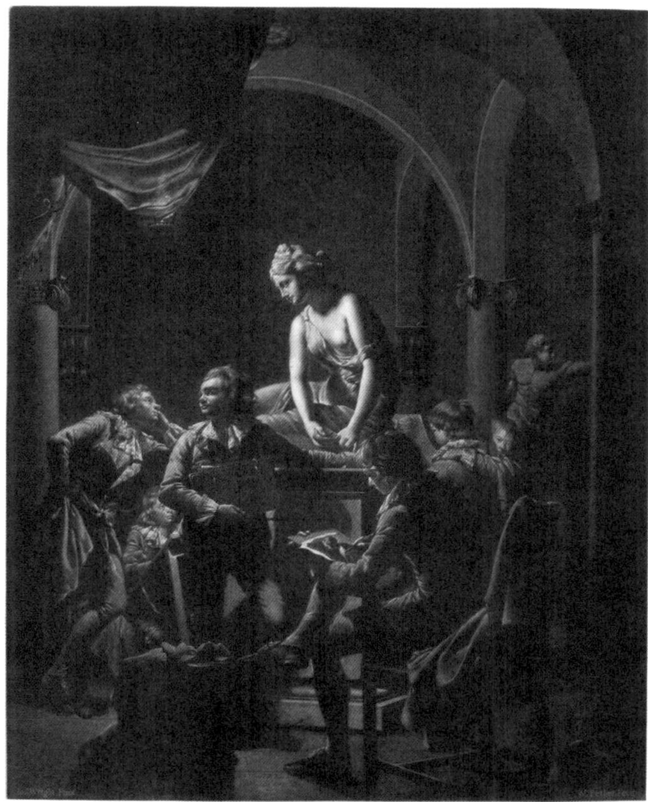

Fig. 4.4 William
Pether, after
Joseph Wright
of Derby, *An
Academy by
Lamplight*, 1772.
Mezzotint.

house that demanded patrons only speak Latin. Once it shuttered, he was unable to pay his creditors and spent time in the notorious Fleet Prison. With no opportunity to pursue the expensive path of a painting apprenticeship, the young Hogarth instead trained with a rather undistinguished silver plate engraver named Ellis Gamble (1712–1733).

A career as a jobbing tradesman might have followed, were it not for the promising artist's unrivalled tenacity. In April 1720, he set up his own enterprise, declaring himself as an engraver of prints. He produced coats of arms, trade cards and plates for booksellers, and used these funds to further his artistic study at the St Martin's Lane Academy (which he would later reform in 1735) and to take classes with the famed history painter James Thornhill (*c.*1675–1734).

As he honed these formal skills, Hogarth also worked on highly original engravings of his own design, which embodied a distinct blend of irreverent satire that was brimming with biting social commentary. In an early work from 1721, he skewers the blind speculation of the South Sea Bubble, which is widely regarded as the world's first financial crash. Gullible investors are depicted astride a carousel, seemingly unaware of the figures being whipped and pummelled below, who are accompanied by preachers and devilish creatures fighting for their souls. Three years later came *The Bad Taste of the Town (Masquerades and Operas)*, a rather unpatriotic indictment of English predilections for continental entertainments. A woman pushing a wheelbarrow of 'waste paper for shops' includes the works of Shakespeare.

These engraved (and partially etched) scenes enjoyed some modest success, but it was Hogarth's debut of an entirely fresh narrative format that truly made his name. In 1730, he set about producing six paintings that depicted the life and untimely death of a fictitious prostitute named Moll Hackabout. Ambitious in scope and

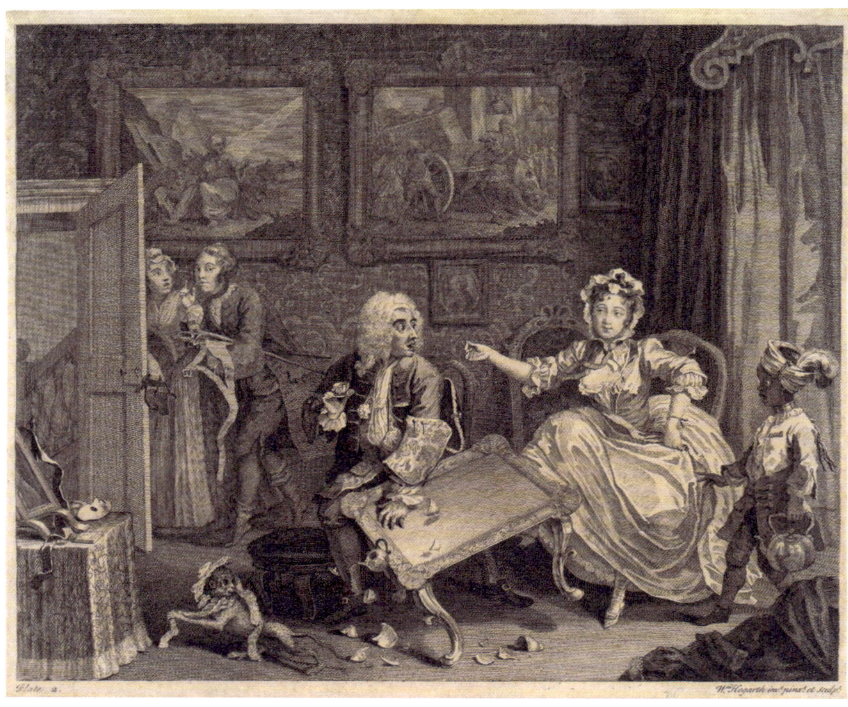

Fig. 4.5 William Hogarth, *A Harlot's Progress*,
Plate 2, 1732. Etching and engraving.

 THE STORY OF PRINTMAKING

undeniably theatrical, *A Harlot's Progress* introduced a moral yet salacious tale of a young woman's downfall, which was anchored in the realities of London life. These canvases were lost in a fire in 1755, but what remains are the exceptional engravings that Hogarth published as a commercially viable counterpart in 1732. The prints were sold as a set, using a straight-to-consumer subscription model that proved an unprecedented hit. In the words of his colleague, the artist George Vertue (1684–1756), it 'captivated the Minds of most People[,] persons of all ranks & conditions from the greatest Quality to the meanest'.[5]

It is clear to see why Hogarth's series proved so popular. Each iteration is packed with extensive narrative detail and symbolism, encompassing scandalous real-life figures among the imagined. In the first plate, Hackabout is presented as a beautiful yet naive country girl who arrives in the city, only to be ensnared by the notorious

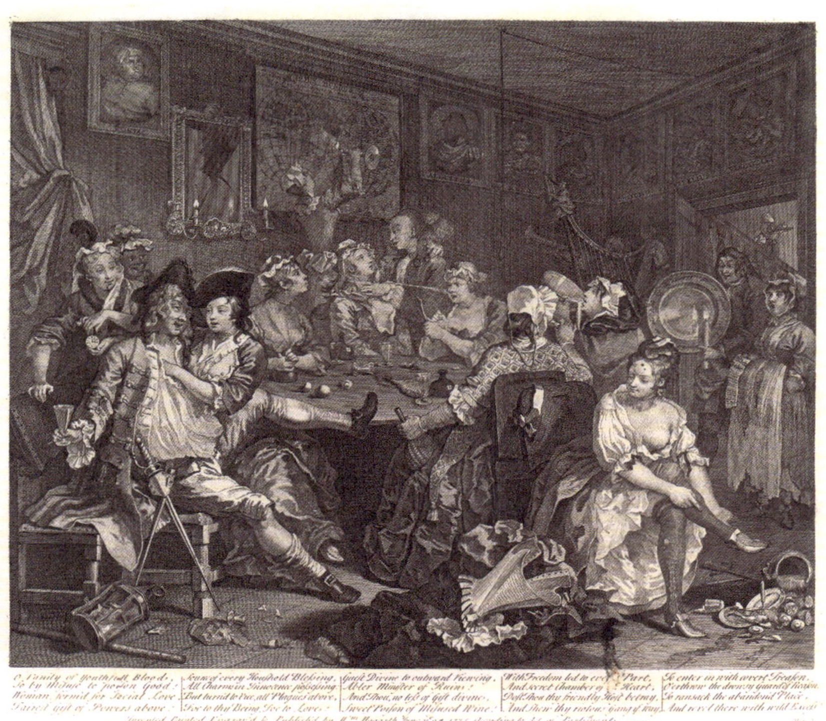

Fig. 4.6 William Hogarth, *A Rake's Progress*,
Plate 3, 1735. Etching and engraving.

real-life brothel keeper Elizabeth 'Mother' Needham, who died after being pelted with stones in the pillory at St James's in 1731. Behind her stands another infamous figure, holding a predatory gaze. Francis Charteris was an aristocrat convicted of raping his maidservant, Anne Bond, only to escape the death penalty following a highly controversial royal pardon.

The frenetic dynamism of Hogarth's lines and dots adds to the rhythm of his storytelling. In Plate 2 (fig. 4.5), dense cross-hatching and sweeping curves detail a luxurious living room replete with all of the trappings of a kept woman. The action centres around Hackabout, who kicks an ornate mahogany tea table in an effort to distract her visiting patron, while her young lover attempts his escape. On closer inspection, her surroundings reveal much about her life and the machinations of Georgian society. Two enormous pictures depicting Old Testament allegories of betrayal are hung against decorative wallpaper featuring an antler pattern – a nod to cuckoldry. The inclusion of a mirror and a mask alludes to this

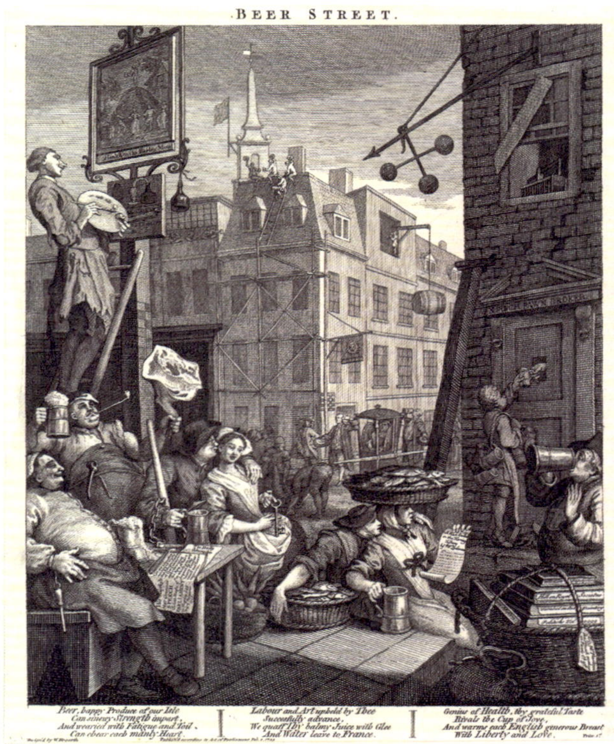

Fig. 4.7 William Hogarth, *Beer Street*, 1751. Etching and engraving.

THE STORY OF PRINTMAKING

young woman's perceived vanity and deception, but also her fashionable social life. More troubling associations come in the form of an exoticised Black pageboy, who is reduced to a mere symbol of colonial wealth and status.[6]

Hogarth capitalised on the success of this project with a sequel: *A Rake's Progress* (1734–5), this time presenting a roguish spendthrift named Tom Rakewell as the central protagonist, while relying heavily on the same sensational motifs (fig. 4.6). He created a fresh series of eight paintings and accompanying engravings, with an elaborate new marketing campaign to match. The price for this new set, to be paid in advance of completion, was one-and-a-half guineas. Hogarth warned his patrons that, once the subscription period was closed, the price would rise to two guineas, thus creating a scarcity market that foretells the introduction of 'editioning' in the mid-nineteenth century.

A numbered edition guarantees that only a limited amount of multiples are printed from a single plate. The lower the total, the

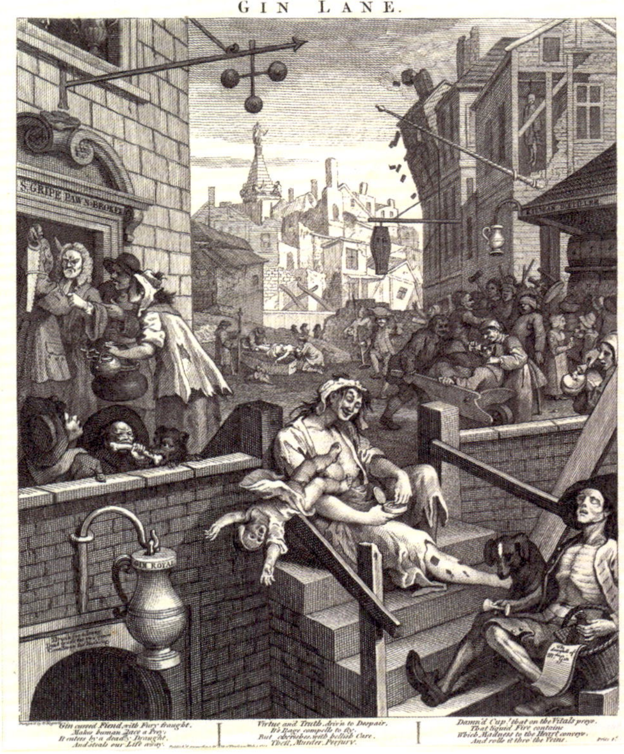

Fig. 4.8 William Hogarth, *Gin Lane*, 1751. Etching and engraving.

higher the value of each multiple, and nowadays most prints will have both these numbers pencilled in the margin of the paper, like a mathematics fraction. This system forms a valuable component of the print marketplace to this day, along with the concept of 'lifetime' impressions, which have proved much more desirable than 'late' versions produced after an artist's death. To prevent any later printing, a plate can be 'cancelled' by defacing it with deep scratches, punched holes or acid, thus destroying the image.

As one might expect, with Hogarth's success came rampant plagiarism, much like the unlicensed copying that befell Dürer centuries before (see p. 37). Pirated editions of *A Rake's Progress* (including a mezzotint series by Elisha Kirkall) were rife, much to the original artist's consternation. To combat this activity, he spearheaded a petition for the Engravers' Copyright Act of 1735 and delayed the publication of his much-anticipated sequel until the day the law was passed.

Despite this rather savvy business decision, other unscrupulous printmakers and publishers found ways to undercut Hogarth's enterprise. They sent spies into his workshop to view the unfinished paintings, claiming to be potential subscribers. They committed the pictures to memory and produced hurried sketches to inform their employers of the work at hand. As a result, unauthorised versions of this new *Progress* appeared on the open market days before the new copyright act came into law. Luckily for Hogarth, these pale emulations did little to temper sales, and might even have promoted his authentic engravings. Certainly, he continued to have great success with his moral scenes in the ensuing decades, not least the partner pieces known as *Beer Street* and *Gin Lane* (figs 4.7, 4.8). These comparative visions of degenerate alcoholism and genteel moderation were prompted by the Gin Act, which was designed to curtail the rampant production and distribution of the potent spirit that had become a scourge on society.

Once again, each print is teeming with symbolism and caricatured vignettes of modern life. In *Gin Lane* – surely Hogarth's most recognisable work – a haggard woman drops her baby from the steps, while, to her left, a deathly skeletal man clutches a bottle. Brawling men, a suicide, and even a skewered infant add to the sense of depravity. By contrast, the consumption of relatively weak beer is depicted as a respectable pursuit that promotes commerce, industry and artistry. The accompanying text extols the virtues of the beverage: 'Labour and Art upheld by Thee / Successfully advance, / We quaff Thy balmy Juice with Glee / And Water leave to France'. This patriotic rhyme alludes to the far-reaching conflict of the Seven Years' War, led by opposing alliances headed by Britain and Prussia, and fought across Europe, South Asia and the Americas. The original plate featured an enemy French soldier being hoisted by a cheery blacksmith. However, by its third state Hogarth had updated the design by adding a romantic sentiment, featuring a couple in an amorous embrace. The young woman receives a kiss from her lover and holds a large key, perhaps alluding to the benefits of a life enjoyed in moderation. The soldier, meanwhile, has been replaced by an enormous haunch of mutton.

The success of these prints was followed by *The Four Stages of Cruelty* (1751), another exercise in ethical instruction, which Hogarth released at two different price points. While his connoisseur collectors paid a similar fee to *A Rake's Progress*, and received impressions on fine paper, a less luxurious edition was made accessible to working people.

The great moral touchstones that Hogarth brought to life were both commercially and critically successful precisely because they mocked contemporary culture. His recognisable themes, famous faces and familiar streets were relatable and thus appealing to a wide audience, who could revel in their erudite irreverence while recognising an element of themselves. The inherent humour that permeates Hogarth's work set the stage for a golden age of British political cartooning that flourished at the end of the eighteenth century and became a true fixture of social commentary and public entertainment. The boom was driven by a prosperous urban society that continued to reap the rewards of imperialism and industrialisation, while the threat of political instability abroad increased an interest in global current affairs.

London's West End was the epicentre of artistic production, where hundreds of print shops created, displayed and sold single sheets that were engraved or etched, and hand-coloured by teams of specialists. Gathering around this fashionable, well-heeled district were publishers such as Samuel William Fores, whose business on the corner of Sackville Street and Piccadilly was deemed a 'caricature warehouse'. William Holland, meanwhile, delighted patrons when he opened an establishment dubbed the Museum of Graphic Genius, at 50 Oxford Street, in 1788.

The actual purchasing of prints remained out of reach for most everyday workers, but passers-by could crowd at these shop windows to take in the latest in topical satire. The genre was dominated by James Gillray (1756–1815) and Thomas Rowlandson (1757–1827), both of whom were published by Fores and Holland. These artists mocked the perceived excesses and exploits of the ruling elite by incorporating comically distorted features and ingenious symbolism. The misdemeanours of the Prince Regent (later George IV) and dealings of political figures, including the statesmen William Pitt, Charles James Fox and Emperor Napoleon Bonaparte, were favourite subjects. For example, in *The Plumb-pudding in Danger* (fig. 4.9), one of Gillray's most celebrated prints, the world is envisaged as a steaming dessert that is carved up by Pitt and a classically diminutive Napoleon (he was actually of average height). Indeed, it has been said that, while banished on the island of Elba, the exiled

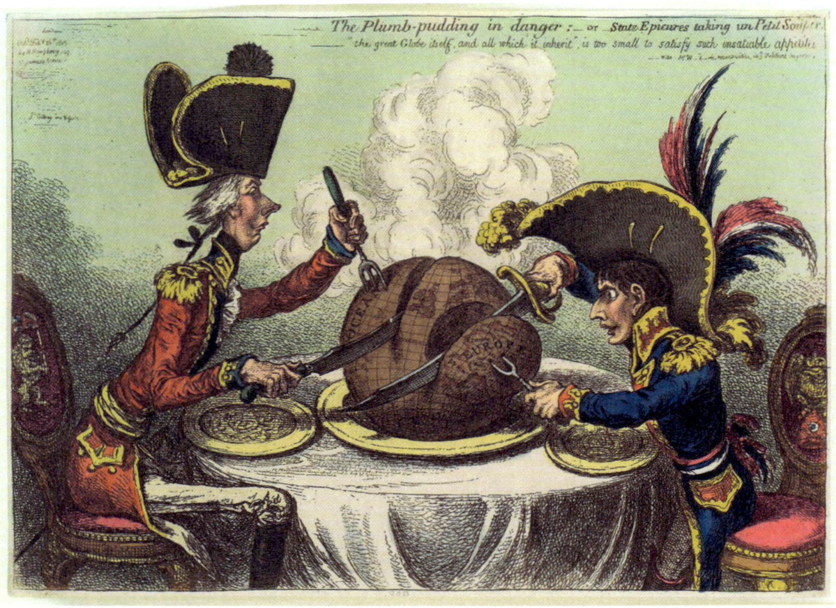

Fig. 4.9 James Gillray, *The Plumb-pudding in Danger*, published by Hannah Humphrey, 1805. Hand-coloured etching and engraving.

 THE STORY OF PRINTMAKING

French ruler declared that Gillray's depictions of him did more damage than a dozen generals.[7]

Nestled at the top of this composition is an accompanying caption that reads 'the great Globe itself, and all which it inherit, is too small to satisfy such insatiable appetites'. Such supplementary texts, which often featured speech bubbles, predate comic books as we know them today and mark the incoming vogue for illustrated periodicals and caricature magazines such as *Punch*, which was first published in 1841. These lines often incorporated witty puns, befitting content which was at times salacious and bawdy.

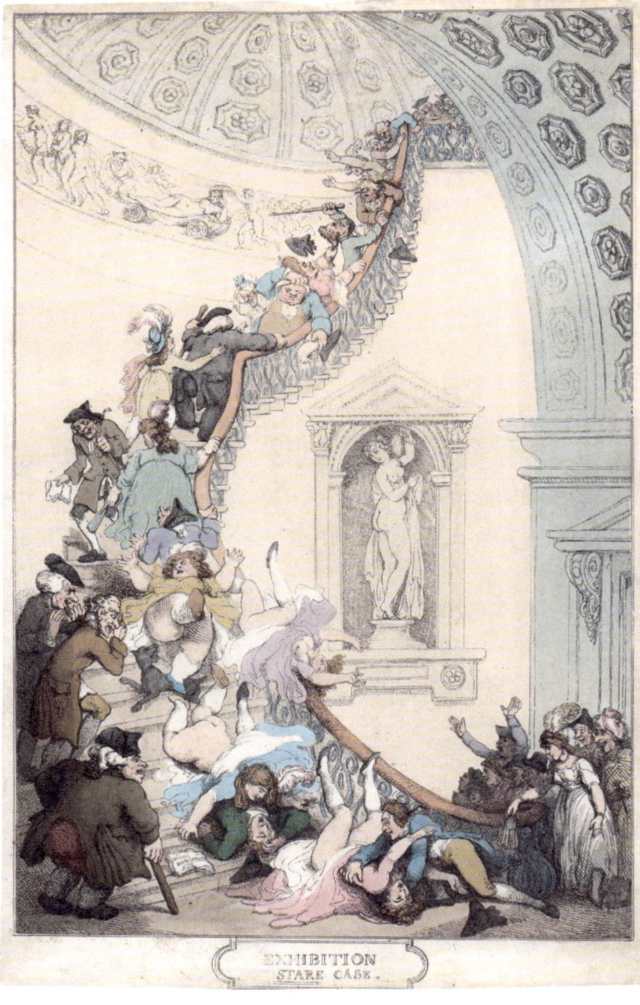

Fig. 4.10 Thomas Rowlandson, *Exhibition Stare Case*, *c*.1811. Hand-coloured etching.

Take *Exhibition Stare Case* (fig. 4.10) by Rowlandson, a brilliant and faintly ridiculous interpretation of the Royal Academy's spring exhibition crowds, who negotiate the steep climb with disastrous consequences. The title's double entendre alludes to society's desire to see and be seen in fashionable settings, while the upended and exposed bodies reference the prevalent nudity found in works of art, which are admired elsewhere.

The context of these satires reveals the social standing of the audiences for which they were intended. Well-heeled readers would have been versed in the political and cultural machinations of the day, and thus able to decode the various symbolisms these artists employed. Far from causing insult, appearing in a caricature was akin to achieving celebrity status, and printers and publishers were often feted by those they ridiculed. This was the case for Hannah Humphrey (*c.*1745–1818), who was one of the most influential publishers of the day. Letters to her shop assistant, Betty Marshall, recall exchanging pleasantries with noblemen while holidaying in Brighton, while other accounts claim Fox entered her establishment personally, to buy copies of Gillray's 1798 work, *The Loyal Toast*. Even the prince himself was a patron. He took out a standing order with Humphrey in 1803, so that he might keep abreast of public opinion, while also buying out complete print runs and original plates to stifle his most unflattering commentary.

Humphrey was undoubtedly an outlier in satirical publishing. Although she was not the only woman in the trade (others include Mary Darly, an early satirist in business with her husband Matthias), most were married or widows, whereas Humphrey preferred to stay single. She also broke from the conventional shop model, which relied heavily on republishing plates by Old Masters, as well as selling sundries including maps, pamphlets, books and stationery. By contrast, Humphrey only sold prints that she had produced, and she became the exclusive publisher of Gillray from 1791.

This rather risky endeavour proved hugely profitable, bolstered in part by the pair's unusual working arrangement. Rather than following the customary business model, in which an artist-printmaker received a fee for a design and a publisher dealt with many upfront costs in exchange for receipt of the final profits, this relationship was more symbiotic. Gillray moved into Humphrey's home in 1793,

THE STORY OF PRINTMAKING

with no evidence of a romance despite an obvious mutual affection. This allowed the artist to concentrate solely on his rapid production of roughly one caricature a week, without interruption, while also receiving support during episodes of poor mental health. Further evidence from ledgers and dockets shows that Gillray had a stake in the shop itself, and was often responsible for its day-to-day running when Humphrey and Marshall were absent.

The satirical publishing industry dominated popular prints of the late Georgian period, at a time when the relationship between print-maker and publisher was deemed valuable and collaborative, at least when it came to the most popular – and therefore powerful – artists. Publishers' names often appeared prominently in prints (as is the case for Humphrey in *Plumb-pudding*), and the famed shops were occasionally subjects in and of themselves. A view of Fores's estab-lishment, for example, features in *Folkstone Strawberries* (1810), attributed to the brothers George (1792–1878) and Isaac Robert Cruikshank (1789–1856), and Gillray's *Very Slippy Weather* (fig. 4.11)

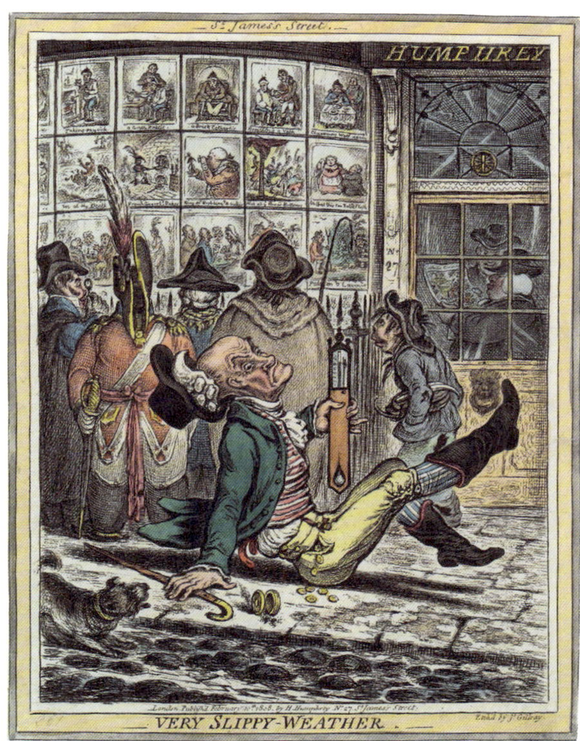

Fig. 4.11 James Gillray, *Very Slippy Weather*, published by Hannah Humphrey, 1808. Hand-coloured etching and engraving.

presents the abundant and illustriously decorated Humphrey store as the backdrop to the comic action.

It seems astonishing, then, that just down the road from the bustling enterprises that populated Piccadilly and St Martin's Lane, an ingenious yet isolated avant-garde printing practice was taking shape, thanks to the experimentation of a unique yet often misunderstood artist, who became a towering figure of British art.

* * *

William Blake (1757–1827) has been described as the first modern artist, calcifying the idea of a singular, inspired genius who works in relative isolation. He was an early titan of Romanticism and an unparalleled printmaker, whose exceptional individualism and creative anachronism were largely overlooked but occasionally ridiculed during his lifetime. His complete unification of poetry and pictures was informed by celestial visions and idiosyncratic theology, which manifested in immensely detailed, labour-intensive printed books. Despite the absolute impossibility of these unique volumes reaching the masses, he believed that a universal appreciation of art could lead to a path of divine redemption.

Blake led a relatively comfortable middle-class existence thanks to the financial assistance of his family, who ran a hosiery shop and haberdashers at 28 Broad Street, in the heart of London's Soho. Apart from a brief sojourn in Sussex, the artist spent his entire life in the city, and lived alongside a cosmopolitan mix of people, from cabinet makers and painters to physicians and clergymen. He attended drawing classes at the nearby Royal Academy and apprenticed to the engraver James Basire (1730–1802), who specialised in fashionable antiquarian subjects.

This relatively conservative training was befitting for a young man of considerable artistic talents who was in need of a respectable trade. He soon set up shop as an engraver and printer, taking on a range of subjects for the influential political publisher Joseph Johnson, who printed the writings of William Godwin, Erasmus Darwin, Anna Laetitia Barbauld and more. Among Blake's commissions was a frontispiece for feminist philosopher Mary Wollstonecraft's text, *Original Stories from Real Life* (1791).

Although this work was progressive in content, the formal qualities of the illustrations were not particularly groundbreaking, and they relay nothing of Blake's truly independent work. Alongside his day job, he developed a mysterious and confounding form of relief etching that combined text and image, while emulating the hand-wrought, medieval illuminated manuscripts that he so deeply admired.

Unlike traditional intaglio practice, Blake used stop-out varnish on a copper plate as one would a paintbrush on paper,[8] both drawing and writing in perfect mirror image. He then built a wax frame around the metal, before filling it with a layer of nitric acid. This allowed the mordant to eat away at the copper, thus creating a plate that was more akin to a chiselled woodcut, where the final design was presented in relief.

Blake's wife Catherine (*c*.1762–1831) played a considerable role in the workshop. Beyond her financial management and record keeping, she often assisted and was occasionally entirely responsible for inking. The Blake palette consisted of limited shades, including Yellow Ochre, Prussian Blue and Madder Lake. A leather dabber and a little linseed oil were used to colour-mix, before applying the concoction to the plate in gentle daubs and running it through a roller press. The result was truly luxurious painterly impressions that feature a textured surface, in which dark mottled shades reveal lighter tones beneath. Colours were often tweaked or completely reworked in subsequent impressions, with additions made in watercolour and even touches of gold.

In his earliest illuminated series, 'Songs of Innocence and of Experience' (1789 and 1794) (fig. 4.12), Blake's looping script appears like bronze lettering against an amalgam of hand-applied watercolour, befitting the dreamlike pastoral setting. Flora, clouds and even entire human figures twist through lines of text in a manner that would have been completely impossible in conventional printing, where letterpress text was printed in blocks, before intaglio images were inserted into dedicated portions of white space.

No one is quite sure how Blake came upon his relief invention. While not entirely novel (there is evidence of Renaissance etchers trying similar techniques), it was by no means commonplace or particularly useful for commercial printers working in considerable volume. Blake stated that the technique was relayed to him by the spirit of his deceased brother, Robert.[9] More likely, he simply built on his experimental capabilities as a seasoned etcher. What is clear is

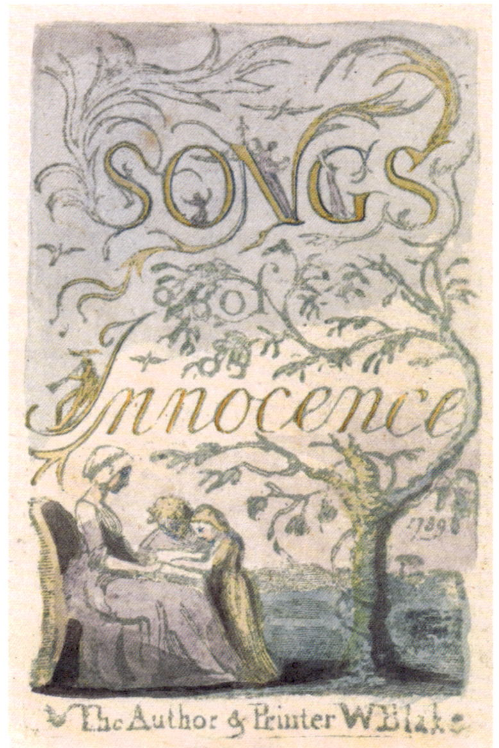

Fig. 4.12 William Blake, 'Songs of Innocence' title page, 1789. Colour-printed relief etching with watercolour.

that the artist considered his illuminated printing process to be just as significant as the final output. In fact, he viewed this caustic world of acids as an allegory for divine transcendence. In *The Marriage of Heaven and Hell* (*c*.1790), of which only nine completed books were ever recorded, Blake wrote:

> But first the notion that man has a body distinct from his soul, is to be expunged; this I shall do, by printing in the infernal method, by corrosives, which in Hell are salutary and medicinal, melting apparent surfaces away, and displaying the infinite which was hid.[10]

Beyond the creative impulse of melding two forms of artistic expression, this technique also allowed William and Catherine Blake to exert complete control over production. According to Alexander Gilchrist, who wrote a biography of the artist in 1863, 'the poet and his wife did everything in making the book – writing, designing,

   THE STORY OF PRINTMAKING

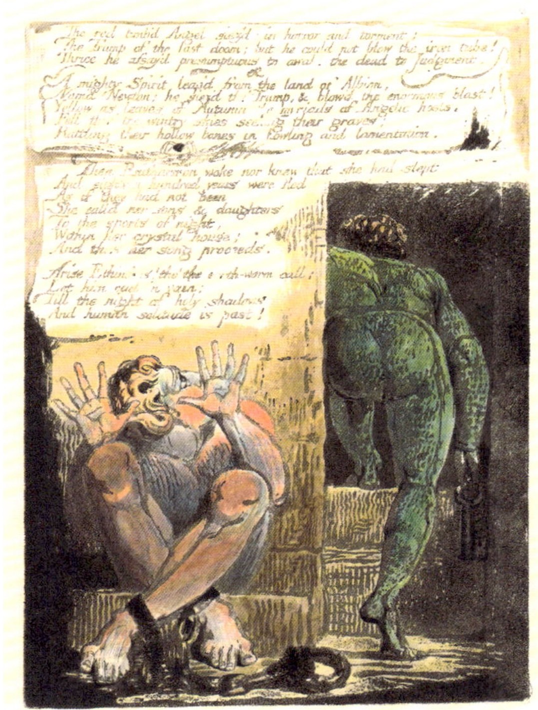

Fig. 4.13 William Blake, *The red limb'd Angel siez'd in horror and torment . . .*, from *Europe. A Prophecy*, 1794. Colour-printed relief etching with oil, watercolour, pen and ink.

printing, engraving – everything except manufacturing the paper; the very ink, or colour rather, they did make'.[11] Such authority shielded them from possible censorship, particularly as Blake embarked on his oracular texts: *America. A Prophecy* (1793), *Europe. A Prophecy* (fig. 4.13), and his epic vision of 'dark Satanic Mills' in *Jerusalem: The Emanation of The Giant Albion* (fig. 4.14).

These books responded to the social and political upheaval of the time, from the urban destruction that was befalling Blake's immediate surroundings at the hands of rapid industrialisation, to the conflicts that arose from revolutions in the soon-to-be-christened United States and in France. British authorities were particularly fearful of an uprising on home soil, as well as the possibility of a Napoleonic naval invasion. In fact, shortly before completing *Jerusalem*, Blake was acquitted on charges of sedition, not for his art, but for supposedly exclaiming 'Damn the King!' in the presence of two soldiers.

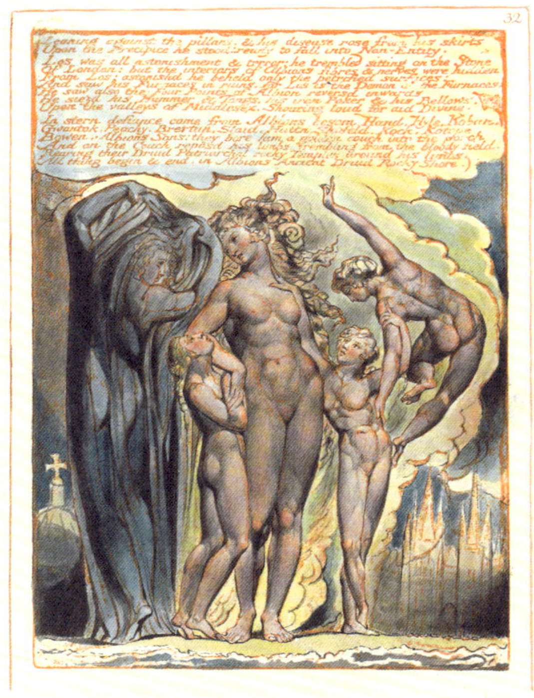

Fig. 4.14 William Blake, *Leaning against the pillars . . .*, from *Jerusalem: The Emanation of The Giant Albion*, 1804–20. Colour-printed relief etching with watercolour, pen and ink.

These breathtaking volumes are filled with tormented souls and transcendent spirits, where raging fires in shades of dark and muddied red singe taut, rippling flesh, or else envelop inky blue skies. They are both glorious and terrifying, embodying frenzied chaos and religious devotion in a manner that feels utterly arcane.

Blake was an artist who seemed to emanate from another time and place. Throughout his life, his work was predominantly bought by collectors of eccentricities, including incunabula (early printed books), who revelled in the perceived 'madness' of their creator. In his disastrous self-mounted show in 1809, Blake was lambasted by critics and failed to sell a single work. Nevertheless, he embodied the reflexive individualism and emotive drama that typified the Romantic period, and he continues to inspire artists to this day. His unwavering conviction has garnered him legions of admirers across the centuries, and the moral underpinnings of his work, along with a steadfast patriotism, held far-reaching influence particularly on the cultural timbre of the ensuing Victorian era.

Shades of these sensibilities are found in the work of another print-maker, Gustave Doré (1832–1883), who produced some of the most enduring images of Dickensian London despite his foreign status as a Frenchman. His success began in Paris, thanks to his exquisite wood engravings that illustrated everything from Dante's *Inferno* to the Bible. This rather confusingly named technique is actually a distinct form of woodblock printing, in which a hard wood is cut across the end grain and carved with a steel rod known as a 'graver'. The close grain of the wood allows the cutter to produce extremely fine lines and to work with the natural pattern of the material. This abundant detail made the medium a popular choice for book illustration, where images were often small-scale, and were produced in increasingly larger runs.

In Doré's hands, a finely articulated mesh of quivering lines might present the macabre outlines of a Satanic council; or the leathery, blackened wings of a devil in flight; or the shadowy recesses of a forgotten prison, all distilled in a manner befitting a diminutive and bound printed page. His prolific output was well documented, and an article in the New York arts journal *The Aldine Press* stated that '[h]e must have exhausted wood enough to have built a temple'.[12]

It was for precisely these reasons that the English journalist Blanchard Jerrold (1826–1884) approached Doré in 1869. He needed an illustrator of considerable acclaim, up to the task of visualising his multifaceted portrait of London. This narrative genre had already proved fortuitous for Rowlandson, whose plates for Augustus Pugin's architecturally minded *Microcosm of London* (1808) were teeming with human life. While these images are joyous in their vibrant colour, Jerrold required an aesthetic that reflected tensions of an industrialised age, in which the luxuries enjoyed by affluent society were at odds with the poverty endured by those worn down by a lifetime of relentless labour.

The resulting title, *London: A Pilgrimage*, was finally published in 1872, following four years of site-specific study from Jerrold, and the enlisting of a ready team of engravers to cut the blocks onto which Doré painted directly. When leafing through a paperback copy, the way both author and artist intended, the reader discovers that each of the 180 engravings is wrought from tightly inscribed marks that depict the fevered pace of life in the city.[13] Densely packed tenements stretch across never-ending streets, cloaked in smoke

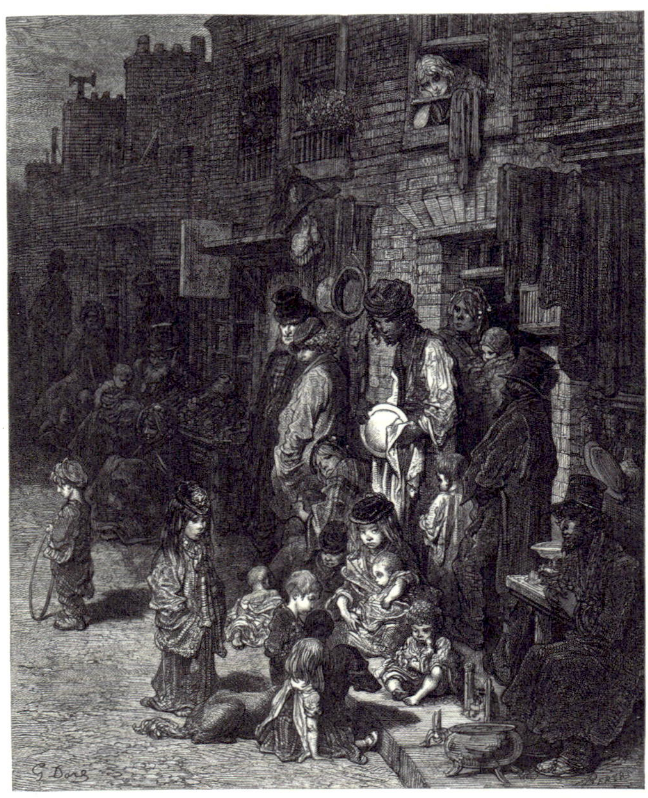

Fig. 4.15 Gustave Doré, *Wentworth Street, Whitechapel*, from *London: A Pilgrimage*, printed by Antoine Valérie Bertrand and published by Grant & Co., 1872. Wood engraving.

belched from trains and factories. Traders, shoppers and thieves jostle among the arches of Billingsgate market, illuminated by gas lights. Destitute families huddle by the roadside in Whitechapel, dressed in rags and clutching tired, despondent children (fig. 4.15). In every scene, regardless of the ascribed hour, there is an inherent darkness, which either creeps among the shadows or threatens to swallow the picture whole.

∗ ∗ ∗

Despite all the developments in tonal printmaking discussed thus far, there is one significant example yet to be explored. Aquatint is probably the most popular and commonly used technique when it comes

   THE STORY OF PRINTMAKING

to creating painterly, tonal effects. Much like mezzotint, it produces gradations as opposed to lines, but offers a semi-translucent effect more akin to watercolour. Its origins can be traced to an Amsterdam printmaker, Jan van de Velde IV (*c*.1593–1641), but the process was widely forgotten in favour of its mezzo rival until the latter part of the eighteenth century, when the French etcher Jean-Baptiste Le Prince (1734–1781) popularised the medium in fashionable Parisian circles.

Aquatint is a form of etching, and it is often used in conjunction with the established line technique. The process comprises of dusting a fine powder, known as 'rosin' (traditionally formed from concentrated pine tree sap), onto the printing plate. Though newer innovations have led to less carcinogenic and explosive substances, inhaling them in any quantity can lead to respiratory problems. Therefore, one must don a mask and protective eyewear before approaching the bespoke aquatint box that is used to contain the dust. Once precautions are in place, an external handle attached to a paddle is spun vigorously to produce a cloud of particles, which then settle on the plate within the box to produce a fine film, not unlike a cake dusted with icing. (It is worth noting that a masterful printmaker might prefer to forgo the box and use a hand-shaker.) The plate is then subjected to extreme heat (often via an open flame) so that the rosin particles fuse to its surface. This will protect areas of the plate from the effects of the acid bath. The result is a densely speckled grain that creates an illusion of painterly shade. It can be masked with stop-out and re-bitten, to produce increasingly dark areas.

The earliest expressions of this medium closely mimicked the formal qualities of the watercolourist's brush. In Le Prince's 1768 print *The Washerwomen* (fig. 4.16), both the gathering clouds and the shadowy forest are articulated in gentle tonal washes, as are the creases of each woman's dress. In a traditional line etching such contours would be rendered through close cross-hatching, but this technique offers a much subtler way of producing convincing depth.

Alongside a fondness for mezzotint, English etchers began to utilise aquatint, and often employed it with such skill that it might seem indistinguishable from the former. In *Two Boys Blowing a Bladder by Candle-light*, Peter Perez Burdett (*c*.1735–1793) reimagines another Joseph Wright of Derby scene (fig. 4.17). Although slightly crude in its execution, this strange illuminated picture is believed

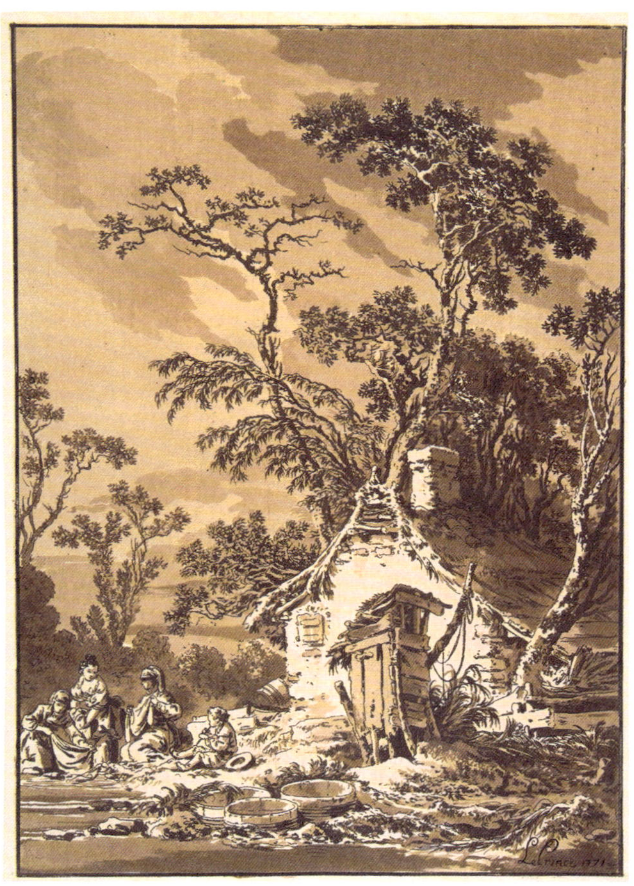

Fig. 4.16 Jean-Baptiste Le Prince, *The Washerwomen*,
1771. Etching and aquatint.

to be the first 'pure' aquatint in Britain, because it does not feature any line work. It was followed by prints by the likes of Thomas Gainsborough (1727–1788) and Paul Sandby (*c*.1730–1809), who perfected his own technique for a liquid rosin that was dissolved in spirits and could thus be applied with a brush.

Although aquatint gained considerable popularity across France, Britain and beyond, there is one artist who harnessed the possibilities of the medium like no other: Francisco de Goya (1746–1828). The painter and printmaker is heralded as one of the greatest Spanish artists ever to have lived, and his seismic influence still reverberates through print workshops and artist studios.

 THE STORY OF PRINTMAKING

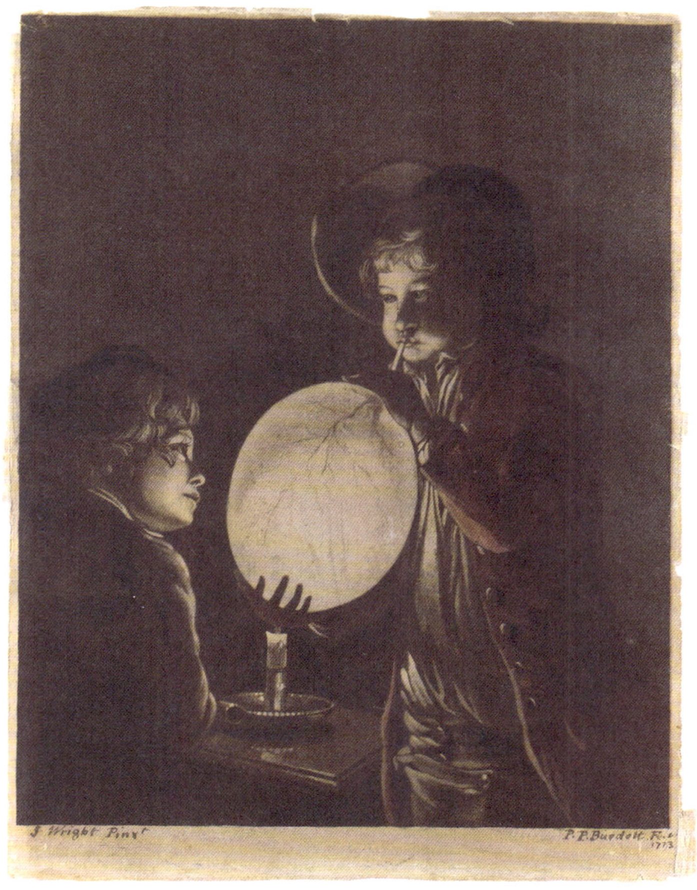

Fig. 4.17 Peter Perez Burdett, after Joseph Wright of Derby,
Two Boys Blowing a Bladder by Candle-light, 1773. Aquatint.

Born in Fuendetodos, and later spending his teenage years in
the more cosmopolitan city of Zaragoza, Goya began nurturing his
artistic talents as an apprentice to the painter José Luzán Martínez
(1710–1785), who is known for his Baroque religious scenes. Later,
Goya joined with brothers Francisco (1734–1795) and Ramón Bayeu
y Subías (1744–1793) at a painting studio in Madrid, which paved
the way for introductions to the royal court. His first commission
was working on preparatory designs for the Royal Tapestry Factory
in Santa Bárbara, specifically a work known as *The Blind Guitarist*
(1778) which was destined for a bedchamber in the Royal Palace
of El Pardo. However, his drafts proved too complicated for the

frustrated weavers, and they returned his work with demands that it be simplified. Before making any changes, he recorded the piece as a large-scale line etching, which never seems to have been printed as an edition. Only a few impressions, including one at the Metropolitan Museum of Art in New York, have ever been recorded.

This rather personal approach to etching would stay with Goya throughout his life, even as the content and context of his work radically shifted. He lived through a period of immense change that brought about an entirely new social order, first through the relatively enlightened ideals of the Bourbon king Charles III and his successor, Charles IV, and then through the brutal conditions of Napoleonic occupation.

Goya's survivalist approach saw him pledge fidelity to various powers, including Joseph Bonaparte (who was ejected following the fall of his brother) and the new Bourbon ruler Ferdinand VII, who took the throne in 1814. This monarch shared none of his forebears' liberal views and instead reinstated the Inquisition, beginning a new reign of terror. Goya demonstrated his allegiance with politically motivated paintings, such as *The Third of May 1808* and the rather more conventional companion piece *The Second of May 1808*, which were both produced in 1814 to commemorate resistance forces. However, it is in his etchings that he truly confronts the physical and psychological torments of his fellow man.

Among his earliest and best-known series is 'Los Caprichos' ('The Fantasies'; 1797–8), a suite of 80 aquatints published in 1799, although it had little commercial success. The title is born from the artist's travels in Italy, where he encountered the *capriccio* style favoured by the likes of Giovanni Battista Tiepolo (1696–1770) and Giovanni Battista Piranesi (1720–1778). It champions imagination and fantasy as a way to demonstrate artistic skill, as opposed to an adherence to realism. Although these Italian artists embraced crumbling ruins and imagined landscapes, Goya reinterpreted the genre as a form of dream-infused satire, where the ills of society – from vice and deceit to witchcraft and superstition – are remonstrated against through comical yet disturbing imagery. In *Here Comes the Bogeyman*, for example, a shrouded figure strikes terror into two shrieking children, while their mother looks faintly amused. This allusion to poor education possibly includes a reference to the presence of the mother's

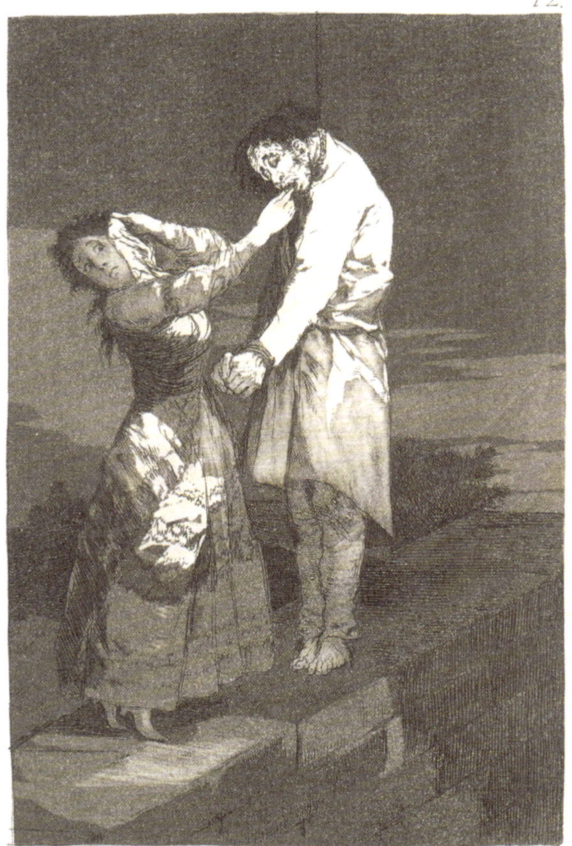

Fig. 4.18 Francisco de Goya, *A Hunt for Teeth*, from
the series 'Los Caprichos', 1799. Etching and aquatint.

illicit lover.[14] By contrast, in *A Hunt for Teeth* (fig. 4.18) the artist
decries both misinformation and sorcery, which is crystallised in a
horrifying image of a young woman pulling teeth from a hanged man.

Perhaps the most famous print in the series, however, is *The Sleep
of Reason Produces Monsters* (fig. 4.19), a semi-autobiographical
image that presents a man slumped at his desk and besieged by
macabre visions. By this time, Goya had largely retired from polite
society following a near-fatal illness that had left him profoundly

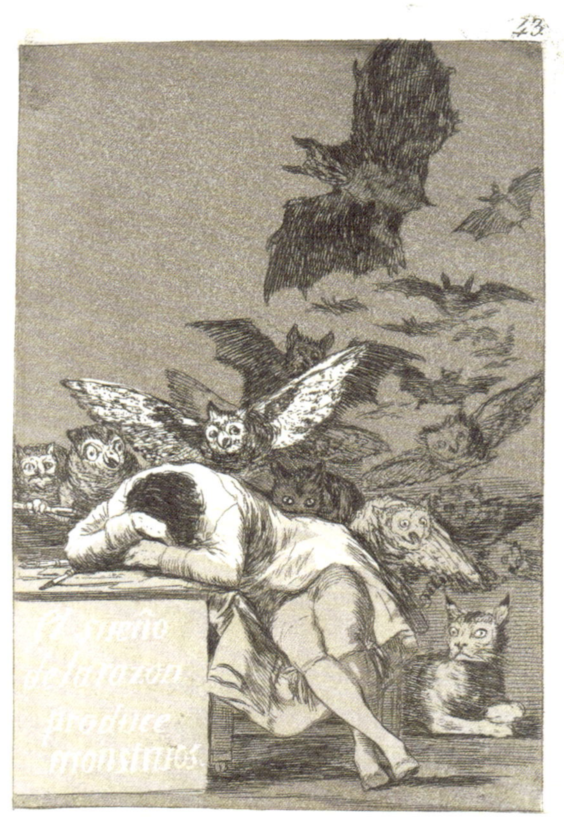

Fig. 4.19 Francisco de Goya, *The Sleep of Reason Produces Monsters*, from the series 'Los Caprichos', 1799. Etching and aquatint.

deaf. The technical proficiency employed here – where a balance of deftly sketched lines reveals each gathering creature that emerges from the shadows – demonstrates the artist's exceptional abilities in both aquatint and line, but also his own isolated emotional state. Although the crux of the work is believed to express the invasion of ignorance and evil when reason is ignored, it has become a broader emblem of mental distress that still holds contemporary relevance.

The inclusion of witty titles, which appeared alongside or else embedded into each plate, has ties with the political cartooning of Hogarth and the Georgian satirists, yet Goya was working in an entirely different landscape. Spanish artists had failed to take up printing with the fervour of their European counterparts, and there was no real printmaking industry in the country. Much of Goya's own exposure to the great printers of art history was through the collection of his friend, the art critic Juan Agustín Ceán Bermúdez (1749–1829), who owned works by Dürer and Parmigianino. He even gifted Goya several pieces by Rembrandt. The lack of any contemporary market was caused in no small part by the rampant censorship that still dominated Spanish society. In fact, Goya prefaced the publication of 'Los Caprichos' with a qualifying statement in the *Diario de Madrid* on 6 February 1799:

> Collection of prints of whimsical subjects, invented and etched by Don Francisco de Goya . . . he has selected from the multitude of stupidities and errors common to every civil society, and from the ordinary obfuscations and lies condoned by custom, ignorance, or self-interest, those he has deemed most fit to furnish material for ridicule, and at the same time to exercise the author's imagination.[15]

He presses the point that these are fictitious analogies, to protect himself from accusations of caricaturing any particular individual. The consequences for offending those in power could be ruinous and, in some cases, even fatal. The realities of this threat are also evident in Goya's later series, 'The Disasters of War' (1810–20). These visceral responses to Napoleonic invasion and the oppressive rules that followed completely upend the prevailing narratives of conflict. In place of grandiose battle scenes and noble deeds are horrifyingly intimate renderings of grisly murder, rape, famine and torture. In *And They Are Like Wild Beasts* (fig. 4.20), the usual language of heroism is eschewed in favour of violent desperation, as women confront soldiers with every weapon at their disposal. Among the crowd, a figure shrouded in aquatint grain lifts a rock above her head, while in front of her, a mother grasps her infant and skewers her attacker with a spear. Furthermore, the utter despair evident in *Bury Them and Keep Them Quiet*, which shows a couple sobbing among a pile of naked corpses, is compounded by the sickening depravity presented in *This Is Worse* (fig. 4.21). Experts have deliberated on whether Goya witnessed this mutilated body impaled on a tree first hand, due to the presence of an inscription on a trial proof, which reads 'The one at Chinchón'.[16]

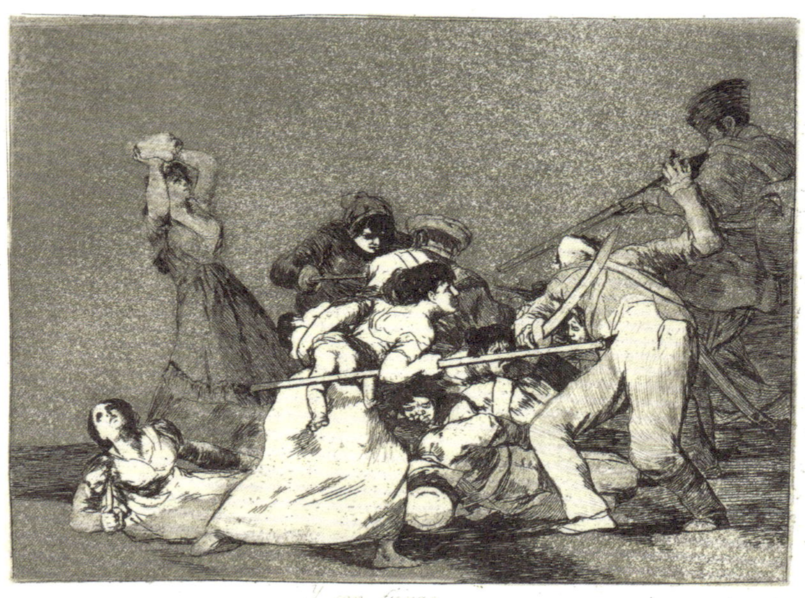

Fig. 4.20 Francisco de Goya, *And They Are Like Wild Beasts*, from the series 'The Disasters of War', 1810 (published 1863). Etching, drypoint and aquatint.

The disturbing nature of these etchings deemed them too dangerous to be published during the artist's lifetime, such was the potency of the condemnation. They only reached the eyes of the public some 35 years after his death, when his son took the plates to the Royal Academy of Fine Arts of San Fernando. While the images evidently speak to the experiences of a particular time and place, they also hold a more universal value that underscores the darker machinations of human existence. Goya's depictions gave voice to unspeakable cruelty and sorrow, but also resilience and fortitude, doing away with the binary codes of heroes and villains in favour of a murkier reality.

By imbuing his prints with a subjective and emotive anguish, Goya reflected a broad change in European attitudes and a reimagining of the social order that reached a crescendo at the tail end of the nineteenth century, heralding the dawn of the so-called 'modern' era. Ultimately, the morality he posed complicates and enriches

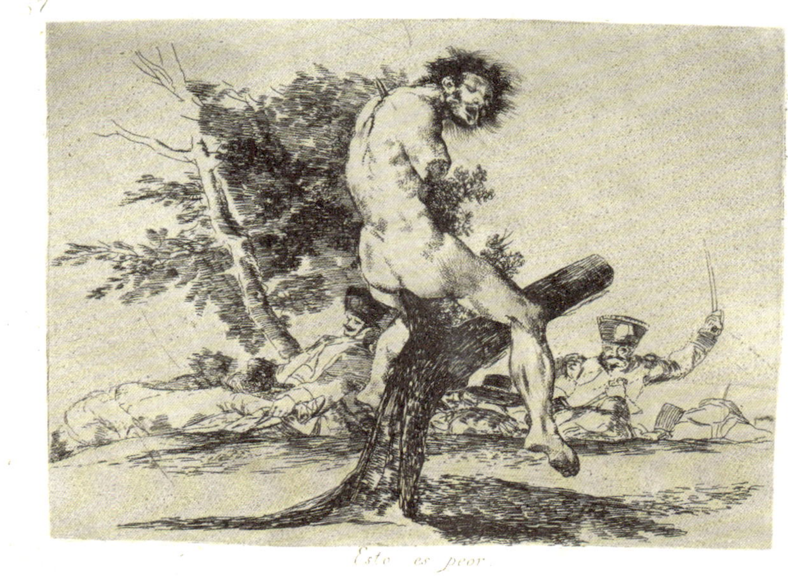

Fig. 4.21 Francisco de Goya, *This Is Worse*, from the series 'The Disasters of War', 1810 (published 1863). Etching, drypoint and aquatint.

the picture built by the plethora of artists discussed in this chapter, and the arc of his oeuvre traces a line from the buoyant, popular satire of Hogarth and the Georgian cartoonists to the physical and metaphorical shadows of printmaking employed by Blake and Doré. The power of Goya's images and the genius of their construction not only changed the language of printmaking, but also art as a whole, the echoes of which can still be felt today.

JAPAN'S FLOATING WORLD

UKIYO-E AND THE PARISIAN POSTER BOOM

You who want to make color prints, you couldn't dream of anything more beautiful

– Mary Cassatt to Berthe Morisot, 1890

THERE IS A handful of artworks in existence that have become so utterly imprinted on the public consciousness that they deserve to be called 'iconic'. The list includes paintings such as Botticelli's *The Birth of Venus* (*c*.1485), Leonardo da Vinci's *Mona Lisa* (*c*.1503) and Johannes Vermeer's *Girl with a Pearl Earring* (*c*.1665), yet there is one print that undeniably makes the grade: *Under the Wave off Kanagawa* (fig. 5.1) by Katsushika Hokusai (1760–1849). This multicoloured woodblock image – also known as the 'Great Wave' – depicts a roaring sea that engulfs both boatmen and Mount Fuji beyond, in swathes of frothing foam. In the centuries since its creation, it has become an international emblem for Japanese culture, adorning everything from book covers and posters to tote bags, mugs and T-shirts.

The intensive proliferation of this image might seem like a modern phenomenon, but it is in fact in keeping with the exceptional rates of print production that dominated the latter half of the Edo era. This was a period of relative peace and economic prosperity that spanned from 1603 to 1867, and it was named after the new capital of Edo (now Tokyo), which supplanted Kyoto as the de facto seat

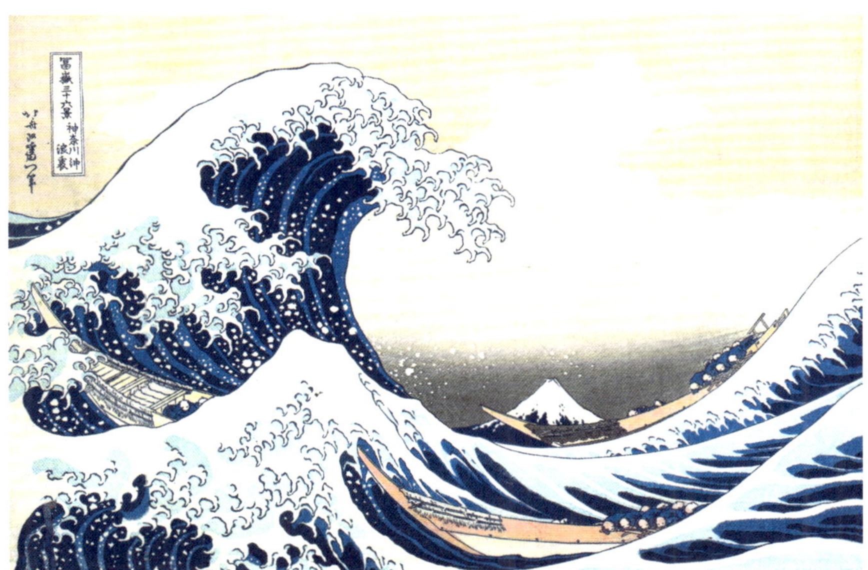

Fig. 5.1 Katsushika Hokusai, *Under the Wave off Kanagawa*, from the series 'Thirty-six Views of Mount Fuji', published by Nishimuraya Yohachi, 1830–34. Woodcut.

of power. All levels of society were constricted by the caste systems and sumptuary laws imposed by the military dictatorship of the Tokugawa Shōgunate, yet the demands of a rising merchant class and cultural elite were met with the introduction of licensed pleasure quarters, where theatres, teahouses, bars and brothels could operate without fear of repercussions.

The most famous of these quarters was Edo's Yoshiwara. This segregated red-light district was established in 1617 and was only accessible through a single, guarded gate. The walled enclave was certainly a place of sexual exploitation, but it was also a hotbed of creativity, where poets, writers, artists and actors all flocked. Its influence was such that the term *ukiyo-e* – derived from a Buddhist term concerning the transience of life in a world of suffering – became synonymous with the art it inspired. These were 'pictures of the floating world', depicting decadence, indulgence and the pursuit of fleeting pleasures.

Although *ukiyo-e* is most often used to describe woodblock prints, it spans a wider cultural phenomenon of painting, poetry and literature that was at odds with the strict traditions of the classical

Japanese style known as *yamato-e*. The more accurate term for these elaborate and abundantly colourful single sheets is *nishiki-e* ('brocade pictures'), named due to their aesthetic similarity to the luxurious, richly decorated fabric.[1]

The innovations that led to these spectacular images began to take shape in the early eighteenth century, when the introduction of new pigments and a brief relaxation of moral edicts (which controlled not only the content of imagery, but also its production and level of colour) led to an expansion of the print market. Both picture books and bound albums of horizontal prints had already enjoyed commercial success, but for the most part these were private commissions enjoyed by the elite. The earliest *nishiki-e* are attributed to Suzuki Harunobu (1725–1770), who is considered one of the earliest luminaries of *ukiyo-e*. He produced an array of New Year calendar prints depicting *bijin-ga* (images of beautiful women) in 1765. These lavish, full-colour posters were originally conceived for private poetry societies, but proved so popular that they were reissued to the buying public through a variety of publishers and booksellers (fig. 5.2).

It was a relatively simple, yet strikingly effective technical device that made Harunobu's multi-chromatic prints possible. The *kento* (or 'pass mark') is a registration guide that is carved directly into the woodblock, beyond the margins of the printing area. It consists of a right-angled recess that allows the corner of the printing paper to nestle perfectly within. A horizontal step is also cut further along the block, which keeps the sheet aligned and in place, with little room for the human error that might come with pin holes or pencil marks. Apprentices might train for months to perfect their mark, listening for the distinct clicking sound that comes with cutting a flawless 90-degree angle.

The process of creating *nishiki-e* has its roots in the earliest forms of relief printing discussed in chapter 1, but it is markedly more sophisticated. Thanks to this advanced registration, it was common for these prints to be formed from five blocks, carved on both sides, thus creating ten surfaces that would usually be inked in single colours. The entire image hangs together with the presence of a 'key' block consisting entirely of black outlines, which is derived from an original drawing by the *eshi*, an artist-designer who worked in consultation with powerful publishers to produce

   THE STORY OF PRINTMAKING

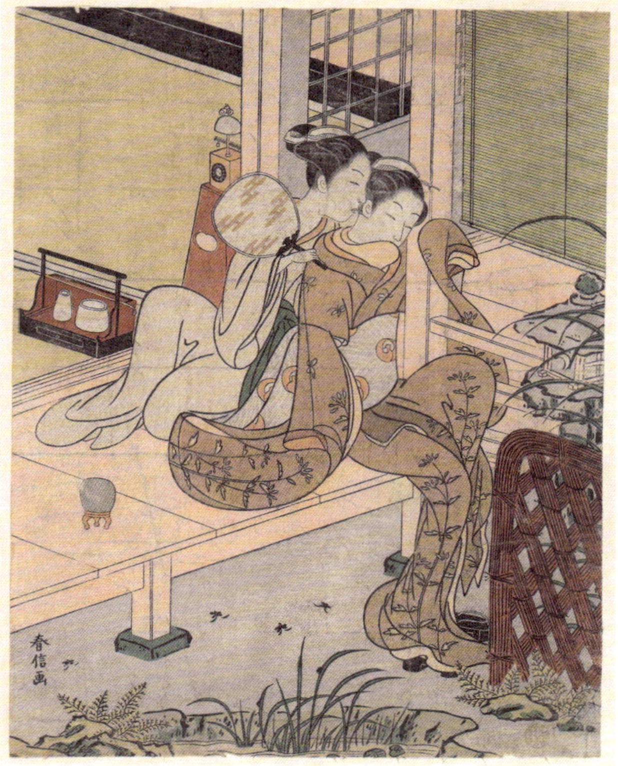

Fig. 5.2 Suzuki Harunobu, *The Gossips*, c.1767. Woodcut.

works on commission. In turn, the publisher funded all material and printing fees, including the labour of carvers and printers. Usually, shopfronts formed part of the studio, so that fresh works could be sold straight to the consumer.

While *eshi* usually designed on demand, the most successful and revered artists – including Hokusai – exercised considerably more creative control and conceived series entirely of their own invention (see pp. 109–12). Unlike their European counterparts, most of these individuals also worked in painting, book illustration and calligraphy, with little regard for woodblock as any kind of inferior or secondary art.

Once the master drawing was perfected, it was passed to the carver, who pasted it directly onto a piece of cherry wood before chiselling away using a *hangi-to*. This dagger-shaped knife features an angled blade that allows for precision-cutting of narrow grooves, quite unlike the U-shaped gouges used to clear away large areas of negative space. The subtleties of a design, including wisps of hair or delicate drapery, were often left to the carver's discretion. Particularly gifted individuals could expect their services to be specifically requested by top designers and renowned artists, which often led to long and fruitful partnerships.

It was the *eshi* who determined the vibrant colour combinations made from the ensuing pigment blocks, with instructions passed on to the printer. The combination of water-based ink and rice paste (which encourages the ink to disperse evenly across the wood surface) is applied with a stiff brush and lightly buffed into the surface of the block. Different layers and consistencies can be used to dramatic effect, most notably in the subtle gradient known as *bokashi*. This technique is achieved by carefully layering pigment in increasingly diluted concentration on a specific area of the block, with the aid of a broader, flatter brush. Other, more luxurious flourishes include the use of iridescent finishing powders made from mica, bronze or crushed seashells, which add a delicate shimmer.

One of the clearest distinctions from European developments is the absence of a press. Traditional Japanese woodblocks are all burnished by hand using a baren, a disk-like pad formed from a coil of twisted cord and covered in a sheath of bamboo. Unlike a machine press, which exerts an enormous amount of even pressure in a single moment, the baren is rubbed in a series of zig-zags to give sharpness and strength to the image, while circular movements allow the pigment to absorb into the paper. This immensely physical task utilises pressure deriving from the printer's shoulder and leading into a flat palm, but it also requires a lighter touch for subtler processes such as *bokashi*, which would be difficult to implement with a press. Other hand-wrought idiosyncrasies include lubricating the surface of the baren with naturally occurring oils, by rubbing it against a cheek or wiry beard, thus saving both time and valuable resources.

* * *

Although the *nishiki-e* process was not mechanised, it was hugely industrious. Prints were produced in their thousands and were so readily available that they could be purchased for the same price as a large helping of noodles. The sensual world of Yoshiwara was ripe subject matter, with *bijin-ga* and *yakusha-e* (portraits of kabuki actors) proving to be some of the most enduring motifs. Erotic encounters were equally sought after, as was the outright explicit imagery found in *shunga*.[2]

As new moral edicts restricted certain forms of image-making, the language of *ukiyo-e* adapted. Once the naming of famous courtesans was banned, coded objects entered their pictures. When warrior portraits were forbidden, kabuki scenes and folkloric tales filled the vacuum. Urban life and fantasy caught the imagination of the buying public in equal measure, with illustrated printed books (where both text and image were carved in relief) telling stories of classical subjects and modern romances. Catalogues of designs for textiles, fans and lacquerware also flooded the market, in a constant and self-sustaining cycle of decadent visual culture.

This cosmopolitan iconography dominated Japan for over a century, but it was in the waning light of the Tokugawa dynasty that print production reached its height and the most celebrated and internationally recognisable names came to the fore. Among them were students of the Utagawa school, an artistic lineage that touched practically every area of *ukiyo-e*. Established by Utagawa Toyoharu (1735–1814) in the late 1760s, this artistic 'family' included Kunisada (1786–1864), Kuniyoshi (1797–1861) and Hiroshige (1797–1858), as well as successors who bore the same name.

These artists went on to develop their own distinct styles and specialisms, yet they also looked to each other for inspiration and collaboration. For example, Kuniyoshi's fantastical triptych *Takiyasha the Witch and the Skeleton Spectre* (1845–6) was informed by illustrations produced by his teacher Toyokuni (1777–1835), who was the second head of the Utagawa school, for a popular novel titled *Biography of the Loyal Utō Yasukata*, published in 1806.[3]

The significance of literary source material is even more apparent in Kunisada's oeuvre. While he enjoyed great acclaim for his intricate portrait pictures, he was also a prolific designer of *gokan*, which are akin to contemporary comics. He collaborated with the celebrated novelist Ryūtei Tanehiko (1783–1842) in his satirical retelling of the eleventh-century text, *The Tale of Genji*. Credited as the world's first novel and written by the noblewoman Murasaki Shikibu, its evocative and romantic sensibility made it perfect fodder for an *ukiyo-e*-obsessed audience. Tanehiko's subsequent volume, *A Fraudulent Murasaki's Rustic Genji* (1829–42), featured densely packed script combined with dynamic monochrome line drawings, and was a veritable hit. It was the first book to sell over 10,000 copies in Japan, and fuelled a 'Genji craze' that infiltrated not only art, but also popular fashion and lifestyle. Genji-themed garments, combs and rice crackers were the must-have accessories of the day.[4]

Kunisada built on this success by creating his own subsequent interpretations, including a collaboration with both Hiroshige and his protégé, Hiroshige II (1826–1869). These ornate single sheets portray not only the action of the text, but also the natural beauty of each setting, which functions as a narrative device in and of itself.

Landscape prints, despite now being one of the most notable forms of *nishiki-e*, did not gain significant traction until the 1820s. The popularity of the genre once again owes a debt to Utagawa Toyoharu, who introduced vanishing-point perspective to his compositions, thus suffusing them with unprecedented depth. He was informed by the gentle trickle of foreign books and prints that reached Japan through the artificial island of Dejima, just off the coast of Nagasaki. This Dutch trading post was the only window to the outside world since the Tokugawa clan implemented a policy of complete isolation in the early seventeenth century, in order to combat Christian colonial powers (particularly the Catholic Portuguese). This policy came to a dramatic conclusion in 1854, when the American naval officer Matthew Perry entered Japanese waters with a squadron of ships, and forced the government to enter into trade and diplomatic relations. Over the next five years, a flurry of further accords was negotiated with the UK, the Netherlands, Russia and France.

Before this seismic shift, government restrictions on domestic travel had already begun to ease. This led artists and designers to capitalise on a renewed public appetite for depictions of the country's vast span. Hiroshige utilised the official stopping points along the Tōkaidō road – a 514-kilometre-long highway trading route that still runs from Tokyo to Kyoto – as inspiration for his series 'The Fifty-three Stations of the Tōkaidō' (1832–3). These images oscillate between the crowded streets of Nihonbashi and the seclusion of the Hakone clifftops, taking in the temporal nature of the changing seasons.

                                    THE STORY OF PRINTMAKING

Hiroshige embraced the same format in 'The Sixty-nine Stations along the Kisokaido' (1834–42). This collaboration with fellow artist Keisai Eisen (1790–1848) – who was best-known for his decadent *bijin-ga* prints – used another commercial thoroughfare as its constant. Both series demonstrate a balance of serene and dynamic narratives, many of which are infused with the subtle complexities of multiple layers of *bokashi* – perfect for articulating grassy hills, icy rivers and melting sunsets. However, these collections are surpassed by the compositional ingenuity, technical discernment and evocative symbolism that underpin Hiroshige's most celebrated series: 'One Hundred Famous Views of Edo' (1856–9).

This compendium (which actually consists of some 120 works) contains some of the most influential prints in the *nishiki-e* genre. Alongside the expansive bird's-eye views one might expect from topographical studies, there are ingenious, tightly framed crops and overlapping pictorial planes that are infused with auspicious symbolism, thus celebrating the various customs of the day.

Much of this is beautifully expressed in *Plum Park at Kameido* (fig. 5.3). The scene is dominated by an unusually shaped tree, which would have been familiar to viewers as the famous *garyūbai*, or 'sleeping dragon'. Both branches and buds crowd the distant visitors who have come to view the blossoms, and who appear amid a verdant gradient of green and red. This print utilises the French concept of *repoussoir*, in which an unusual object appears in the foreground, thus playfully pushing the intended subject into the middle distance.[5]

The same technique is employed in *Mannen Bridge, Fukagawa* (fig. 5.4). Here, a dangling turtle is foregrounded as a viewing accomplice, who looks out across the water. It was common for aquatic creatures to be sold underneath the bridge, so that people might purchase them and set them free, in an exercise designed to bring good karma.

There are more subtle allusions in *Asakusa Rice Fields and Torinomachi Festival* – one of the only images to be set entirely in an interior space (fig. 5.5). The scene is cut in two by a sharp diagonal delineating the wooden framework of a teahouse, while the remnants of recent patronage can be spotted in the discarded towel and selection of hairpins lying on the floor. The white cat is a stand-in for the courtesan who has briefly left the room. This

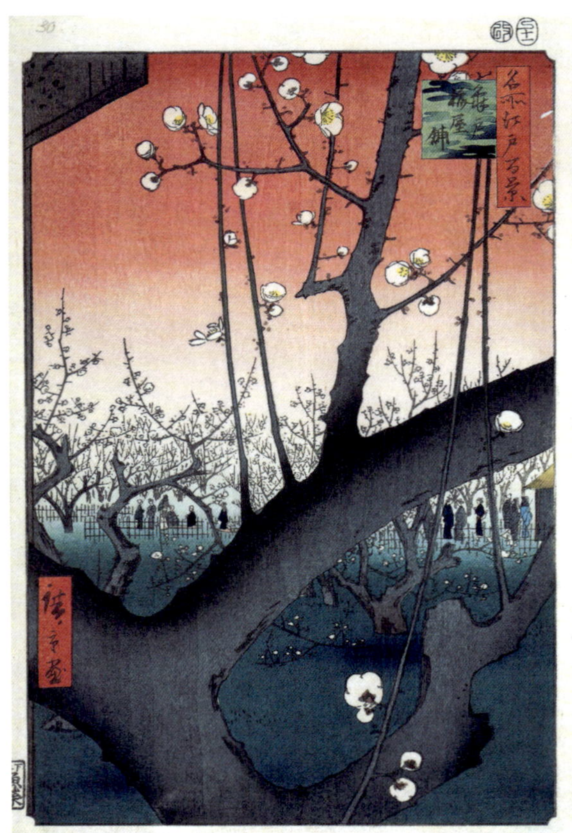

Fig. 5.3 Utagawa Hiroshige, *Plum Park at Kameido*, from the series 'One Hundred Famous Views of Edo', published by Uoya Eikichi, 1857. Woodcut.

slightly melancholy scene, with its sunset bleeding into the surrounds of Mount Fuji, might well be regarded as a commemoration of Yoshiwara itself. The notorious pleasure district was razed to the ground in 1855 by the devastating Ansei earthquake, which killed over 10,000 people.

* * *

Along with Hiroshige, Hokusai stands tall as a master of landscape views. Although he did not descend from the Utagawa school (he trained with another *ukiyo-e* master, Katsukawa Shunshō, and began his career as an apprentice woodblock carver), he incorporated similarly bold experiments with perspective, and enjoyed considerable celebrity during his decades-long career. His most famous series is 'Thirty-six Views of Mount Fuji' (1830–34), which incorporates the 'Great Wave'. One of the most novel aspects of these prints was

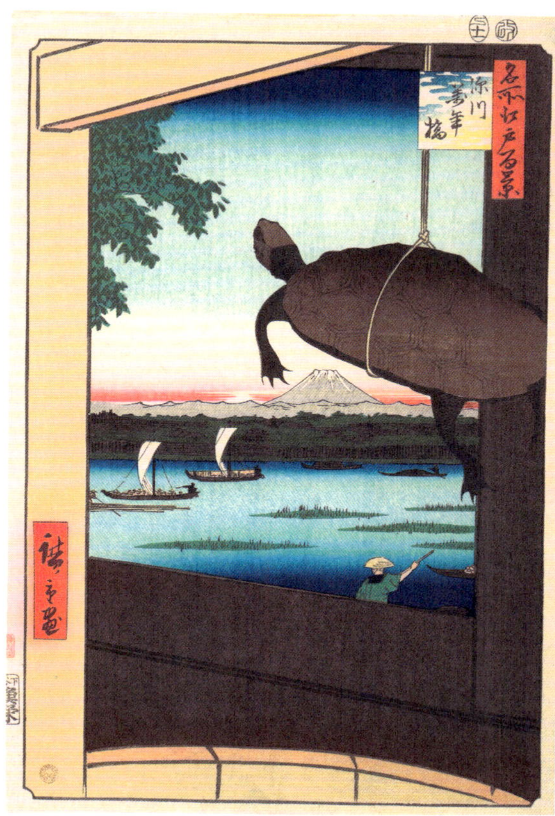

Fig. 5.4 Utagawa Hiroshige, *Mannen Bridge, Fukagawa*, from the series 'One Hundred Famous Views of Edo', published by Uoya Eikichi, 1858. Woodcut.

the treatment of Japan's greatest natural monument, which appears not only as a looming presence of astonishing scale and beauty – as demonstrated in *Fine Weather*, *Clear Day* and *Rainstorm beneath the Summit* – but also as a background player amid the everyday machinations of Japanese life. In *Noboto Bay*, for example, labourers gather shellfish beneath the frame of an enormous temple gate, which outlines the snowy peak far beyond. In *Kajikazawa in Kai Province* (fig. 5.6), the mountain's presence is defined by a single line, which gives way to the sea mists that surround the spectacle of a fisherman and his child, who are attempting to pull in their catch on a stormy day.

The same sense of peril is evident in the 'Great Wave' (see fig. 5.1), where the violent, cresting curls threaten to upend the boatmen below. With the employment of the same palette of deep, cool blue and crisp

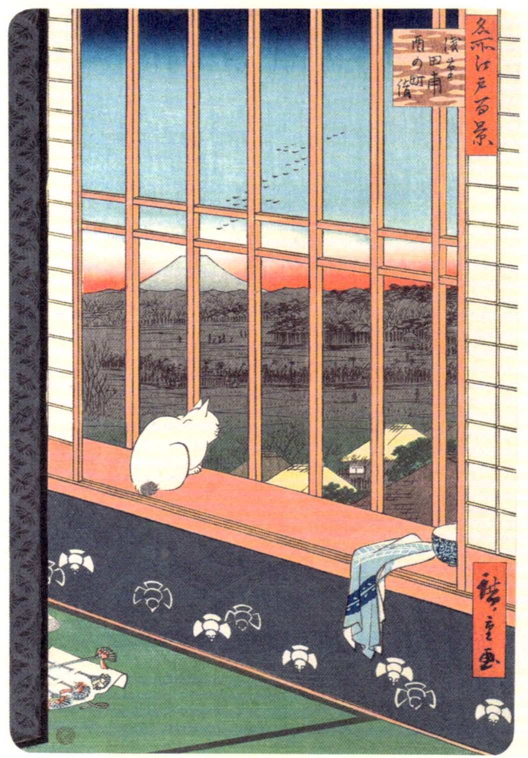

Fig. 5.5 Utagawa Hiroshige, *Asakusa Rice Fields and Torinomachi Festival*, from the series 'One Hundred Famous Views of Edo', published by Uoya Eikichi, 1857. Woodcut.

white throughout, the mountain practically becomes one with the ocean that surrounds it. This heavily stylised composition demonstrates Hokusai's ability to convey the emotive power of water, which he explored in his wondrous, lesser-known series 'A Tour of Waterfalls in Various Provinces' (*c*.1832). Here, he articulates an array of shimmering cascades and lustrous ripples in elegant detail (fig. 5.7).

Another unifying element across both of these series is the continuous use of a distinct hue known as Prussian Blue. This was the first truly synthetic pigment, which was first introduced to Japan in 1829 as another tightly regulated European import. It was markedly more stable than indigo, and far cheaper than ultramarine (which is made from lapis lazuli stones mined from ancient deposits in Afghanistan), thus giving artists a brilliant new colour with which to articulate both sea and sky.

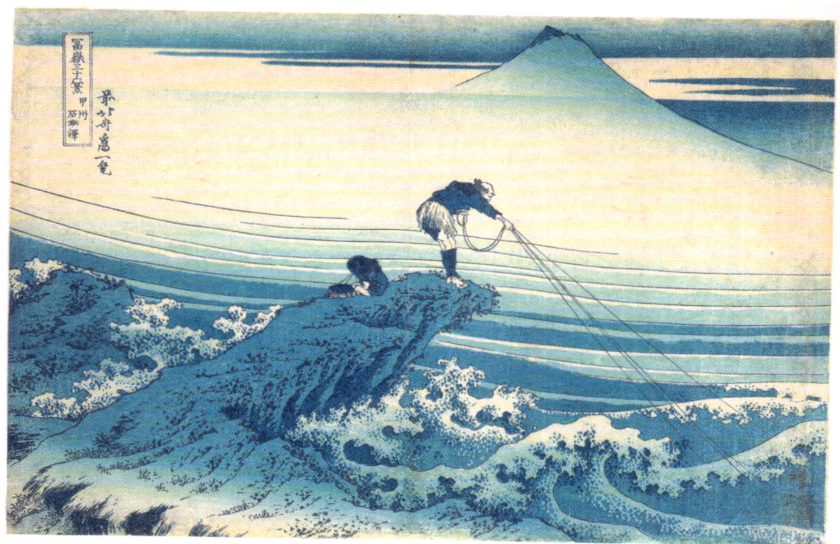

Fig. 5.6 Katsushika Hokusai, *Kajikazawa in Kai Province*, from the series 'Thirty-six Views of Mount Fuji', published by Nishimuraya Yohachi, 1830–34. Woodcut.

Original adverts for 'Thirty-six Views' state that the earliest impressions were printed entirely in blue, and there are indeed extant prints of these first runs, complete with a coloured key block. The success of the series led Hokusai to add another ten views, all of which were keyed in black, with subsequent prints featuring both monochrome outlines and full-colour detailing.

The artist was in his early 70s when he conceived this series, at a time when he had already afforded himself the title of 'old man mad about painting'. Indeed, it was his skill with the brush that he was best-known for during his lifetime. He even entertained the shōgun with live demonstrations of his talents.[6]

Far from being protective of his methods, he also set about producing instructional books for artists and craftsmen, which naturally relied on heavily illustrated printed manuals. These included designs for combs and tobacco pipes, and a compendium of 'tasty morsels' tackling subjects that jobbing artists might struggle with, including birds, plants and utensils. In the preface to his pattern book from 1836, his sincerity is marked: 'If, on occasion, you find this book

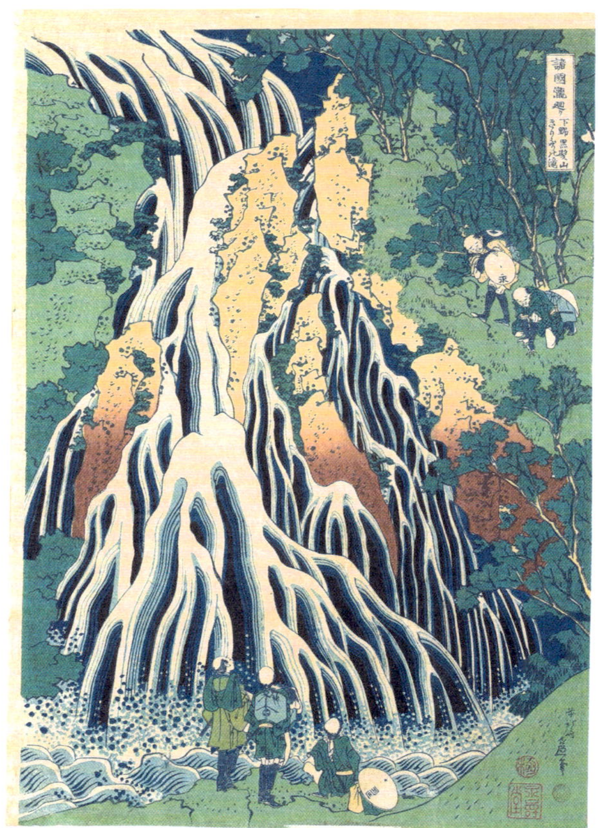

Fig. 5.7 Katsushika Hokusai, *Kirifuri Waterfall at Kurokami Mountain in Shimotsuke*, from the series 'A Tour of Waterfalls in Various Provinces', published by Nishimuraya Yohachi, *c.*1832. Woodcut.

useful, I will feel only pride that it has been one gem in the Crystal Mountains, one branch in a forest of cinnamon trees.' A rather more playful sensibility can be found in the second volume of his enormously popular *All about Painting in Colour* (1848), thus relaying his multifaceted creative temperament: 'Even those who cannot be in Hokusai's proximity long to learn his style of painting, like infants yearning for their mothers.'[7]

The artist grew more prolific as he aged, ultimately producing thousands of single-sheet prints, manuals, picture books and paintings during his long career. He also changed his name some thirty times, in keeping with the Japanese tradition for a new designation with each creative evolution. Although his brilliance is indisputable, recent scholarship has uncovered the sizeable support of his third daughter, Katsushika Ōi (1800–1866). Known officially as Eijo, she has been

     THE STORY OF PRINTMAKING

described as his 'ghost brush'. Her rather unusual name stems from a family joke: her father's incessant yelling to grab her attention (quite literally shouting 'Oi!') led her to take on the moniker.[8]

Following her divorce from a fellow painter, Ōi moved in with her father, but rather than fulfilling domestic duties she set about assisting in his art production, as she had done in her youth. Much has been made about the relative squalor that Hokusai spent his final decades in, such was the dedication to his craft. An aversion to housework was shared by his daughter, and there are suggestions that they would move house rather than clean up.

Despite the relative erasure of Ōi's contributions (which included adding figures to designs and colouring various works), research is now being done to unearth paintings she assisted with, as well as those she produced alone. Though investigations into her printed oeuvre are nascent, *An Illustrated Handbook on Daily Life for Women* (fig. 5.8) is attributed to her as sole designer.[9] In a poignant

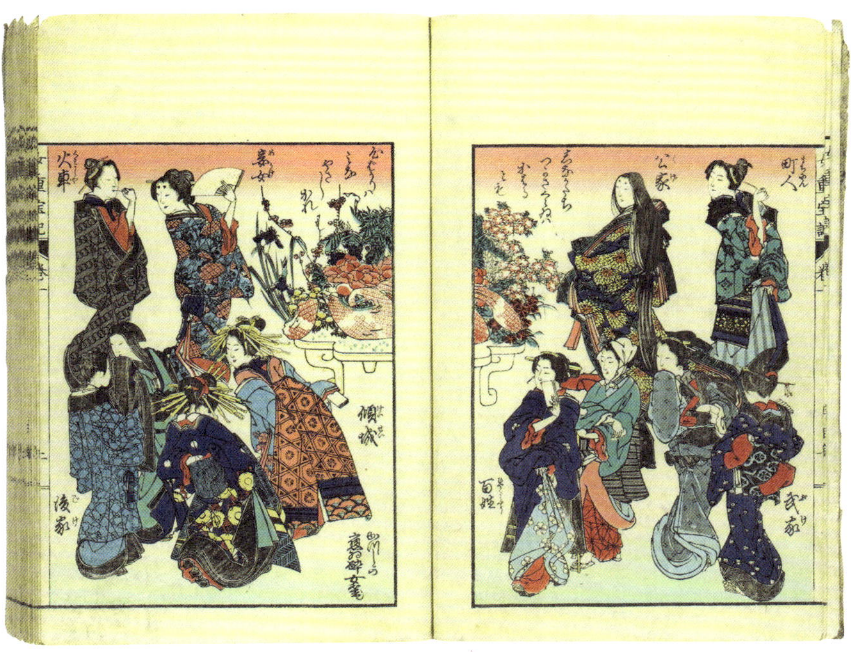

Fig. 5.8 Katsushika Ōi, pages from *An Illustrated Handbook on Daily Life for Women*, 1847. Woodcut.

irony, it relays appropriate etiquette and pursuits such as spinning and sewing, depicted both in full-page visual narratives and within the margins of the text.

This reference book is in keeping with the vast number of printed publications issued by Hokusai, which, although less widely celebrated than his single-sheet prints, probably had the biggest influence on the creative culture of *ukiyo-e*. The distinct graphic style of his book *One Hundred Views of Mount Fuji* (*c.*1834) – the blocks of which were cut by one of his favourite carvers, Egawa Tomekichi – makes for an instrumental work, despite being eclipsed by his comparable *nishiki-e* series in subsequent years. Across these three bound volumes, the rectangular borders of each page act as a frame for his narrative visions, but on occasion his images break free of these margins, as if nature itself cannot be contained.

This publication also features a text by the very same celebrated novelist who penned *A Fraudulent Murasaki's Rustic Genji*, and his astute preface captures the evocative essence of Hokusai's art:

> He has glimpsed the slopes through willow branches and gazed up at the peak through trembling stalks of rice. He has traced true views of the vast ocean breaking in rough waves against the rocks, of valleys filled with white clouds, of ascents through winding mountain passes and descents through perilous ways – his spirit resides in this volume.[10]

** * **

This spirit went on to capture imaginations far beyond Japanese shores. In 1868, the Emperor Mutsuhito (posthumously known as Meiji) usurped the final Tokugawa shōgun and restored absolute imperial rule, thus igniting a sociopolitical revolution that would have unprecedented influence on the aesthetic language of late nineteenth- and early twentieth-century Europe. While his predecessors had reluctantly accepted some foreign influence, Meiji welcomed change with open arms. He encouraged international trade and industrial modernisation, and even demanded that his courtiers wear French fashions such as bowler hats and neck ties. A fascination with all things foreign was also evident in the brief vogue for *Yokohama-e* prints, named after the port city that served as the first official global

　　　　THE STORY OF PRINTMAKING

trading port. These *nishiki-e* focused on non-East Asian incomers and the various curiosities associated with their customs and costumes.

The Meiji Restoration's cultural policy built on a rich export market that had already found footing in the previous decade. Kimonos, lacquerware, painted screens, ceramics, books and prints were all shipped abroad in an effort to promote the country's artistic prowess and usher in a new era of commercial prosperity. What followed was a fashion for all things related to *Japonisme*, a term coined by the critic Philippe Burty[11] to describe an obsession with goods originating from the formerly isolated archipelago, as well as a thirst to replicate them, particularly within France. In an intensive cultural exchange that was undoubtedly inflected with exoticism, specialist dealers and antique shops soon dominated the French capital. Siegfried Bing was among the most famous, as was Hayashi Tadamasa, a Japanese native who arrived in the city as an interpreter for the Paris Exposition, in 1878.

With their alluring and transient subjects, compositional flatness and vibrant pigments, it was prints of the floating world that proved revelatory for the artists of the Parisian avant-garde. The Impressionists, a group that included Claude Monet (1840–1926), Auguste Renoir (1841–1919), Edgar Degas (1834–1917), Berthe Morisot (1841–1895) and Mary Cassatt (1844–1926), were captivated by the great number of *ukiyo-e* exhibitions that soon proliferated. Another member, Camille Pissarro (1830–1903), described the deep affinity he felt with the emotive sensibilities of the masters in a letter to his son Lucien in 1893: 'Hiroshige is a wonderful impressionist. Monet, Rodin and I are enthusiastic. How glad I am to have painted the effects of snow and floods; these Japanese artists have confirmed us in our visual judgement.'[12]

One account has it that French artists first encountered *nishiki-e* prints when they were used as packing material for crates of porcelain that had been shipped from Japan, but Monet claimed to have discovered one in a junk shop in Le Havre when he was just a teenager, and he noted that he later saw examples on display in a Dutch tearoom.[13] While these prints were celebrated in European exhibitions as distinct art objects, they were far more ephemeral and of little value back home, which may have been due to changes in taste, as well as the abundance of sheets that remained readily available.

The painter and etcher Félix Bracquemond (1833–1914) was equally enamoured by a book of Hokusai's *manga* (or sketches), which was owned by the influential and astute intaglio printer Auguste Delâtre (1822–1907). He refused to sell the rare export despite the artist's pleas, instead preferring to share the pictures at his shop, among his wider circle of patrons.

Artists soon incorporated their newfound fascinations into their work. Bracquemond's designs for tableware, which adorned the tables of the Jing-lar Society (a private members' club founded by Burty, dedicated to discussions of Japanese culture), borrowed motifs from the works of Hokusai and Hiroshige. Prints also appeared as distinct objects, as is the case in Édouard Manet's (1832–1883) depiction of Émile Zola, which features a woodblock impression by his Japanese contemporary Utagawa Kuniaki II (1835–1888), pinned to the wall in the background.

Vincent van Gogh (1853–1890) had his own impressive selection of *ukiyo-e*, and was the most devout copyist.[14] He made several facsimiles of his favoured prints, including Hiroshige's *Plum Park at Kameido* and an image of a courtesan by Eisen. He supposedly moved to Arles because he believed the landscape possessed a light similar to that found in Japan. He was more than a little guilty of indulging in the fantasy of rural existence and primitivism peddled by *Japonisme*, which was completely at odds with the realities of a complex nation that boasted one of the biggest metropolises the world had ever seen. Van Gogh's feelings concerning the emotive power of *nishiki-e* are expressed in a passionate letter to his brother Theo, in 1888, comparing the 'Great Wave' to Eugène Delacroix's allegorical seascapes: 'Hokusai wrings the same cry from you – but he does it with his *line*, his *drawing*; as you say in your letter – these waves are *claws*, and the ship is caught in them, you feel it.'[15]

A striking element of the avant-garde obsession with the language of woodblock is that few actually attempted to utilise the medium. Notable exceptions include Auguste-Louis Lepère's (1849–1918) multicoloured print *Convalescent, Mme Lepère* (fig. 5.9), which depicts his wife in a soft ombré of muted shades, achieved through *bokashi* experiments. Henri Rivière's (1864–1951) ambitious 1891 series depicting views of the Eiffel Tower's construction was designed as a homage to Hokusai's views of Mount Fuji. However, the woodblock

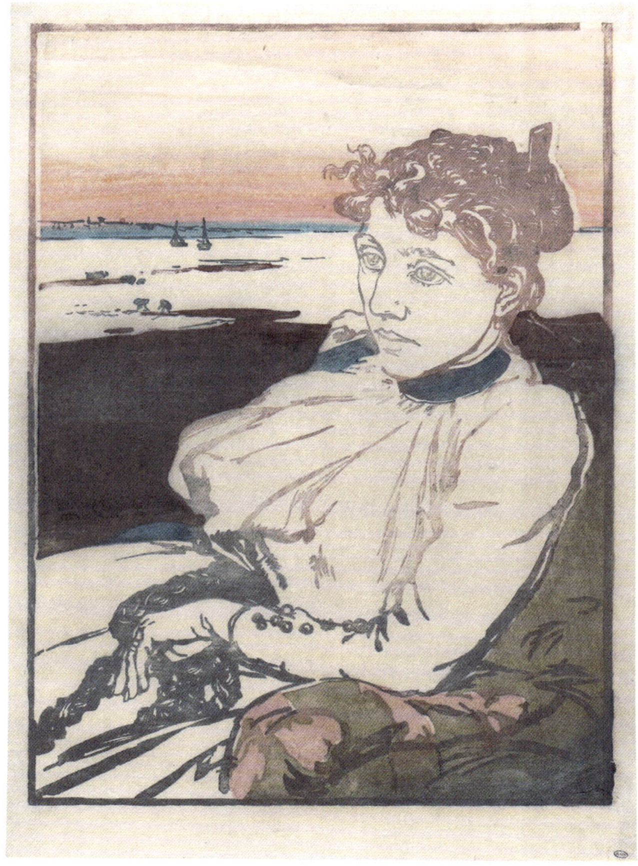

Fig. 5.9 Auguste-Louis Lepère, *Convalescent, Mme Lepère,* 1892. Woodcut.

technique proved so laborious that only six were produced in this manner.

There was one artist who deftly translated the qualities of colourful relief prints through intaglio techniques. Mary Cassatt's suite of ten colour aquatints are among the most celebrated examples of Impressionist printmaking, regarded as much for their content as for their technical acumen. They detail the quotidian domestic activities of ordinary upper-class women, both embodying the motifs that characterised the *bijin-ga* beauties and channelling them through the artist's distinct female gaze.

Cassatt was an American expat of considerable talent, who came from an affluent industrial family in Philadelphia. She escaped the constraints of high society to make her own way in Paris. She worked first as an official copyist at the Louvre and honed her skills in both paint and print, with notable support from Degas. It was he who first suggested she take up etching, in order to contribute to his ill-fated portfolio publication *Le Jour et la nuit* (which never materialised). Nevertheless, Cassatt became fascinated by the process, and a major exhibition of *nishiki-e* at the École des Beaux-Arts in 1890 opened her eyes to the possibility of something far more experimental. Following her visit, she wrote to her fellow Impressionist Berthe Morisot:

> Seriously, you must not miss that. You who want to make color prints, you couldn't dream of anything more beautiful. I dream of it and don't think of anything else but color on copper. . . . You must see the Japanese – come as soon as you can.[16]

Cassatt not only embraced the distinct palette that had so inspired her; she also emulated the specific compositional framework of Kitagawa Utamaro (*c.*1754–1806), who was a virtuoso of the 'beauties' genre, following in Harunobu's footsteps. Both *The Bath* (1890–91) and *The Letter* (fig. 5.10) directly reference Utamaro's work, with the latter print presenting a delicately folded missive that is near identical to the one featured in *Portrait of Hinazuru of the Keizetsuro* (fig. 5.11). In another alluring image, of a woman washing herself at a basin (fig. 5.12), the gentle curve of an exposed back mirrors a preoccupation with the nape of the neck and slightly revealing clothing, which epitomised the idealised vision of Japanese womanhood.

Producing such complex prints was no easy feat. Despite her own expertise, Cassatt sought out the assistance of a professional printer, Modeste Leroy, to produce 25 impressions of each work.[17] To begin, the composition was sketched out on paper, and then traced onto a copper plate that had been covered in a 'soft ground'. Unlike the hard ground discussed in chapter 3 (see p. 46), this surface does not solidify, meaning that subtler marks can be rendered with waxy crayons, producing marks that appear more akin to pastel. It was a favourite among the Impressionists, who sought to emulate the expressive nature of their *en plein air* sketches.

Once the marks were traced, the artist used drypoint to produce the dark lines similar to a *nishiki-e* key block, followed by both aquatint and stop-out, to produce pattern and gentle tonality. The

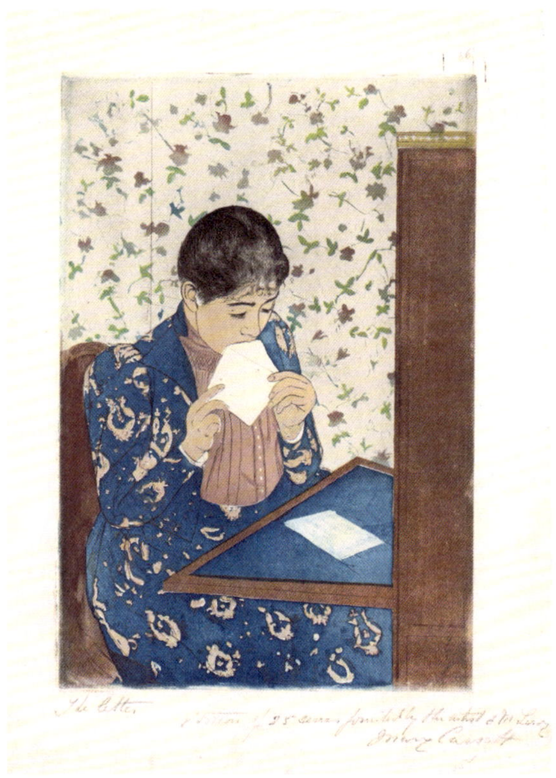

Fig. 5.10 Mary Cassatt,
The Letter, 1891. Etching,
drypoint and aquatint.

final stage was to introduce colour, using a hand-applied technique
called *à la poupée*, meaning 'with the doll', in which multiple pigments
are applied to the same plate with the aid of small fabric-wrapped
tools. When the surface is polished, subtle blending between the
various shades can occur.

Rather than aiming for a consistent set of editions, Cassatt experimented liberally with colour, especially when it came to intricate
decorative surfaces such as wallpaper and fabric. She closely mimicked
the luxurious complexities of *ukiyo-e* pictures in various iterations of
The Fitting (1890–91). Both the patterned walls and carpet appear
in differing shades of taupe, green, red and blue, effectively rendering
each print unique.

These aquatints were rarefied objects, designed to be admired
in an intimate setting or else exhibited to a discerning public, as

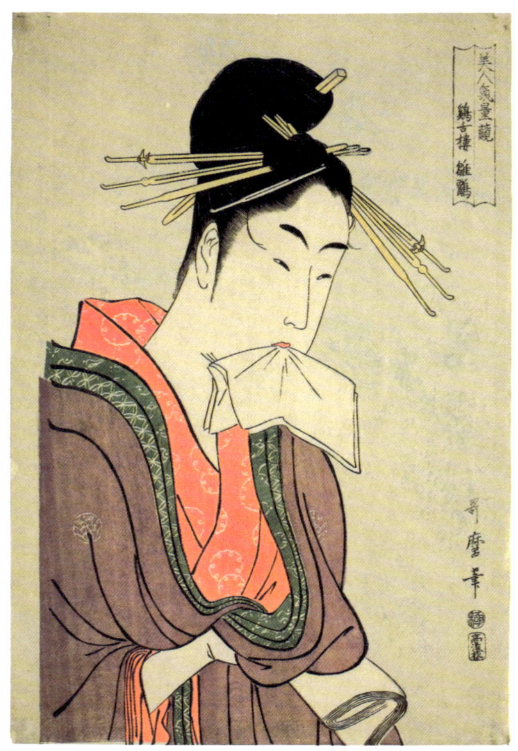

Fig. 5.11 Kitagawa Utamaro, *Portrait of Hinazuru of the Keizetsuro*, from the series 'Comparing the Charms of Beauties', *c*.1794–5. Woodcut.

independent works of art. Indeed, an 1891 solo show of Cassatt's prints mounted by her dealer and champion of Impressionism Paul Durand-Ruel (1831–1922) was widely acclaimed, and allusions to the great Utamaro were not lost among the critics.

The printed culture of Paris, however, extended far beyond the realm of any artist studio or gallery wall. Just as Japanese urban life was enwreathed in images of Edo's floating world, so the French Belle Époque was replete with decadent imagery that blurred the line between elegant artistry and commercial enterprise. The streets of Montmartre were covered with the seductive assignations of the *demi-monde*, where posters for salacious cabarets, cafés-concerts and circuses fought for attention against the clamour of advertisements proclaiming the wonders of everything from cigarettes to cold cream. The abundance of imagery was so great that in the 1860s an industrious printer named Gabriel Morris invented attractive cylindrical columns specifically designed to display his posters. These

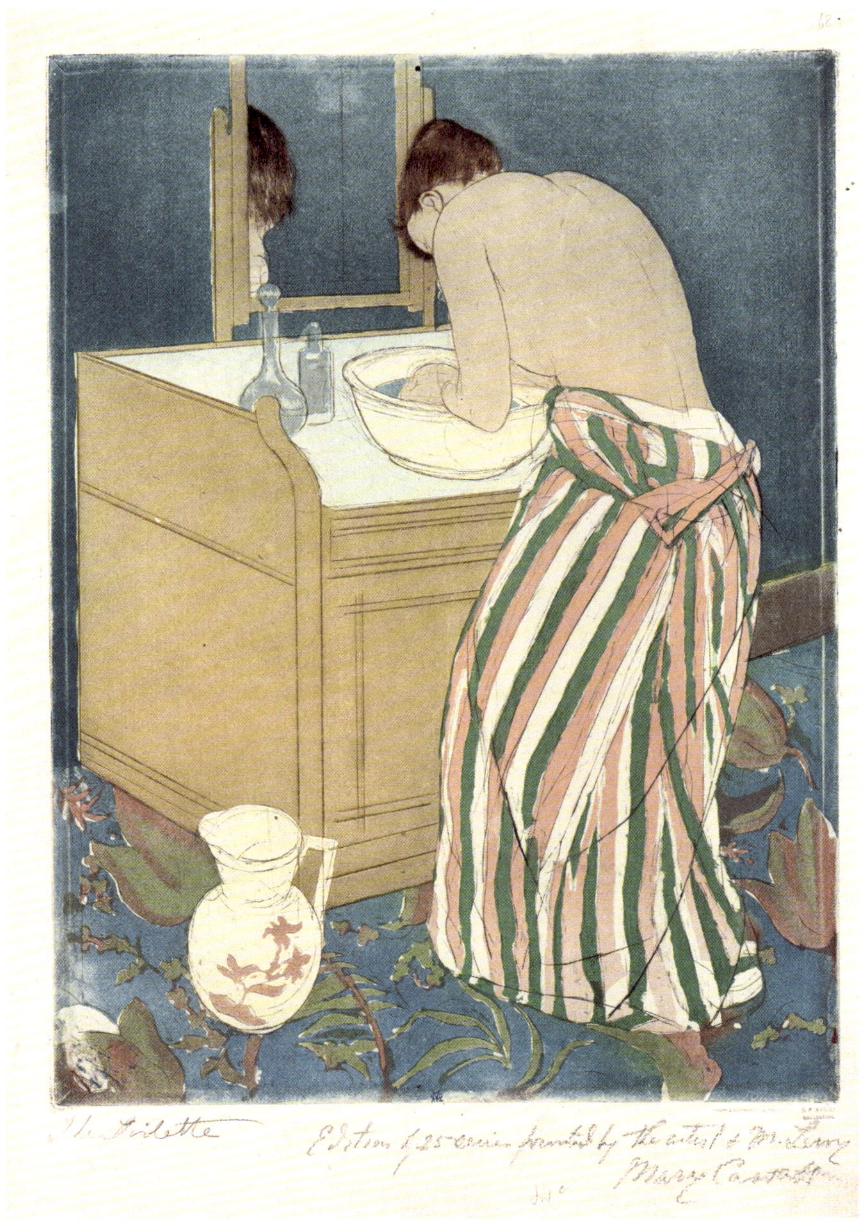

Fig. 5.12 Mary Cassatt, *The Toilette*, 1891. Etching, drypoint and aquatint.

'Morris' columns proved so popular that hundreds were installed in the ensuing two decades, and they remain a beloved feature of Parisian life.

This was not the only innovation to symbolise a new dawn of image-making during the *fin de siècle*. In a significant departure from the printing techniques discussed thus far, this ceaseless production was made possible not by the meticulous carving of woodblocks, nor even a combination of engraved and etched lines, but through an entirely new process that works on the simple premise that oil and water do not mix.

* * *

Lithography, a process named from the Greek for 'stone scribing', was first patented by the German playwright Alois Senefelder (1771–1834) in around 1799.[18] His quest to find a cheap and effective alternative to intaglio and letterpress – which left him at the mercy of commercial printers when he wished to reproduce his scripts – led him to experiment with a system that did not rely on incising a surface, but rather processing chemical repellents that rest on the same plane.

Traditionally, the lithographic process utilises heavy slabs of limestone. This hard yet fine-grained rock serves as the perfect surface on which to embed an image by means of wax and water. First, the surface must be ground down and levelled to ensure accurate printing. This is usually achieved by grinding a fine carborundum (silicon carbide) grit beneath another piece of stone, and polishing with intensive circular motions. Far from simply assuring a quality image, a balanced surface will stop any disastrous cracking that could occur under uneven pressure, rendering the stone useless.

Once prepared, an image can be drawn directly onto the surface using greasy materials including specialist crayons and an oil-based liquid known as 'tusche'. It is both the immediate, expressive qualities of this process, along with the abundance of experimental methods, that makes it appealing for so many artists. It is possible to mimic the hard lines of a pencil and the fluidity of watercolour, a spatter of ink or otherworldly folds of texture known as 'reticulation', all on the same stone.

The next step is to fix the design with a number of processes using chemicals, including a layer of gum arabic to protect negative space, and rosin powder which effectively bonds the greased design to the stone. Once fixed with solvent, the drawing appears

                    THE STORY OF PRINTMAKING

as a ghostly image, which is known as an 'etch' (this is an entirely different process from that of intaglio etching).

To bring this ghost to life, the stone is dampened and printing ink is applied with a large double-handed roller (akin to an enormous rolling pin). Because the greasy ink is repelled by water, it will only affix to the areas that have been etched. The key to effective rolling is consistency, and most expert lithographers can determine the correct level of ink by the subtle, sticky sound that emanates with each pass. If needed, adjustments can still be made at this late stage, by scraping back layers of ink with specialist tools or acids. Once the lithographer is satisfied, the stone might be passed through the press multiple times before the first official impression is taken, in order to push the ink deeper into the surface and obtain the appropriate tonal effects.

The press itself sits somewhere between a mangle and a stamp. A pressure bar is set using a screw-and-wheel mechanism, before the stone is placed on the printing bed with damp paper positioned on top. The scraper bar (akin to a stiff squeegee) is then lowered by means of a lever, so that it can make contact with intense force once the stone is passed beneath it. The immense weight of the stone means that it is usually re-inked and dampened for subsequent impressions while remaining on the printing platform.

The capabilities of lithography to faithfully reproduce painted and sketched marks proved revelatory for artists who wished to replicate existing pieces as well as create entirely new works. Among the early French adopters were Théodore Géricault (1791–1824), Eugène Delacroix (1798–1863) and Honoré Daumier (1808–1879), who took to the medium to express both romantic sentiments of revolutionary independence and satirical sociopolitical commentary.

Although artists embraced lithography as a means of independent creative production, it was the poster that truly flourished. It began as an adjunct commercial printing enterprise, before gradually becoming a focal point, not least when innovations in colour took hold. The invention of steam-powered and 'offset' presses – which allowed a design to be imprinted on a rubber cylinder instead of stone or metal to speed up production – dramatically increased output. This, coupled with an age of prosperity that took hold following the end of the Franco-Prussian War in 1871, signalled a golden era of exquisitely illustrated bills and banners, known as *affichomanie* or 'poster mania'.[19]

A true giant of this genre was Jules Chéret (1836–1932), who had apprenticed as a lithographer from the age of 13 and first found success as a packaging designer for the Rimmel makeup brand. He went on to set up his own shop in 1866, and perfected a three-stone process that offered an as-yet-unseen prism of colour. Just as with *nishiki-e*, he used a black key stone, which was accompanied by a pure red, as well as a multi-hued 'rainbow roll' background.

It was not only colour, but also form that cemented Chéret as the pre-eminent poster designer of the period. His cascading letters appeared among the swirling skirts and kicking legs of performers at infamous establishments including the Moulin Rouge and the Folies-Bergère. In his 1893 poster depicting the American dancer Loïe Fuller (fig. 5.13), the outline of her body is only thinly veiled by a whirl of gossamer fabric, which appears like a roaring flame against a background of jet black.

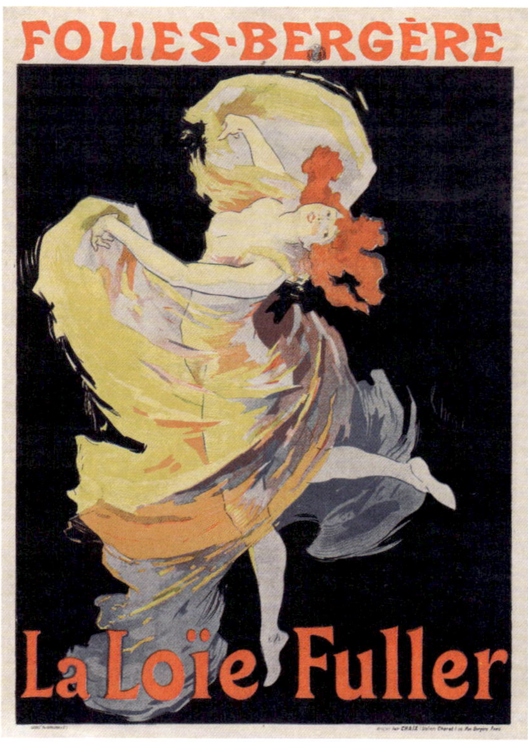

Fig. 5.13 Jules Chéret, *Loïe Fuller at the Folies-Bergère*, 1893. Lithograph.

                    THE STORY OF PRINTMAKING

Chéret elevated the essence of the poster, from something derivative and throwaway, to something cutting-edge and collectable. Astute enterprises such as Mourlot Studios and Imprimerie Edward Ancourt capitalised on this commercial viability, and were just as influential as the artists with whom they collaborated.

If Chéret was the forefather of lithography, then Henri de Toulouse-Lautrec (1864–1901) was his undisputed heir. This troubled aristocrat – whose absinthe-tinged pictures have become an icon of the Belle Époque – was just as inspired by Japanese prints as his Impressionist peers. He saw the flat planes of colour and concise, fluid lines as the perfect medium with which to convey the spirit of Paris's bohemian underbelly. Much like Cassatt, Lautrec had a particular affinity with the work of Utamaro, and created his own portfolio of lithographs based on the Japanese artist's depictions of courtesans in 'The Twelve Hours of the Green Houses' (*c.*1795). Lautrec's compendium, showcasing the rather mundane aspects of everyday life in a brothel, encompassed sketched marks, spatters and stipples that demonstrate a subtler approach towards the possibilities of lithography than the vivacious posters for which the artist is best known.

Some of his prominent examples include *Divan Japonais* (fig. 5.14), named after the famed drinking establishment, which presents the dancer Jane Avril enjoying a refreshment next to the writer Édouard Dujardin. Another recognisable figure comes in the form of the singer Yvette Guilbert, who is identified only by her trademark black gloves. Beyond the distinctive title, hints of Japanese influence can be felt everywhere. The surprising crop of Guilbert's body is reminiscent of the unusual compositions favoured by Hokusai and Hiroshige, and the specific symbolism used to denote each celebrity (whether it be fashion or physical appearance) is similar to the encoded visions of Japanese courtesans and kabuki actors. Flat slices of citron and fiery orange are set against Avril's inky black dress, which is redolent of a particularly dominant key block.

This latter technique appears time and again in Lautrec's oeuvre, as well as that of other artists, including Théophile-Alexandre Steinlen (1859–1923). His celebrated depiction of a pitch-black feline in *Tournée du Chat Noir de Rodolphe Salis* (1898) comprises another poster that sits tall within the Belle Époque canon. Given the

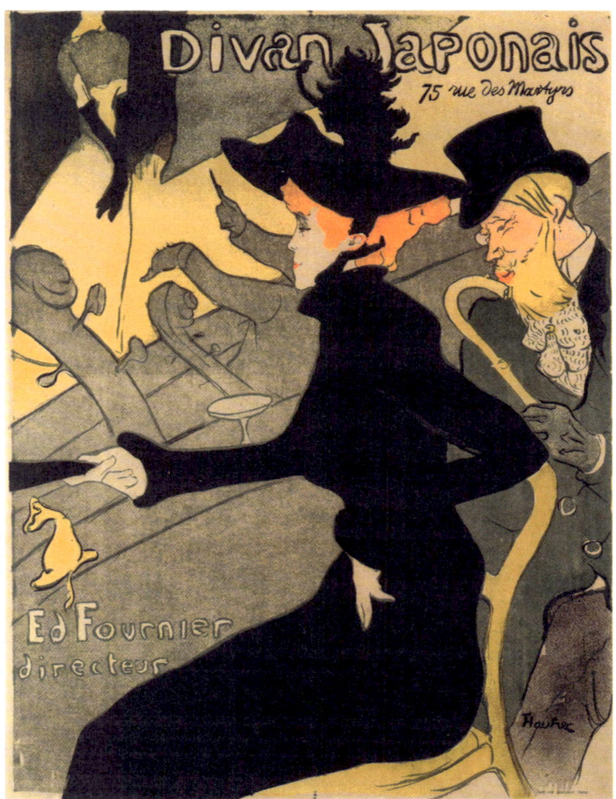

Fig. 5.14 Henri de Toulouse-Lautrec, *Divan Japonais*, 1892–3. Lithograph.

propensity for lashings of black, it should come as no surprise that artists looked not only to *nishiki-e* but also to Japanese calligraphy for inspiration. Pierre Bonnard's advertisement for France-Champagne (which was printed by Ancourt) stands as another testament (fig. 5.15). The quivering froth of sparkling wine has hints of the 'Great Wave' about it, while the expressively painted letterforms hold the dynamism – if not quite the finesse – of a calligrapher's brush.

Bonnard (1867–1947) was so enchanted by the aesthetics of *Japonisme* that he was afforded the nickname of 'the Japanese one' among the Nabis. This group, which included Paul Sérusier (1864–1927) and Édouard Vuillard (1868–1940), championed pattern and ornament above all else. These artists believed they could revitalise painting with a new modernist sensibility, while collapsing the perceived barrier between 'decorative' and 'fine' art. The flattened

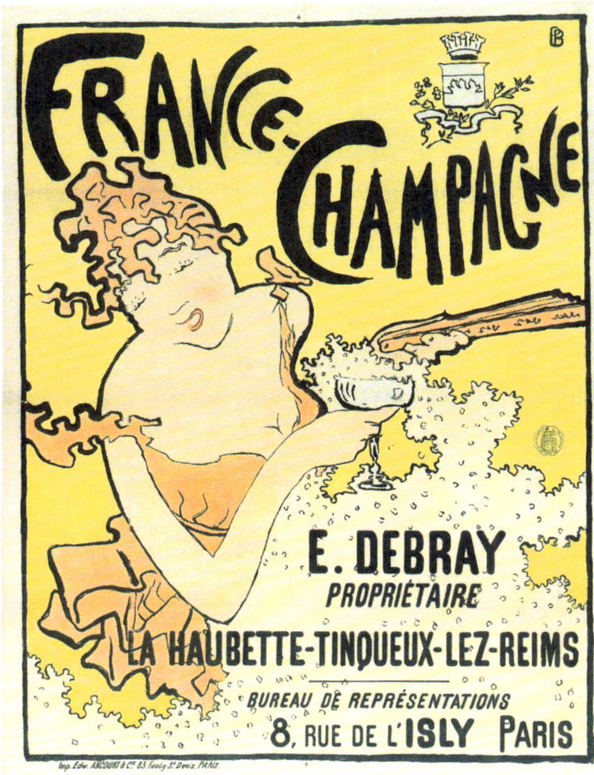

Fig. 5.15 Pierre Bonnard, poster for France-Champagne, 1889–91. Lithograph.

perspective and vibrant hues they favoured once again owed a debt to *nishiki-e* and wider *ukiyo-e* imagery, and paved the way for Art Nouveau. This movement represented a synthesis of art and craft that extended to elaborate advertising and poster design, and was dominated by the Czech émigré Alphonse Mucha (1860–1939). With his devotion to natural forms, love of sinuous outlines and a veritable obsession with beautiful women, the spectres of Edo's pleasure quarters lived on.

CHAPTER 6

ARTISTIC IMPULSE

EXPRESSIONISM, SURREALISM AND PSYCHOLOGICAL PROCESS

[It is in] the imminent risk of destruction, that the greatest result may occur

– Stanley William Hayter, 1949

VIOLENCE, POVERTY, CARNAL desire and emotional torment: these were the subjects that transfixed the Expressionists, who were far more concerned with feeling than formalism. These artists strove to unpick the workings of the inner psyche and deconstruct the perceived social order, by doing away with bourgeois affectation and replacing it with innate forms of art-making that could articulate life amid conflict and urban chaos.

This loosely associated movement came into being through the dominance of two German groups at the outset of the twentieth century. Die Brücke (The Bridge) formed in 1905 in Dresden, as a bohemian collective that favoured communal working – at least for a time. It counted Ernst Ludwig Kirchner (1880–1938) and Erich Heckel (1883–1970) among its original members, neither of whom had any formal artistic training. They strove to convey the essence of a subject as opposed to producing any accurate depiction, and favoured bold, gestural marks and extreme colour palettes.

In much the same vein, the Russian émigré Wassily Kandinsky (1866–1944) declared that 'the painter must train not only his eye but also his soul', in his manifesto *Concerning the Spiritual in Art*

(1911).[1] It was published the same year that he founded Der Blaue Reiter (The Blue Rider) with Gabriele Münter (1877–1962) and Franz Marc (1880–1916) in Munich, which laid out his path towards pure abstraction. In his essays, he argued that true art should be free of any material reality. Instead, it should reflect the essential spirit of its creator.

The significance of the psychological within the burgeoning Expressionist movement was informed by new lines of scientific and philosophical thought across Germany, Austria and beyond. Friedrich Nietzsche's critiques of morality and religion preceded the theories of Sigmund Freud and Carl Jung, both of whom demanded in-depth explorations of the subconscious. These propositions – along with the Symbolist pursuit of pure subjectivity – had a profound effect on the visual language of the late nineteenth and early twentieth century, where an exploration of interiority replaced a preoccupation with surface.

The earliest seeds of this hybrid sensibility can be traced to Max Klinger (1857–1920), a Leipzig-born artist who produced socially critical art that laid bare the darker aspects of urban life, including poverty and prostitution. He is credited with spearheading a revival in artistically minded intaglio printmaking at a time when printed matter in Germany had come to represent rather uninspired pictures produced on a mass scale. Klinger understood the evocative nature of a more intimate print process, and was equally enamoured by the country's strong graphic lineage. He spent time poring over works at the Kupferstichkabinett (Museum of Prints and Drawings) in Berlin, which counts compositions by Dürer, Rembrandt and Goya among its holdings.

Klinger's deeply emotive images – in which the familiar is undercut by the phantasmagoric – demonstrate his interest in French naturalist authors such as Émile Zola and Gustave Flaubert, as well as the allegorical subjects favoured by the Symbolists. His ever-more experimental prints often combined several intaglio techniques, including etching, drypoint, aquatint and mezzotint, all of which served to achieve a dramatic range of line and tone that allude to a collision of the physical and celestial planes.

His love of music, too, is most evident in the 1894 series 'Brahms Fantasies' (fig. 6.1), which was designed to be viewed while listening to the composer's scores. This notion followed the theory of the

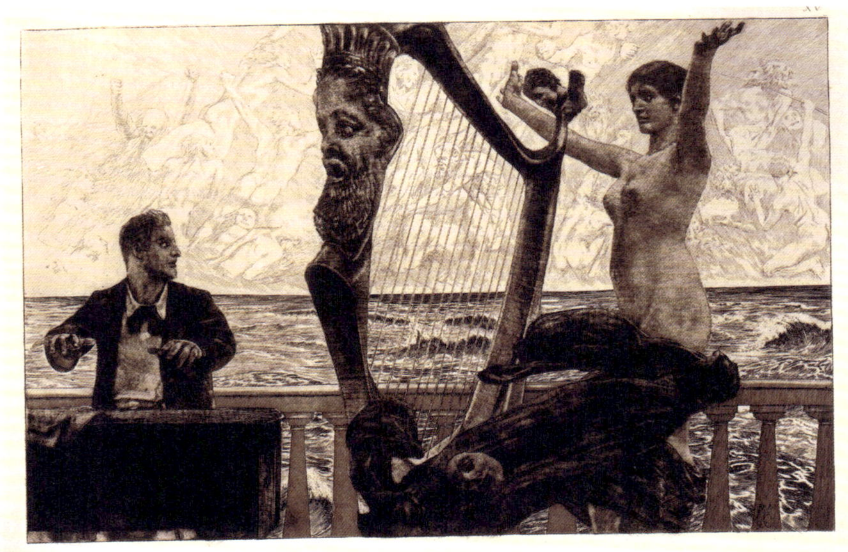

Fig. 6.1 Max Klinger, *Evocation*, from the series 'Brahms Fantasies', 1894. Etching, engraving, aquatint and mezzotint.

Gesamtkunstwerk or 'total work of art', which focused on synthesising every facet of creativity, including visual art, music, poetry, architecture and film. It went on to become a core tenet of German Expressionism.

Klinger's influence is evident in the deeply emotional imagery of Edvard Munch (1863–1944). The Norwegian artist spent time in Berlin from 1892 to 1895, and in turn he had a significant influence on the younger Expressionists who followed in his wake. His haunted visions were informed by the trauma of losing both his mother and sister at a young age, and his own struggles with mental health. The artist had a habit of returning to specific motifs, notably in his infamous *Scream*, which he reproduced both in oils and lithography. This practice was as much to do with earning money as it was with exploring process, but there is no doubt that Munch saw printmaking as a way of unlocking complex visual problems that could trouble him for decades.

This was the case in his eerie images of the Madonna, who appears not as a chaste and venerated mother of Christ but as an alluring, self-possessed nude, who dwarfs a quivering foetus cowering below (fig. 6.2). This lithograph features painterly strokes that are undercut with feverish scratches across the woman's face and torso,

   THE STORY OF PRINTMAKING

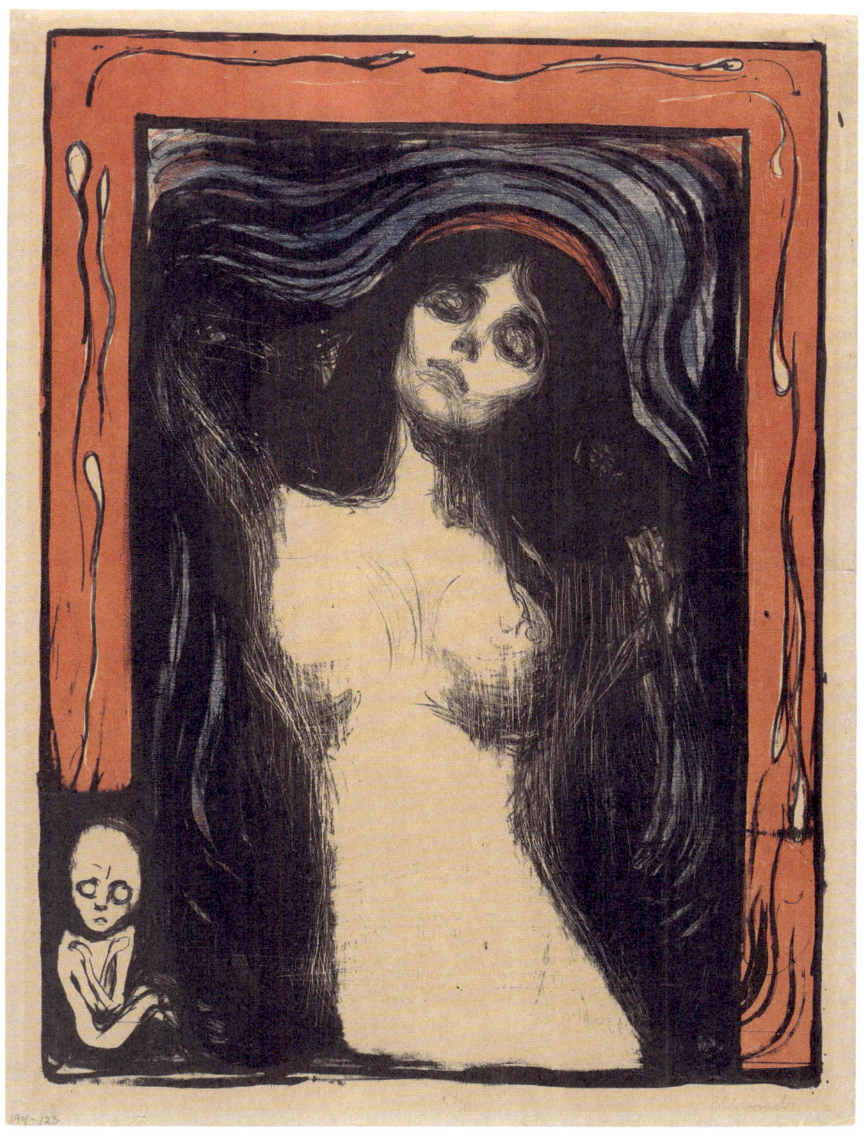

Fig. 6.2 Edvard Munch, *Madonna*, 1895–1902. Lithograph.

and various impressions see her surrounded by combinations of red, blue and black. In fact, the rather controversial sperm-covered frame proved too salacious for some collectors, and Munch produced a black-and-white version with this detail omitted.[2]

The artist also turned to the material qualities of woodcut to express both anguish and longing. The violent act of gouging served as an apt reflection of his mental state, and his habit of incorporating the grain of the block into his compositions celebrated the physical properties of the form. Such treatment was a world away from the meticulously cut and registered prints that had been perfected in *ukiyo-e* and demonstrate just how malleable a technique can be, depending on the hand that commands it. In impressions of *Moonlight I* (fig. 6.3) and *Moonlight II* (1896–1902), it is clear that Munch is just as concerned with process as he is with outcome.

This combination of the physical and the cerebral proved hugely attractive to members of Die Brücke and Der Blaue Reiter, who had largely convened in Berlin by 1910. Kirchner revelled in all kinds of printmaking, stating: 'The technical procedures doubtless release energies in the artist that remain unused in the much more lightweight processes of drawing or painting . . . . There is no better place to get to know an artist than in his graphic work.'[3]

In an account from Gustav Schiefler (an art historian and collector known as a 'passive' member of Die Brücke, thanks to his ongoing

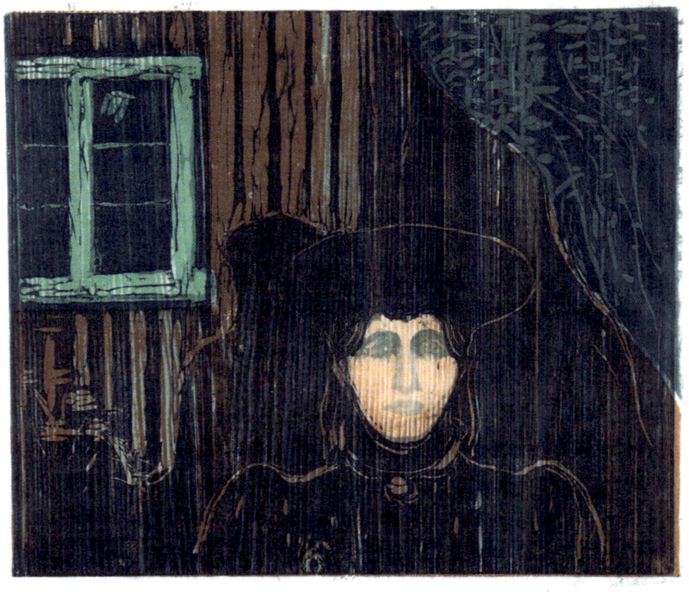

Fig. 6.3 Edvard Munch, *Moonlight I*, 1896. Woodcut.

   THE STORY OF PRINTMAKING

support), he describes a similar joy felt by Heckel, who immersed himself in the seemingly magical properties of lithography: 'As a valuable possession he had got hold of a stone and told me how, often at night, spurred by the creations of his fantasy, he would leap up to put down on the stone the visions of his inner eye; he would etch it, pull a few impressions and then grind off the image again so that he could make another one.'[4]

Despite this evident praise, it was woodcut and drypoint that proved to be the most vital methods with which to articulate the sharp angles and exaggerated forms that typified the movement's aesthetic. These expressions countered any notion of an idealised body and replaced it with grotesque flesh. Formal preparation was rejected in favour of instinct and improvisation. Gone were the preparatory sketches that might have foregrounded traditional printmaking. This was raw creativity, which artists enacted themselves, thus conveying a perceived crudeness – even naivety – that was worlds away from the practice of expert, professional printers.

Although plenty of Expressionist artists did produce prints with limited and rudimentary resources, the results could appear anything but. Marc evoked extraordinary dynamism in pieces such as *Tiger* (1912) and *Riding School after Ridinger* (1913), which are filled with the same exhilarating action found in Kandinsky's *Sounds* series (1907–12). The anguish apparent in Emil Nolde's (1867–1956) *Prophet* (1912) is also a feat of acute compositional balance, portraying a grizzled face that seems to be pulled down by the jagged gestures of every cut. The artist briefly joined Die Brücke, but remained something of an outsider, with a lingering preoccupation with mysticism. His fascist sympathies – he was a member of, then denounced by, the Nazis – have troubled historians for years.[5]

* * *

When considering the lasting impact of Expressionist printmaking, there is no figure that looms larger than Käthe Kollwitz (1867–1945). Her images of grief and violence transcend the specific sociopolitical contexts in which they were originally wrought, and relay an urgent bodily despair that cuts right to the heart of what it means to be human.

Kollwitz was born in Königsberg, in what was then East Prussia, to a progressive, middle-class family who supported her artistic talents, even when opportunities for women were minimal. While studying art at several *Damenschulen* (women's schools), she encountered the work of Max Klinger, which proved influential in her decision to do away with oils and instead pursue drawing, printmaking and sculpture. It was not only his images, but also his rhetoric, that inspired this move. In his 1891 treatise *Painting and Drawing*, he made an argument declaring drawing media – in which he included prints – as the most appropriate means of social commentary and reportage.

This struck a chord with Kollwitz, who moved to Prenzlauer Berg (then one of Berlin's poorest districts) that same year with her husband, Karl Kollwitz, who was a doctor. His consulting rooms abutted her studio and they lived in a flat above, leading her to come into contact with the harsh realities of life below the poverty line, particularly the hardship of women.[6] This experience is recorded in a diary entry from 1908:

> The longer [I examine the situation] the more I understand the typical plight of working-class families. Once the man starts drinking or becomes ill and unemployed, it always leads to the same results. He either hangs round his family's neck like a millstone . . . or he takes his own life.[7]

Kollwitz had little formal training in printmaking, which makes her body of work all the more impressive. Years before the foundation of either Die Brücke or Der Blaue Reiter, she produced a series of exceptional works that married politically minded critique with more intimate renderings of despair. 'A Weavers' Revolt' (1893–7) consisted of three etchings and three lithographs, and was inspired by a theatrical drama penned by Gerhart Hauptmann, which recounted the events of an uprising in 1844 in the Prussian province of Silesia (now in Poland). Its provocative debut invoked the ire of imperial censors, and the play was soon banned.

Rather than focusing solely on the workers' riotous destruction of machinery and attacks on wealthy merchants' homes, Kollwitz looked to the abject misery that drove them to such action. In *Need* (fig. 6.4), for example, a mother brings her hands to her head and watches over her sick and starving child, whose pallid complexion is illuminated with only the softest of marks. By contrast, their

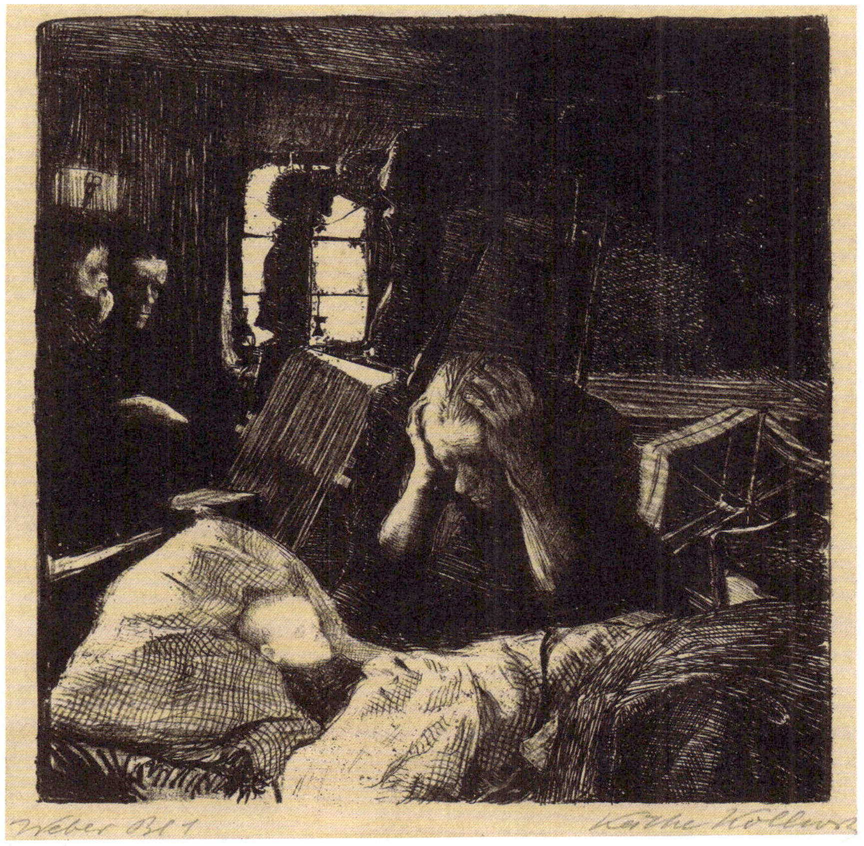

Fig. 6.4 Käthe Kollwitz, *Need*, from the series 'A Weavers' Revolt',
1893–7. Early impression printed before edition published in 1920
by Emil Richter. Lithograph and chine collé.

gloomy surroundings reveal a home dominated by the demands of
industry, while other family members appear crouched in the shadows. Kollwitz further consolidated her oppressive scene by using a
technique called chine collé, in which a piece of coloured paper is
fixed with glue and run through the press at the same time as the
plate, thus producing another hue that does not require alternate
inks. The grey-ochre shade employed here adds to a sense of crushing oppression.

Death depicts another cramped home, but this time realism is
undercut by the eerie presence of a skeleton, whose boned hand reaches
out to touch a malnourished woman. Once again, this macabre scene

directs light upon a child's face, whose wide-eyed stare suggests they might perceive the phantom before them.

The series was exhibited at the Grosse Berliner Kunstausstellung (Great Berlin Art Exhibition) in 1898 and caused something of a sensation. Kollwitz's work so struck painter and printmaker Max Liebermann, who was a member of the award jury, that he suggested she be nominated for a medal. Kaiser Wilhelm II – who, as royal sponsor of the event, had absolute veto – vehemently rejected the suggestion, on the grounds that she was stoking class warfare. Nevertheless, her fame was set, and she soon joined the Berliner Secession group, who worked beyond state-approved salons in a form of subversive precursor to the more radical Expressionism that followed.

Despite her series' acclaim and the evident skill involved in producing such works, Kollwitz remained frustrated. When explaining her reasoning for executing three prints in lithography, she stated the following: 'My technical ability in etching was still so slight, that my first attempts failed. It was for this reason that the first three plates of the series were lithographed and only the last three etchings succeeded technically.'[8]

In spite of this, she persevered with her technical inquiry. In another cycle of historically minded prints titled 'Peasants' War' (1902–8), which focused on a German uprising begun in 1522, she executed the images in etching, aquatint and drypoint, and even scratched them with sandpaper. This experimental approach to the intaglio plate is yet more evident in the standalone piece *Woman with Dead Child* (fig. 6.5). This harrowing depiction is among the artist's best-known, and marks a shift towards more intimate scenes dominated by huddled embraces, as well as the specific icon of maternal loss. To achieve the subtle texturing that forms the basis of each figure's gnarled and mottled skin, Kollwitz impressed textured paper onto the soft ground, and experimented with various different states, including another blend of greenish-grey chine collé.

She used her youngest son, Peter, as a model for the composition, which she sketched while clutching him and looking into a mirror. In a devastatingly prophetic turn of events, he died in action in Flanders only a few months after the outbreak of the First World War. She never recovered from this loss, and the enormity of her grief is evident in another diary entry, from 22 August 1916: 'Made

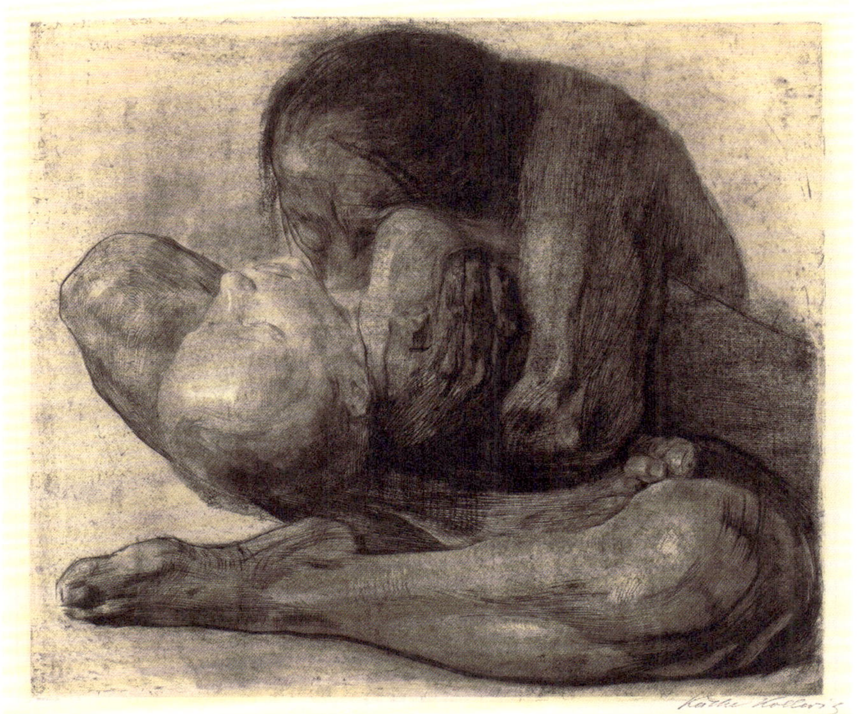

Fig. 6.5 Käthe Kollwitz, *Woman with Dead Child*, 1903.
Etching, drypoint, sandpaper and soft ground.

a drawing: the mother who takes up her dead son in her arms. I could make a hundred pictures like this but they still wouldn't bring me closer to him.'[9]

The devastation wrought by the conflict marked a turning point in Kollwitz's process, which was soon dominated by woodcut. Gone were the subtleties of the etching needle, which were replaced by stark, graphic scenes that are dominated by swathes of black. In her ensuing series titled 'War' (1921–2), her isolated figures are pulled from any contextualised scene, as if floating in a netherworld of their own torment. This is most keenly felt in *The Mothers* (fig. 6.6), where a huddled mass of women join together in an effort to protect their children from harm (Kollwitz was explicit in saying that she represented herself and her two sons in the work). Her succinct gouges articulate terror, resilience and kinship in a manner that feels

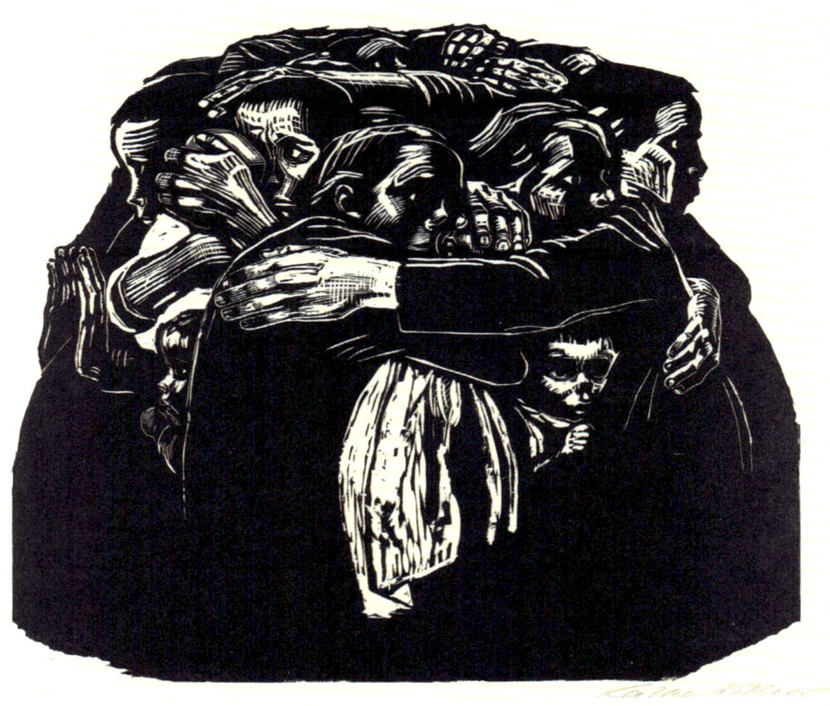

Fig. 6.6 Käthe Kollwitz, *The Mothers*, from the series 'War', 1921–2. Probably printed by Fritz Voigt, published by Emil Richter, 1923. Woodcut.

utterly relatable, and she professed her own pride in the series in a letter to the writer and historian Romain Rolland on 23 October 1922: 'I have tried again and again to represent war. I was never able to capture it. Now, finally, I have finished a series of woodcuts that come close to expressing what I have always wanted to express.'[10]

* * *

The ramifications of the First World War had a profound effect on the language of Expressionism as a whole, even among those who had initially welcomed the conflict as a means of violently rebuilding the social order. Franz Marc was killed by a shell splinter during the battle of Verdun, Kandinsky was forced to return to Russia, and Kirchner was discharged following a nervous breakdown. Meanwhile, Heckel – who enjoyed the rare privilege of being permitted to print and paint while stationed in Belgium with the Red Cross – was deeply shaken by the suffering of wounded soldiers, which he recorded in

THE STORY OF PRINTMAKING

woodcuts gouged with a pocket knife, on planks recovered from a destroyed shipping terminal.

Throughout the conflict, print continued to serve as a cheap and readily available form of art-making, particularly as other materials such as paint and canvas became scarce. Beyond artists' independent bodies of work, group portfolios and publications were used to convey first nationalistic, then pacifist messaging. The influential dealer and publisher Paul Cassirer (1871–1926) produced a patriotic journal titled *Wartime* (1914–16), which included lithographic interpretations of the conflict by various artists. Following his disillusionment after serving as a military ambulance driver, he changed the title to *The Picture Man* (1916), featuring an antiwar sentiment which included an image of a praying figure by Ernst Barlach (1870–1938), called *Give Us Peace!* (1916).

Any optimism that might have followed the Armistice was eclipsed by the political violence of the November Revolution (1918–19). Following the abdication of Kaiser Wilhelm II, various German factions entered a power struggle, resulting in an uneasy coalition between socialist parties and political players from the former imperial order, which led to the founding of the Weimar Republic.

Many artists felt betrayed by this re-establishment of a ruling class, which compounded the lasting trauma of war. They turned away from the subjective and fantastical elements of Expressionism and replaced the aesthetic with a caustic realism that became known as 'New Objectivity'. These individuals depicted their experiences of the conflict, as well as the conspicuous decadence and urban corruption that defined post-war existence.

Among the most explicit denouncements was George Grosz's (1893–1959) 'God with Us' (1918; published 1920). This portfolio of lithographs relies on austere, cartoonish lines to recount the rife corruption and inequity within the military (the artist served as an infantry soldier). In *German Doctors Fighting the Blockade* (fig. 6.7), a rotting skeleton is declared fit to fight, while portly officers laugh and joke beyond. Similarly, in *Blood Is the Best Sauce*, those of high rank enjoy a luxurious meal while unarmed protestors are attacked without mercy.[11]

Both Grosz and his publisher Wieland Herzfelde were tried for defamation and forced to surrender all copies of these prints to the

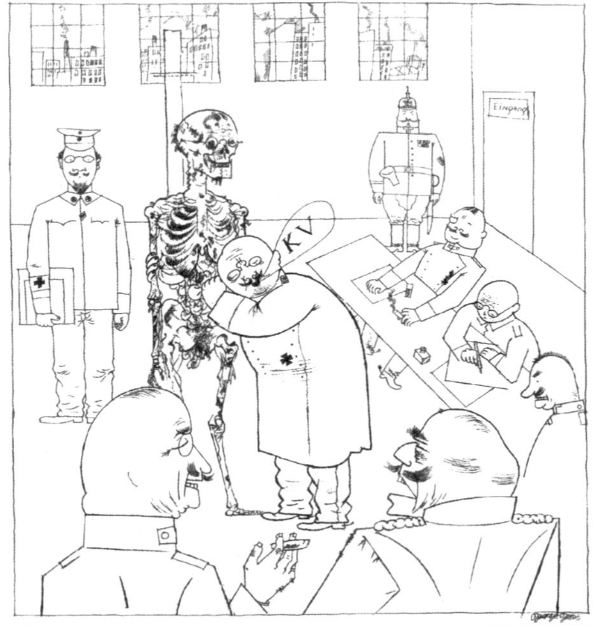

Fig. 6.7 George Grosz, *German Doctors Fighting the Blockade*, from the portfolio 'God with Us', 1918; published 1920. Printed by Hermann Birkholz, published by Wieland Herzfelde, 1920. Lithograph.

army. The fact that the accompanying captions were produced in three languages (French, German and English) suggests that Grosz wished his disdain to connect with as broad an audience as possible. Once again, it was only through print publishing that such strides could be made, as a powerful counterpart to depictions on canvas.

The same can be said of Otto Dix (1891–1969), whose huge oil-on-tempera panels titled *The War* (otherwise known as the 'Dresden Triptych') were completed from 1929 to 1932. He invoked the Old Masters in this epic battlefield narrative, yet it is his series of 50 etchings of the same title that truly conveys the intimate horrors of the conflict. Published in 1929, these prints feature gruesome and at times claustrophobic depictions inspired by his own experience in the trenches at the Somme and the Eastern Front (fig. 6.8). He used aquatint, drypoint and stop-out to articulate burned flesh, bleached-out bones, and the screams of terrified soldiers.

✳ ✳ ✳

The physical act of printing and its psychosomatic associations were a defining element of Expressionism, but it was not the only movement

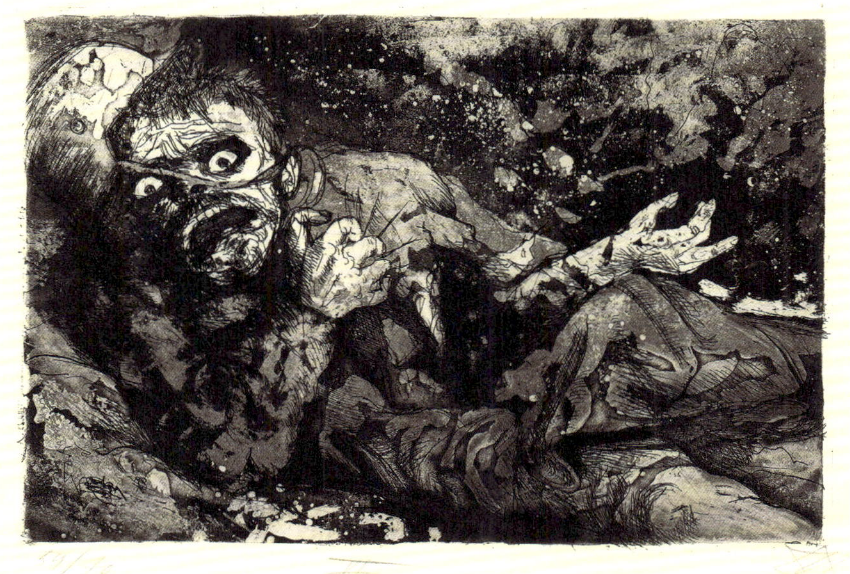

Fig. 6.8 Otto Dix, *Wounded Man (Autumn 1916, Bapaume)*,
from the portfolio 'The War', 1924. Printed by Otto Felsing, published
by Karl Nierendorf, 1929. Etching and aquatint.

to cherish the connection. Beyond Germany and Austria, a parallel
pull was felt in Paris, where a wealth of established printing workshops continued to span both mass-produced commercial enterprise
and a renewed interest in the creative possibilities of experimental,
process-driven works, particularly among the Surrealists.

This evolution is particularly evident within the work of Pablo
Picasso (1881–1973), the giant of modernism who continually rein-
vented the vanguard. While best-known as a painter and sculptor, he
was also a prolific printmaker, and his work with the block, stone
and plate had a considerable influence on his wider oeuvre. His
interest intensified as he reached the final decades of his practice,
and his print archive eventually numbered over 2,400 unique
designs.

His earliest celebrated print, and the first that he made in
the French capital, is a line etching known as *The Frugal Repast*
(fig. 6.9). Made in 1904 and printed by Auguste Delâtre,[12] it depicts
the sharp violence of poverty and the emotional distance of a couple
enduring a stiff embrace. These were common themes throughout

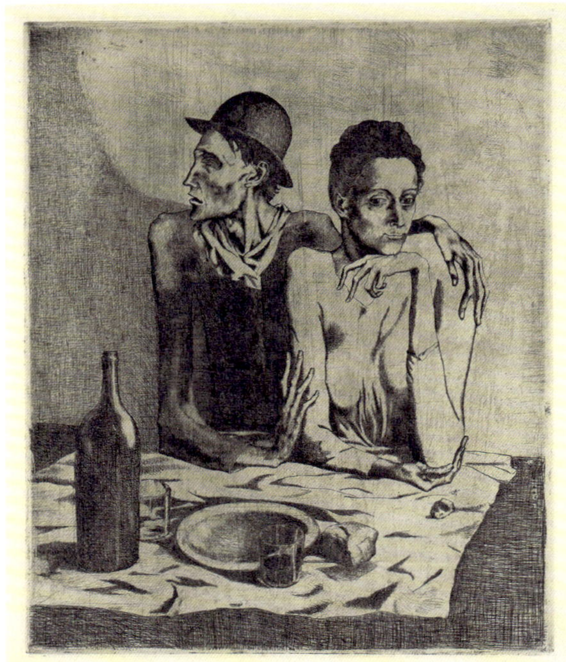

Fig. 6.9 Pablo Picasso, *The Frugal Repast*, 1904. Printed by Auguste Delâtre, 1913. Etching.

Picasso's Blue Period, which was marked by the death of his close friend Carles Casagemas and the deprivation he encountered while eking out an existence in Montmartre.

The skeletal bodies are rendered in the same awkward, angular lines of Picasso's Expressionist counterparts, where shadows fall both on bony hands and the strangely grotesque folds of fabric that cling to the woman's breasts. By contrast, her partner's concave chest is almost indistinguishable through the dark net of densely hatched lines from which it is formed. The unusual ripples that appear in the background of this composition were not deliberate, but remnants of a landscape etching by a fellow artist, Joan González (1868–1908). Picasso was so impoverished that he recycled the gifted zinc plate, but failed to fully eradicate the marks of his predecessor.

It would be another nine years before this print was finally published, thanks to the attentions of Ambroise Vollard (*c.*1866–1939). This wildly successful art dealer offered Picasso his first Parisian solo show in 1901, and, although it was only moderately successful, it cemented a fruitful partnership. Vollard was himself an outsider

                    THE STORY OF PRINTMAKING

who had arrived in the French capital from the tiny colonial island of Réunion. By the time he met Picasso, he had already established himself as a perennial tastemaker who valued not only works on canvas, but also prints that could be sold as part of collectable portfolios or appear in luxurious illustrated books. He established a gallery in 1893, and championed the likes of Renoir, Bonnard and Paul Cezanne (1839–1906). He also supported Cassatt in her pursuit of printmaking, when her main dealer, Durand-Ruel, showed an initial lack of interest.

The most ambitious and arguably most famous of his projects with Picasso was the 'Vollard Suite', a collection of 100 etchings made between 1930 and 1937. This compendium was not a straightforward commission, but rather a dialogue between dealer and artist that involved conversations about the success of particular impressions, after a long day in the studio. This relationship is an exemplar of how dealers, working as independent individuals, had begun to collaborate closely with artists on high-calibre print compendiums.

The naming of the suite was afforded by subsequent critics and historians, and it was never referred to as such by either artist or dealer. In fact, Picasso rarely labelled his prints, and the various complexities of his subject matter have troubled those who wish to create broad thematic readings. In the suite, he encompasses a vibrant tangle of symbolism that reaches from within the inner psyche and the annals of art history to the sociopolitical context of the day. He depicts the artist's studio and the role of the muse (which was particularly striking, given his new affair with Marie-Thérèse Walter), as well as the act of convening with and creating sculpture. A large expanse also explores the coupling of eroticism and animalistic violence (including disturbing depictions of rape) through the classical figure of the Minotaur. The artist's obsession with creative mythos is also introduced in his rather derogatory renderings of Rembrandt, who appears as caricatured versions of his own aged self-portraiture.

The push and pull between sensuality and depravity within this series mirrors the visual language that had developed through German Expressionism. Other examples beyond the works of the 'Vollard Suite' are more explicit in their denouncement of war, as well as the rise of fascism in Spain. Designed much like a set of comic strips,

Dream and Lie of Franco (1937) consists of a satirical depiction of an obscene authoritarian, followed by the devastation that befell the Basque town of Guernica when it was bombed by Franco-allied German troops (the same subject that inspired his famed colossal canvas). In this version, the greyscale oils are replaced with etched lines and watery aquatint.

Picasso was a self-taught printmaker, but he cherished the advice and guidance of experts. Delâtre had nurtured his nascent interest in intaglio with both *The Frugal Repast* and the subsequent drypoint series 'The Acrobats' (1904–6). Roger Lacourière (1892–1967) was another great teacher. His atelier was renowned for its technical expertise in etching, and counted Henri Matisse (1869–1954), Joan Miró (1893–1983) and Salvador Dalí (1904–1989) among its habitués. He introduced Picasso to the painterly effects made possible with sugar-lift, a form of aquatint in which a sugar, soap and ink solution is painted directly onto a clean plate, creating marks that are closely aligned with the fluidity of a painter's brush. Once a ground is applied, the plate is immersed in boiling water, and the soluble solution lifts off the ground with the aid of some gentle disturbance with a brush. The possibilities for subsequent layers of aquatint and stop-out are endless, but the real ingenuity behind this process lies in enabling gestural brush marks that would be nigh-on impossible to achieve with an etching needle.

To this day, many printmakers swear by their own unique sugar-lift concoctions. Some prefer corn syrup, or a mixture containing the chicory and caffeine compound known as Camp Coffee. Plenty of pilgrims to Atelier Lacourière, including the great British etcher Norman Ackroyd (1938–2024), recall being shown the exact recipe favoured by Picasso, thanks to the generosity of Madeleine Lacourière (Roger's wife). She used to mix his sugar-lift while preparing her morning coffee, and would occasionally cook steaks on the etching hot plates.[13]

Picasso paired the technique with other aquatint approaches to great effect in select prints within the 'Vollard Suite', which otherwise features a commanding scarcity of line. In *Faun Uncovering a Sleeping Woman* (1936), for example, an enormous variety of tone and gestural mark-making is made possible through rosin layers, etched lines and scratched textures. In *Blind Minotaur Led by a Little Girl in the Night* (fig. 6.10), arguably one of the most technically

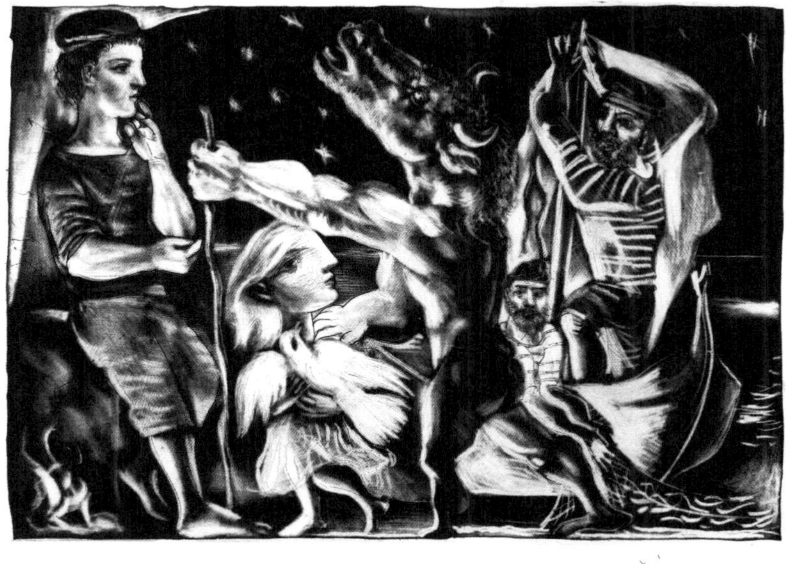

Fig. 6.10 Pablo Picasso, *Blind Minotaur Led by a Little Girl in the Night*, from the 'Vollard Suite', 1935. Printed by Roger Lacourière, *c.*1939. Aquatint and drypoint.

complex and dream-like prints in the series, a deeply etched aquatint ground is scraped back to reveal vibrant highlights, emulating the dramatic effects of a mezzotint. This constant experimentation within the workshop was chronicled by the artist's friend and secretary, Jaume Sabartés, who stated: 'At six the printers left. To please Picasso, Lacourière would remain, and then precisely as if he were in his own studio and quite independent of anyone Picasso would begin new experiments.'[14]

Vollard would never see the publication of this project, nor the great critical reception and market it subsequently generated. He died suddenly in 1939, when his chauffeur-driven car crashed upon leaving his country estate. Rumours suggested that he died due to the impact of a heavy copper etching plate, or else a bronze sculpture. Thousands of recently delivered impressions of the suite were found at his Parisian property, which accounted for roughly 313 copies of this large-scale edition. They finally entered the public realm after several exchanges among Parisian dealers, with complete sets first sold by Henri Petiet in the 1950s, and the name of their late originator soon attached.

Picasso never ceased printmaking, even after this tragedy. Much in line with the rest of his practice, he continued to innovate and seek out those who could bring his vision to life. This was clear in the remarkable relief prints he produced with the printer Hidalgo Arnéra (1922–2007), which were conceived not through woodcut, but through commercially available linoleum. This rubbery material is still used as a cheap and effective form of floor tiling, which is much more malleable than wood. When warmed on a hot plate it becomes surprisingly supple, and small gouges – even scalpels – can be used to create lines of varying thickness. The impermeable surface is quite unlike naturally textured woodgrain, which makes it perfect for producing flat, slick layers of colour and crisp, high-contrast imagery.

Although Picasso first began experimenting with the technique known as 'linocut' in the 1930s, it was not until the 1950s that he truly mastered its properties. He started by designing several posters advertising his ceramics exhibitions in Vallauris, but it was his large-scale piece *Still Life with Glass under the Lamp* (fig. 6.11) that set a new precedent. With Arnéra's guidance, he chose not to produce a different plate for every one of his four colours, but instead to use a system known as 'reduction'. This involves progressively cutting away the design from a single plate, and printing at intervals in between. It is a technique that demands acuity and confidence, because, once carved, the design cannot be undone. Moreover, it means only a limited edition can be produced, as each layer is obliterated with every development.

Fortunately, the process is demonstrated clearly by the trial proofs Picasso produced to test each coloured layer. What begins as a rather detailed image of a lamp illuminating a dinner table, articulated in lemony yellow, becomes increasingly simplistic as further areas of linoleum are cleared away. It is only when these states are brought together that the brilliantly vivid scene comes to life in additional green, red and black. The technical calculations and creative complexity needed to produce such a work show just how accomplished a printmaker Picasso had become and also the huge debt he owed master printers, who not only sought to articulate his ambitious visions, but also afforded him the tools to do so himself.

   THE STORY OF PRINTMAKING

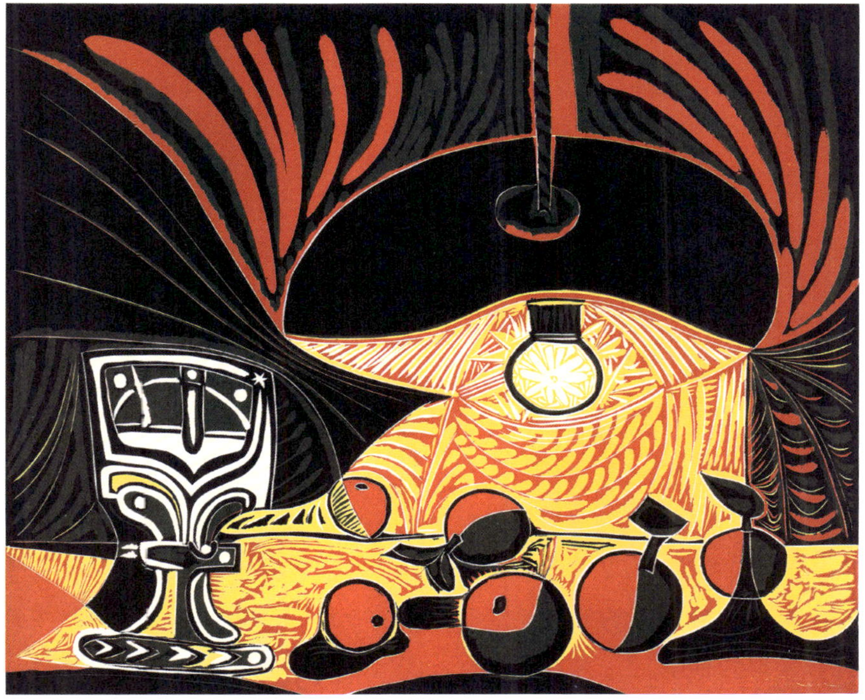

Fig. 6.11 Pablo Picasso, *Still Life with Glass under the Lamp*. Printed by Hidalgo Arnéra, published by Galerie Louise Leiris, 1962. Reduction linocut.

The artist's formidable output additionally allowed him to become something of a patron to those whose talents he both admired and demanded. This was certainly the case with Aldo Crommelynck (1931–2008), a gifted printer who first worked with Picasso at Lacourière's atelier, before partnering independently with the artist during the last decade of his life. This intaglio expert set up shop in the town of Mougins in 1963 (with assistance from his brother, Piero, 1934–2001), and ostensibly operated as an extension of the Picasso studio. This proximity allowed the pair to collaborate on celebrated series such as the '347 Suite' (1968) with unprecedented speed, while managing Picasso's exacting expectations.

Crommelynck's considerable skills led him to work with a host of other artists on his return to Paris, following Picasso's death in 1973. Here he nurtured a younger generation, including Pop artists such as Jim Dine (b. 1935), Richard Hamilton (1922–2011) and Jasper Johns (b. 1930), before relocating to New York, where his talents were sought after by the likes of Claes Oldenburg (1929–2022) and Ed Ruscha (b. 1937; see also chapter 8). and Ed Ruscha (see also chapter 8). Many of these artists have stated that it was Crommelynck who first truly showed them the possibilities of intaglio, acting as teacher, mentor and collaborator. For the printer himself, the ultimate objective was always to aid artists in the best expression of their work, 'by finding the appropriate methods and implementing them well. More than well – perfectly.'[15]

* * *

The authority of process, as opposed to any premeditated outcome, was at the heart of Stanley William Hayter's (1901–1988) teaching. This hugely influential printmaker was dedicated to the artistry of intaglio, and had a considerable impact on the language of abstraction. Although born in London, he established himself among the Surrealists in Paris. His arrival in 1926 followed a brief career as a chemist and geologist, which informed his rigorous pursuit of invention and experimentation in the printing studio. It was during this first year that he trained in engraving under the artists Joseph Hecht (1891–1951) and Jacques Villon (1875–1963), while honing his innate skills as a painter. He soon had such a command of intaglio processes (including engraving, etching and aquatint) that he set up his own workshop, known as Atelier 17.[16]

This name has become synonymous with the history of twentieth-century printmaking, and few enthusiasts will be a stranger to its influence. Unlike other operations, which were chiefly concerned with representing pre-existing concepts, Hayter believed that a process-driven approach defined by the subconscious could offer up entirely new ideas, which only came into being once a print was complete. In fact, it was only through accident and error that the mind could be truly set free.

Hayter's proposition aligned with Surrealist ideas of 'psychic automatism', in which conscious control is given over to unconscious thought. He encouraged individuals to arrive at their own solutions through extensive experimentation, and counted Picasso, Miró, Max Ernst (1891–1976) and Alberto Giacometti (1901–1966) among his earliest students.

While most studios still embodied something of a facilitatory role, Hayter championed a collaborative atmosphere that did away with traditional hierarchy, and he inducted his students through techniques that were designed to break old habits. Preparatory drawings were forbidden, as were any attempts to replicate the qualities of a painting. He favoured non-representational art, and insisted on printing proofs at every state and stage, so that the artist could make sense of developments and follow their own creative impulse. As he explains in his book *New Ways of Gravure* (1949): 'It is in the exposure of his idea and his plate to the accidents of a method, to the imminent risk of destruction, that the greatest result may occur in a work and the most valuable experience in the artist.'[17]

Hayter is credited with revolutionising intaglio not only in Europe, but also in the USA. Following the outbreak of the Second World War, he travelled to New York with his wife (the American sculptor Helen Phillips, 1913–1995) after a brief stint designing camouflage patterns back in the UK. He established another iteration of his famed atelier in association with the New School for Social Research in 1940. It soon became a meeting place for Surrealist émigrés and a younger cohort of artists who had begun to build a new visual vocabulary that was distinctly American.

Many of the Abstract Expressionists,[18] as they became known, had developed an understanding and appreciation of the so-called 'graphic arts' while training as part of the Federal Art Project of the Works Progress Administration (WPA). This groundbreaking government initiative was set up as part of President Roosevelt's New Deal and ran from 1935 to 1943. It introduced a range of new arts centres with a strong focus on education, and employed artists to produce public works of art, propelling a fresh creative sensibility that stretched throughout the ensuing decades.

Hayter's atelier, far from being a place of mere technical instruction, offered rarefied access to the heroes of the Parisian avant-garde. Miró, Ernst, Roberto Matta (1911–2002) and Yves Tanguy (1900–1955) had all escaped to New York. They congregated at the studio and experimented with intaglio alongside younger peers such as Robert Motherwell (1915–1991), Louise Nevelson (1899–1988), Willem de Kooning (1904–1997) and Jackson Pollock (1912–1956).

The latter's distinct form of action painting shares an affinity with his tutor's messaging, not to mention the very specific treatment of an intaglio plate. Unlike a traditional approach to a canvas mounted onto a wall or easel, Pollock approached his surface from every angle, dripping house paint directly from the can to make marks. The technique is similar to how one turns a piece of metal in order to better incise or ink it. Pollock's move towards complete abstraction has links to the influence of Hayter, who encouraged his students to experiment with line, form and composition before attempting to ascribe a deeper meaning in their work. He even eschewed any sense of orientation, preferring instead to consider a completed image before making a definitive decision on how it should be presented.

During the decade that it was based in New York, Atelier 17 became a gathering place for all kinds of creative minds, whether artists, poets, philosophers or scientists. Debate on any subject was encouraged, but a more fastidious approach to printmaking began to emerge, along with Hayter's position as supreme head of his enterprise. For one, he never relented in his bias towards intaglio and was particularly dismissive of lithography, which he deemed too akin to reproduction despite evidence against this viewpoint.[19] He could also be overbearing, despite his original intent to allow artists to find their own way. Nevelson, who is best-known for her sculptural assemblages, recalled, in a 1968 interview, being stifled by Hayter's well-meaning gaze: 'Mr. Hayter was so sweet. He gave me a great deal of attention and every time I took a breath he was taking one. And that defeated me because I didn't want to be what you call an expert on all those tools.'[20]

Nevelson also had an outright altercation with fellow workshop member Boris Margo (1902–1995), who informed her that her heavily slathered inkings were unacceptable and untidy. She remained unmoved, and the various iterations of *Moon Goddess* (1952–4) demonstrate her unbridled application of a heavily inked brush in directional swirls and swipes that varied with every impression. Indeed, when printed, the pigment occasionally bled beyond the plate, resulting in carbon-black dribbles.

By the time of this quarrel, Hayter had already moved his principal workshop back to Paris, but not before he began developing a novel form of 'viscosity' printing (also known as 'simultaneous colour'). By using a textural variety of soft and hard grounds on a single plate, along with coloured inks formulated at different levels of viscidity, multiple areas can be inked in several hues without the fear of merging or the need to accurately register several single-colour plates. This technical mastery was pioneered with considerable input from Krishna Reddy (1925–2018), an expert printer from Andhra Pradesh who had studied at the eminent Santiniketan fine arts school in West Bengal (which focused on traditional Indian practices) and the Slade School of Fine Art in London. Following his arrival in Paris in the early 1950s, he became Hayter's right-hand man and eventually a director of Atelier 17. These advancements in intaglio opened up entirely new possibilities for expressive colour printing, which is evident in Hayter's own works. Among them is the early piece *Maternity* (fig. 6.12), which was made in New York to commemorate the birth of his son,[21] and *L'Escoutay* (1951) which features vibrant, gestural shapes achieved through etching and stencils.

This complex methodology was more than likely informed by the printer's investigations into William Blake's relief etchings, at the behest of the poet and Blake scholar Ruthven Todd (1914–1978). After acquiring a fragment from an original plate, the pair tried to

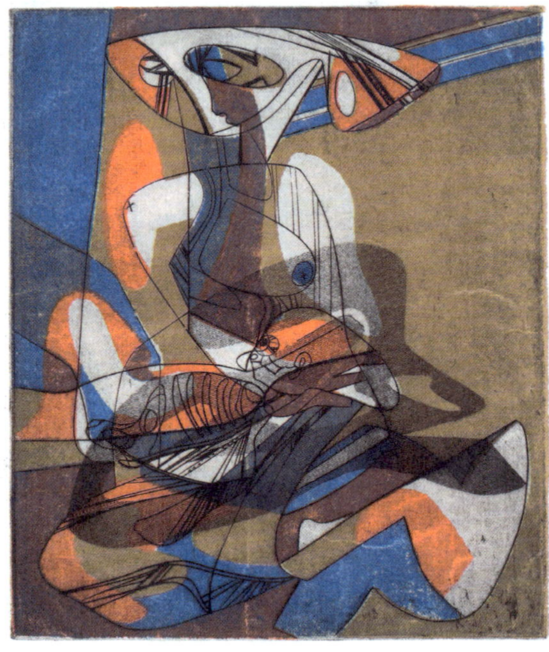

Fig. 6.12 Stanley William Hayter, *Maternity*, 1940. Engraving, etching and screenprint.

ascertain how it was created, with the help of other Atelier 17 artists including Miró and Ernst. Although far from conclusive, these tests went some way to replicating the artist's remarkable mirror writing with the aid of stop-out varnish, and the subsequent portfolio included abstract compositions informed by his celestial illustrations. Although the visual language differs, there is an inherent connection between Blake and Hayter's championing of process. While the former found spirituality and higher meaning, the latter favoured automatism and accident. Ultimately, both understood the potential of printmaking as a means to articulate something that lies beyond conscious understanding.

CHAPTER 7

RESISTANCE AND REVOLUTION

MEXICAN METAL CUTS AND THE TALLER DE GRÁFICA POPULAR

A work of art . . . does not need revolution as its subject in order to be revolutionary

— Elizabeth Catlett, 1975

DURING A TRIP to New York in 1933, Frida Kahlo (1907–1954) was feeling homesick. After several years touring the United States with her husband, the revered muralist Diego Rivera (1886–1957), she longed for the sights and sounds of Mexico City and set about creating her own colourful haven in their hotel room. She covered the walls with a series of brightly pigmented pieces of paper, which were printed with sensational news stories, scurrilous gossip and satirical political imagery.

These broadsides were the work of José Guadalupe Posada (1852–1913), a prolific printmaker who enjoyed modest success during his lifetime, only to be heralded as a hero of revolutionary Mexican aesthetics a decade after his death. His *calaveras* (skeletons) have become synonymous with a form of vernacular cultural identity known as *mexicanidad*, which renounces colonial Spanish influences and embraces indigenous tradition to articulate a distinct form of 'Mexicanness'. These motifs shared a close association with Día de los Muertos (Day of the Dead), a holy festival that briefly reunites the living with the souls of the deceased.

Posada was born in the city of Aguascalientes, the son of a baker and a homemaker who were both of indigenous heritage. He studied at the Municipal Academy of Drawing before embarking on a career as a lithographer in the workshop of José Trinidad Pedroza (1837–1920), in the early 1870s. This was a healthy trade for a young man of considerable artistic talents, and employment was practically guaranteed thanks to a strong commercial printing tradition that championed 'popular prints' among a litany of other visual ephemera.

Posada was originally tasked with creating cartoons for Pedroza's political periodical *El Jicote* (The Wasp), which often criticised the government and ruling class. Such critique came with considerable risk, as growing authoritarianism gradually eroded the liberal promises of President Benito Juárez's La Reforma.[1] Political pressures might well have encouraged Posada to follow his employer to the city of León, where he eventually took over the newly established workshop and produced all kinds of printed material, including flyers, religious devotional cards and catalogues. He also tutored lithography at a local high school.

By 1888 he had relocated to Mexico City, in search of new commercial opportunities and to foster connections with like-minded printmakers. The vibrant metropolis was fertile ground for revolutionary sentiment amid the discontent of Porfirio Díaz's dictatorship, which took hold after his second successful presidential election in 1884. It was in this milieu that Posada found his signature style, thanks in no small part to Antonio Vanegas Arroyo (*c.*1850–1917), an influential and prolific publisher who specialised in cheap gazettes and broadsides that catered to the popular imagination. His imprint produced tales of lurid crimes, devastating disasters and celebrated folk heroes, as well as political discourse and a variety of hobbyist books. An advertisement for the business reads as follows:

Founded in the year 1830 of the nineteenth century,
this ancient firm stocks a wide choice:
Collections of Greetings, Tricks, Puzzles, Games, Cookbooks,
Recipes for Making Candies and Pastries,
Models of Speeches, Scripts for Clowns, Patriotic Exhortations,
Playlets Meant for Children or Puppets, Pleasant Tales,

  THE STORY OF PRINTMAKING

Also: the Novel Oracle, Rules for Telling the Cards,
a New Set of Mexican Prognostications, Books of Magic, Both
  Brown and White,
a Handbook for Witches.[2]

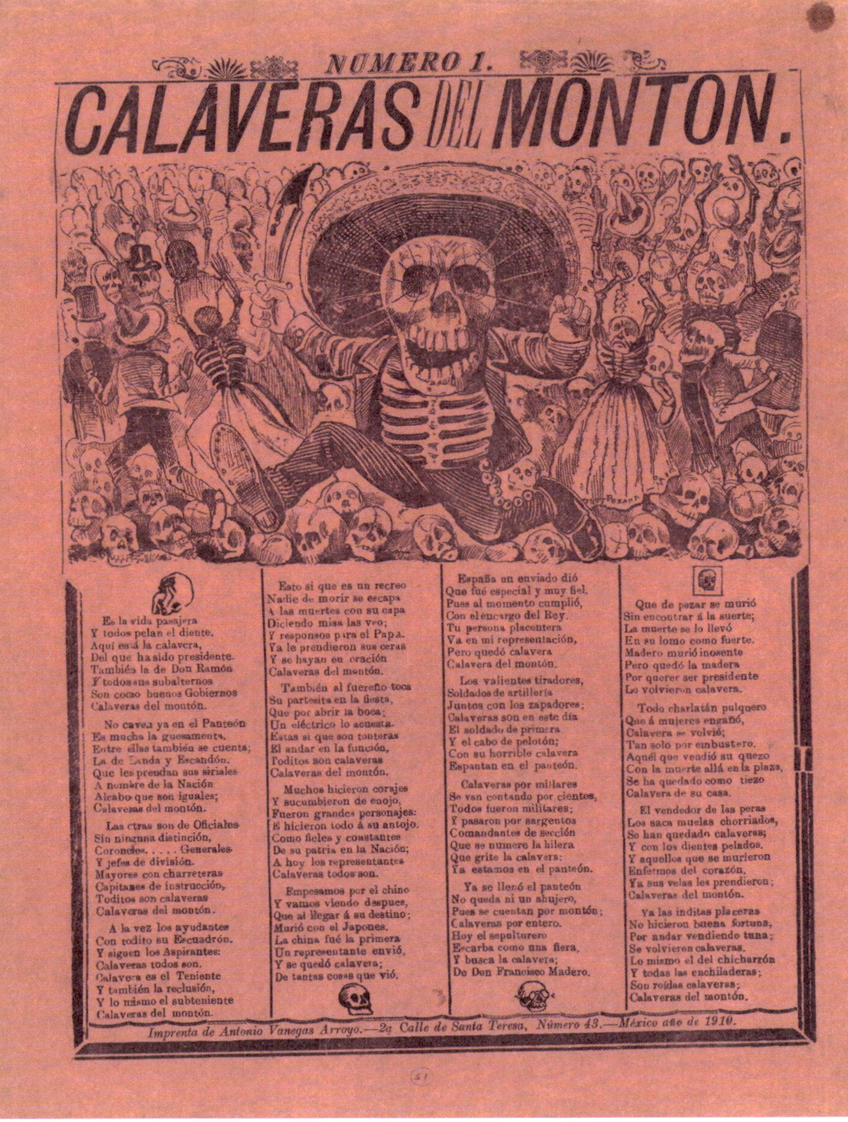

NÚMERO 1.
CALAVERAS DEL MONTON.

Es la vida pasajera
Y todos pelan el diente.
Aquí está la calavera,
Del que ha sido presidente.
También la de Don Ramón
Y todos sus subalternos
Son como buenos Gobiernos
Calaveras del montón.

No cavea ya en el Panteón
Es mucha la guesamenta,
Entre ellas también se cuenta;
La de Landa y Escandón.
Que les preudan sus siriales
A nombre de la Nación
Alcabo que son iguales;
Calaveras del montón.

Las otras son de Oficiales
Sin ninguna distinción,
Coroneles..... Generales
Y jefes de división.
Mayores con charreteras
Capitanes de instrucción,
Toditos son calaveras
Calaveras del montón.

A la vez los ayudantes
Con todito su Escuadrón.
Y siguen los Aspirantes:
Calaveras todos son.
Calavera es el Teniente
Y también la reclusión,
Y lo mismo el subteniente
Calaveras del montón.

Esto si que es un recreo
Nadie de morir se escapa
A las muertes con su capa
Diciendo misa las veo;
Y responsos para el Papa.
Ya le prendieron sus ceras
Y se hayan en oración
Calaveras del montón.

También al fuereño toca
Su partesita en la fiesta,
Que por abrir la boca;
Un eléctrico lo acuesta.
Estas si que son tonteras
El andar en la función,
Toditos son calaveras
Calaveras del montón.

Muchos hicieron corajes
Y sucumbieron de enojo,
Fueron grandes personajes;
É hicieron todo á su antojo.
Como fieles y constantes
De su patria en la Nación;
A hoy los representantes
Calaveras todos son.

Empesamos por el chino
Y vamos viendo despues,
Que al llegar á su destino:
Murió con el Japones.
La china fué la primera
Un representante envió,
Y se quedó calavera;
De tantas cosas que vió.

España un enviado dió
Que fué especial y muy fiel,
Pues al momento cumplió,
Con el encargo del Rey.
Tu persona placentera
Va en mi representación,
Pero quedó calavera
Calaveras del montón.

Los valientes tiradores,
Soldados de artillería
Juntos con los zapadores;
Calaveras son en este día
El soldado de primera
Y el cabo de pelotón;
Con su horrible calavera
Espantan en el panteón.

Calaveras por millares
Se van contando por cientos,
Todos fueron militares;
Y pasaron por sargentos
Comandantes de sección
Que se numere la hilera
Que grite la calavera:
Ya estamos en el panteón.

Ya se llenó el panteón
No queda ni un ahujero,
Pues se cuentan por montón;
Calaveras por entero.
Hoy el sepulturero
Escarba como una fiera,
Y busca la calavera;
De Don Francisco Madero.

Que de pezar se murió
Sin encontrar á la suerte;
La muerte se lo llevó
En su lomo como fuerte.
Madero murió inosente
Pero quedó la madera
Por querer ser presidente
Lo volvieron calaveras.

Todo charlatán pulquero
Que á mujeres engañó,
Calavera se volvió;
Tan solo por enbustero.
Aquél que vendió su quezo
Con la muerte allá en la plaza,
Se ha quedado como tiezo
Calavera de su casa.

El vendedor de las peras
Los saca muelas chorriados,
Se han quedado calaveras;
Y con los dientes pelados.
Y aquellos que se murieron
Enfermos del corazón,
Ya sus velas les prendieron;
Calaveras del montón.

Ya las inditas placeras
No hicieron buena fortuna,
Por andar vendiendo tuna;
Se volvieron calaveras.
Lo mismo el del chicharrón
Y todas las enchiladeras;
Son roídas calaveras;
Calaveras del montón.

Imprenta de Antonio Vanegas Arroyo.—2ª Calle de Santa Teresa, Número 43.—México año de 1910.

Fig. 7.1 José Guadalupe Posada, *Calaveras from the Heap, Number 1.*
Published by Antonio Vanegas Arroyo, 1910. Relief engraving or photo-
relief etching with letterpress.

Arroyo employed Posada as his chief illustrator, capitalising on his inherent wit and eye for graphic simplicity, which was soon dominated by crowds of skeletal figures (fig. 7.1). Although the symbol of the *calavera* was not original (another employee, Manuel Manilla (1830–1900), had already executed plenty of designs in this fashion), Posada's dynamic compositions and vivid imagination set him apart. Among his most famed examples is a depiction of the literary hero Don Quixote, who appears astride a cadaverous, galloping horse (fig. 7.2). Perhaps even better known is 'La Catrina' (fig. 7.3), a much beloved yet darkly humorous take on the affectations of the bourgeois

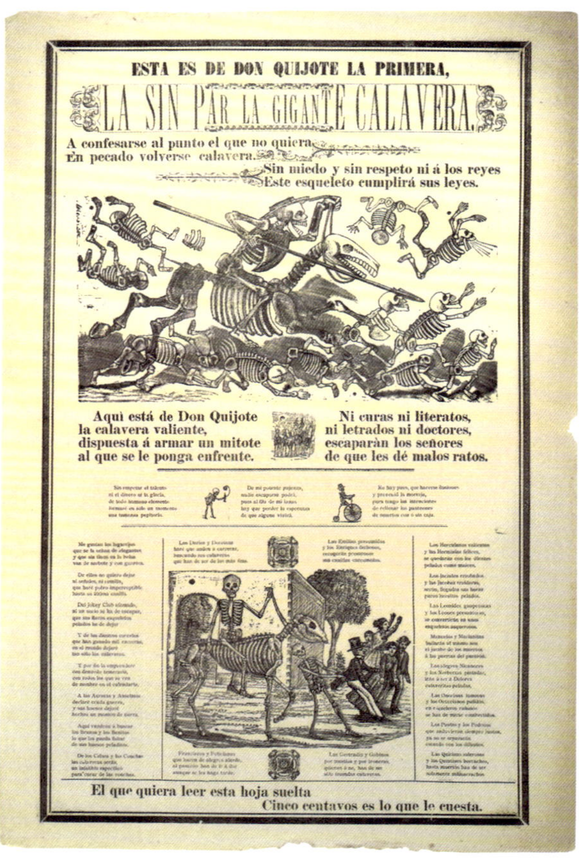

Fig. 7.2 José Guadalupe Posada (top) and Manuel Manilla (bottom), *This Is Don Quixote, the First, the Matchless, the Giant Calavera without Equal.* Published by Antonio Vanegas Arroyo, 1872–1913. Relief engraving or photo-relief etching with letterpress.

   THE STORY OF PRINTMAKING

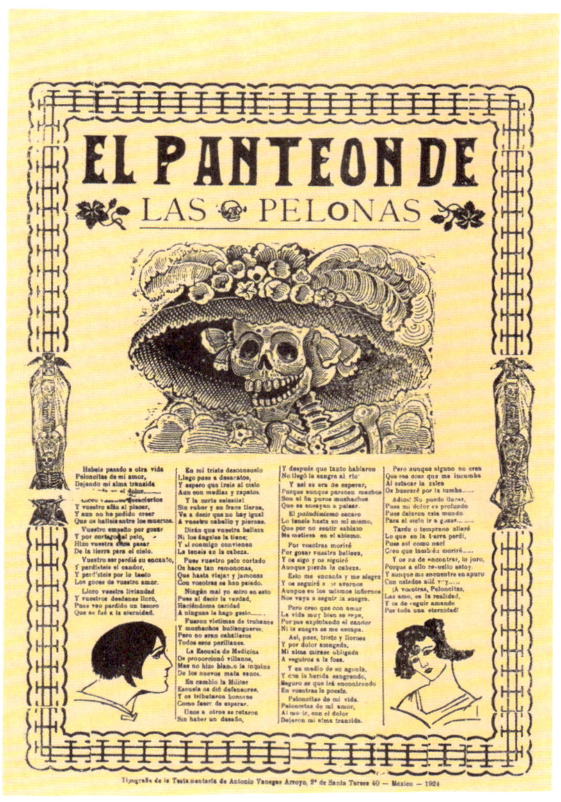

Fig. 7.3 José Guadalupe Posada, *Graveyard of Bald Women*,
featuring 'La Catrina'. Published by Antonio Vanegas Arroyo, 1924.
Relief engraving or photo-relief etching with letterpress.

Mexicans who adopted European airs. This figure wears an elaborate feathered – and obviously foreign – bonnet, as well as a wide grin.

These popular motifs were continually reused with new texts and reimagined layouts, on colourful sheets ranging from red and yellow to purple and green. Although the artistry of these prints is undeniable, Arroyo was chiefly concerned with production and profits. Rather than attempting to disguise the flaws born from hasty and relentless production, his workshop embraced them. Cracks from worn-down plates were used for emphasis, heightening the drama of a knife attack or a flash flood. Inky blotches caused by nails used to reassemble broken blocks were incorporated into scenes of fatal rail crashes and other calamities, while mismatched typography served as dynamic exclamations that conveyed a sense of urgency, even to those viewers who could not read.

***

Although Posada's visual style is instantly recognisable, exactly how he went about creating his plates is more complicated. Early accounts suggest that he engraved directly into metal blocks used for typesetting, creating a relief as opposed to an intaglio plate. José Clemente Orozco (1883–1949), who was one of the stars of the Mexican muralist movement and formed one third of *Los Tres Grandes* (The Big Three) alongside Rivera and David Alfaro Siqueiros (1896–1974), recalled passing Posada's workshop on the way to school. He stated in his 1945 autobiography:

> Posada worked in full view of the public behind the shop window . . . where I used to stop enchanted for a few minutes on my way to and from school to observe the printmaker. . . . Sometimes, I was bold enough to filch a few of the metal shavings that fell as the *maestro* moved his burin over the typemetal plate coated with red lead. . . .[3]

The number of skilled engravers required to keep up with such arduous production surely became prohibitive as his workload increased, which might well explain why researchers have found evidence of acid processes on original Posada plates. It seems he used a form of photo-relief etching, in which a design was drawn onto white card with black ink, before being photographed to produce a high-contrast negative. This image could then be exposed onto a zinc plate that had been covered in light-sensitive gelatin, effectively producing stopped-out lines that were protected from a subsequent dip in the acid bath.[4] The result is a metal relief block akin to a traditional woodcut, produced without the need for the time-consuming expertise of artisan cutters, and not unlike the experimental medium developed by William Blake and investigated by Stanley William Hayter (see pp. 155–6).

Photomechanical printing was commonplace in Mexico by the 1870s. By coating a copper plate in a light-sensitive gelatin, a negative could be exposed onto its surface and etched, allowing for an accurate reproduction that could be printed. With such technology

THE STORY OF PRINTMAKING

available, there is no reason to suggest that both illustrator and publisher would not have harnessed its cost-effective utilities. However, the mythology surrounding Posada's 'authentic' style has led to the prevailing idea of a more vernacular craftsmanship, which continues to permeate today. Much of this has to do with his veneration by *Los Tres Grandes*, who sought to rescue his legacy after an unassuming death in 1913, when he was buried in a pauper's grave. Despite him not living to see the outcome of the Mexican Revolution (which spanned from 1910 to 1920), his legacy was soon painted as one that could define the visual force of a new, modern republic.

Rivera's spurious claims that he both knew, and was taught how to print by Posada do not diminish his observations concerning this printmaker's brilliance. As he reveals in this critique from his autobiography *My Art, My Life* (first published in 1960):

It was he who revealed to me the inherent beauty in the Mexican people, their struggle and aspirations. And it was he who taught me the supreme lesson of all art: that nothing can be expressed except through the force of feeling, that the soul of every masterpiece is powerful emotion.[5]

Rivera went on to immortalise the artist in his 1948 mural *Dream of a Sunday Afternoon in Alameda Park*, which presents the figure of 'La Catrina' with her creator to one side and a childlike depiction of Rivera on the other. Kahlo, in her preferred traditional dress, stands behind the skeleton's shoulder. This enormous 15-metre fresco chronicles the key events of recent Mexican history, and places Posada at the indisputable artistic centre.

* * *

It was not Rivera, but a Frenchman of Mexican ancestry who first sought to revive Posada's legacy. Jean Charlot (1898–1979) had gone to Mexico City, to work on a mural with Rivera, in 1920. He was immediately struck by the printed penny-sheets sold in every corner of the city. They came with no name, and were so ubiquitous that it seemed no one had cared to remember who had designed them. He eventually located the Posada workshop, where the artist's son continued to operate, and took hand-burnished prints of all the remaining plates and blocks. Many of these were reprinted in *Mexican*

Folkways, a bilingual magazine founded in 1925 by the American anthropologist Frances Toor, to promote Mexican artistry across the border. Charlot, who sat on the editorial board with Rivera, wrote a number of articles for this title and beyond, hailing Posada as the ultimate printmaker of the Mexican people.

Another decidedly more radical publication reprinted the same blocks as a way to connect with everyday working people, as opposed to craft connoisseurs. *El Machete* (fig. 7.4), named after the distinct blade, was a newspaper born from the Union of Technical Workers, Painters and Sculptors, which counted *Los Tres Grandes* among its members. Its first issue in August 1924 featured Posada's image of Zapatistas (followers of the revolutionary agrarian leader Emiliano Zapata) ambushing federalist soldiers.

This socialist gazette was handed out on the street and fly-posted under the cover of night. With scarce funds, artists including Siqueiros and Xavier Guerrero (1896–1974) exploited cheap materials such as discarded planks of wood to produce roughly hewn relief prints, following Posada not only in graphic style, but also in economic sensibility. The activist Graciela Amador (1898–1961) penned a brief poem to would-be patrons, with a nod to the limited palette of key black and bloody crimson: 'For that heavenly red to stay, pay.'[6]

El Machete was eventually shut down by the government due to its close affiliation with the Mexican Communist Party. Its

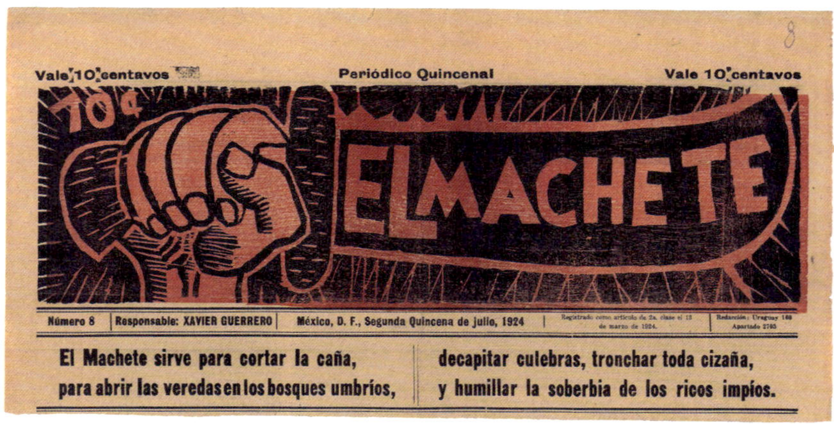

Fig. 7.4 David Alfaro Siqueiros, title page masthead
for *El Machete*, 1924. Photo-relief and letterpress.

pronouncements on workers' rights and social reforms proved too dangerous for an administration that was still grappling with factionalism, rebellion and the assassination of some of the revolution's key leaders. Support for commissioning public murals did, however, remain an integral form of creative employment, and a new generation of artists committed to social change owed much to federal commissions they worked on.

Among them was Leopoldo Méndez (1902–1969), who was to become one of the most influential printmakers of twentieth-century Mexico. He was born and raised in the capital and enjoyed a comprehensive arts education, before founding the League of Revolutionary Writers and Artists (LEAR) with the influential Siqueiros and younger muralists Luis Arenal (1909–1985) and Pablo O'Higgins (1904–1983). This loosely connected group was founded in 1934, the same year the liberal president Lázaro Cárdenas came to power. The group encompassed practically every member of the creative avant-garde and resisted any specific party allegiance. Its raison d'être was to form a united front against the threat of fascism both at home and abroad, through a marriage of art and politics that was underpinned by progressive literary voices and powerful imagery. The group's flagship periodical *Frente a Frente* (Face to Face) used both photomontage and traditional print techniques to condemn right-wing oppressors and directly satirise dictators including Adolf Hitler and Benito Mussolini.

The sheer size of LEAR, and Méndez's opinion that it had been overrun by opportunistic artists who were not suitably dedicated to the cause, led him to set up a more focused printmaking coterie known as El Taller de Gráfica Popular (the People's Graphic Workshop, or TGP) in 1937. He entreated the same founding members to join the project – alongside other eminent painters such as Alfredo Zalce (1908–2003) and Raúl Anguiano (1915–2006) – with an inspired yet romantic vision of Posada's workshop in which egalitarian, communal production worked to create images dedicated to the dignity and freedom of the Mexican people.

The TGP first found a home in a rented room offered by the master lithographer Jesús Arteaga (who counted Orozco and Siqueiros among his clients). After receiving donated equipment from a local university, the workshop was able to go about producing both relief and lithographic prints. It originally created posters, handbills and newspapers aimed at promoting antifascist organisations and trade unions, all of which were designed and produced collectively. Every artist played to their strengths, whether it be drafting, designing or printing, and many built sizeable graphic outputs alongside completing commissions for murals, making paintings and assuming teaching posts. Méndez recalled these early days with deep pride, stating, 'This workshop . . . gives an idea of what it was like to be an artisan in the golden age of graphic arts in Mexico.'[7]

Posada's influence stretched further than the guiding principles of the workshop. He was presented as an emblem of historical pride that validated both the TGP's mission and its artistic lineage, not least in Zalce's fantastical woodcut *José Guadalupe Posada and Calaveras* (1948). Here, Posada is depicted tossing his famed broadsides into a crowd of skeletons while carving at his bench, where he is surrounded by the admiring figures of Rivera, Orozco and Méndez.[8]

The inescapable motif of the *calaveras* continued to endure within the TGP's output, too. In anonymous, collectively produced papers and broadsides these satirical renderings were rife, and they even appeared as morbid, hand-wrought typography assembled from femurs, spines and daggers. Reprints of original Posada plates continued to prove popular, but it was Méndez's distinct compositions and dynamic relief cuts that rendered the connection most potent. His ability to combine topical sociopolitical events and the ongoing language of revolution was influenced by Posada, as is evident in his enduring portrait of the printmaker from 1953 (fig. 7.5). This large-scale linocut depicts the master in his workshop, surrounded by his tools, a typesetter and the Flores Magón brothers, who were revolutionary activists. In this imagined scene, Posada looks up from his printing plate to witness the state-sanctioned violence playing out on the street beyond.

This fictitious, but otherwise realistic, portrayal is eclipsed by an altogether more macabre vision in *What May Come* (fig. 7.6). Méndez presents himself lying on top of sheafs of Posada prints, at the bottom of a scene that twists the symbols of the Mexican flag into a nightmarish vision. The eagle, usually poised triumphantly on a nopal cactus, appears crucified against a cross that has been transformed into a swastika through the addition of four blades.

     THE STORY OF PRINTMAKING

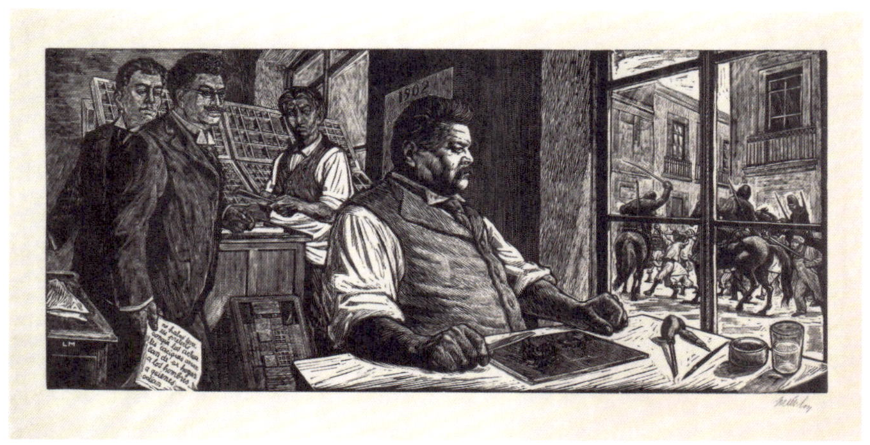

Fig. 7.5 Leopoldo Méndez, *Posada in his Workshop (Homage to Posada)*,
1953. Linocut.

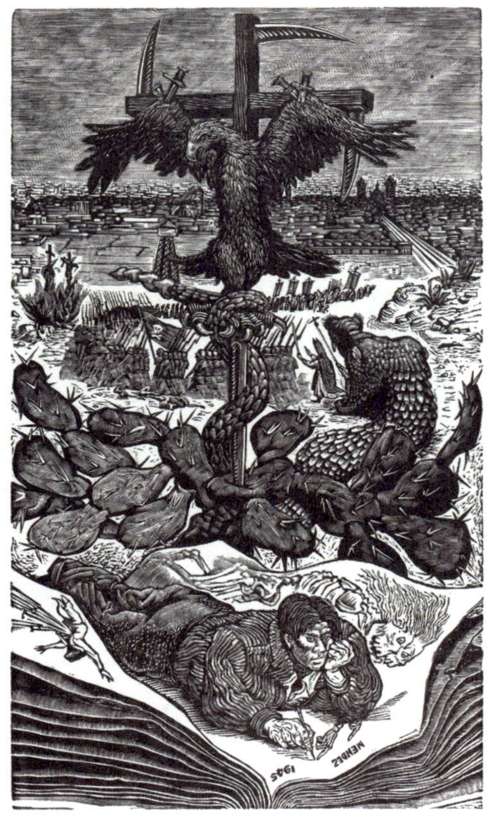

Fig. 7.6 Leopoldo Méndez,
What May Come, 1945.
Woodcut.

Rather than overpowering a snake in its claws – in an allusion to the mythic founding of the Aztec city of Tenochtitlán – the bird of prey is bound by the reptile's body as it slithers towards the modern landscape of Mexico City, which is being overrun by fascist troops with the aid of the Catholic Church.

This disturbing image was produced at the culmination of the Second World War, at a time when Mexico's own future remained uncertain. It was commissioned and purchased by the Art Institute of Chicago, and was distributed among members of the museum's prints and drawings club, as well as being sold to the general public. This overseas collaboration was hardly unusual for the TGP or its artists. The workshop's international outlook and reach was such that an array of exhibitions was mounted in Chicago and New York, buoyed by the two nations' increasingly friendly relationship in the fight against fascism. Unfortunately, the group's endeavours to ingratiate its work within the Soviet Union were greeted less enthusiastically. In 1940, a portfolio of over 100 prints was sent to Moscow, but was met with disapproval for its perceived expressionistic tendencies and a relationship to Cubism, as well as for failing to fully glorify the lives of the peasantry and industrial workers.[9]

Although these Russian officials seemingly had little understanding of Meso-American visual history (which had a strong influence on Cubism), or the merits of realistic portrayals of class struggle, suspected associations with the German Expressionists and the broader European avant-garde were well founded. The cross-pollination of liberal ideas and authoritarian resistance had long inspired LEAR members, as is evident in the Dada-inflected photomontages published in *Frente a Frente*. As political refugees from Europe found safety in Mexico City, the impetus to produce a chronicle of the terror that had befallen much of the continent took hold. The most significant example was *The Black Book of Nazi Terror in Europe* (1942–3). This compendium of writing, photographs, drawings and prints was organised by Hannes Meyer (1889–1954), the Swiss-born architect and former director of the Bauhaus, who joined the TGP in 1942 following his forced departure. Its publication was supported by the governments of Mexico and Peru, and the exiled president of then-Czechoslovakia, with an introduction that reads as follows:

Here the reader will find the fundamentals of Nazism in their most despicable applications, in Germany as well as in the rest of the occupied countries. . . . They are the work of [those] who succeeded in escaping from the claws of Nazism, often from one country to another, and who, in spite of belonging to different political sectors, represent all – in diverse shades of meaning – antifascist opinion.[10]

In fact, the book contained not only contributions by Europeans, but also Americans and Mexicans, including O'Higgins, Zalce and Méndez. The latter's *Deportation to Death (Death Train)* (fig. 7.7) is considered to be one of the earliest images of the concentration camps to be produced outside of Europe, and is perhaps the first print of the subject. In a testament to the enduring relevance of Käthe Kollwitz's emotive realism, several of her prints were also included. Her influence among Mexican printmakers of the period was keenly felt, particularly by Méndez, who produced several woodcuts inspired by her work. He depicted mournful women who appear hunched in their grief, with their heads in their hands, in a vision of austere domesticity. One of these pieces appeared on the cover of *Freies Deutschland*, a newspaper published by German exiles in Mexico, as an analogy for the psychological horrors of war.

* * *

Through the international reputations of its most famed members, and a nascent business acumen that was seemingly at odds with socialist ideals, the TGP's renown grew. The latter evolution was revitalised by Meyer, who had understood the commercial potential of more rarefied portfolios of work, following the success of the anti-Nazi *Black Book* and Méndez's American collaboration. He set about establishing the TGP's official publishing house, La Estampa Mexicana, which produced beautifully designed and authored editions printed on expensive papers. They were aimed not at a broad public, but at a burgeoning collectors' market that was becoming established in the United States. Among its output was Zalce's 'Estampas de Yucatán' ('Prints of the Yucatán'; fig. 7.8), a series of lithographs that celebrated contemporary Mayan culture in the southeastern region, and the ambitious 'Estampas de la Revolución Mexicana' ('Prints of the Mexican Revolution', 1947) which featured single-sheet prints from 16 artists and glorified heroes such as Zapata and Pancho Villa.

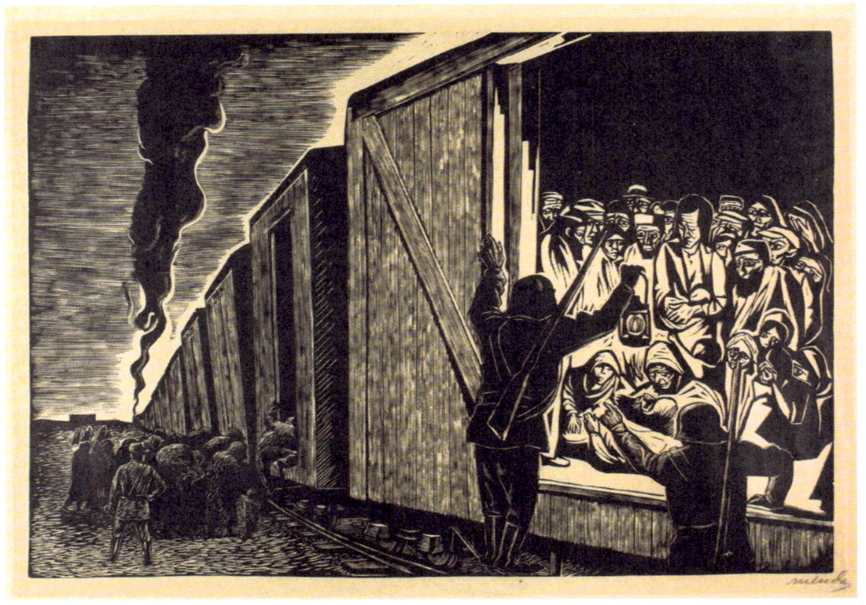

Fig. 7.7 Leopoldo Méndez, *Deportation to Death (Death Train)*, 1942, published as part of *The Black Book of Nazi Terror in Europe*, 1942–3. Linocut.

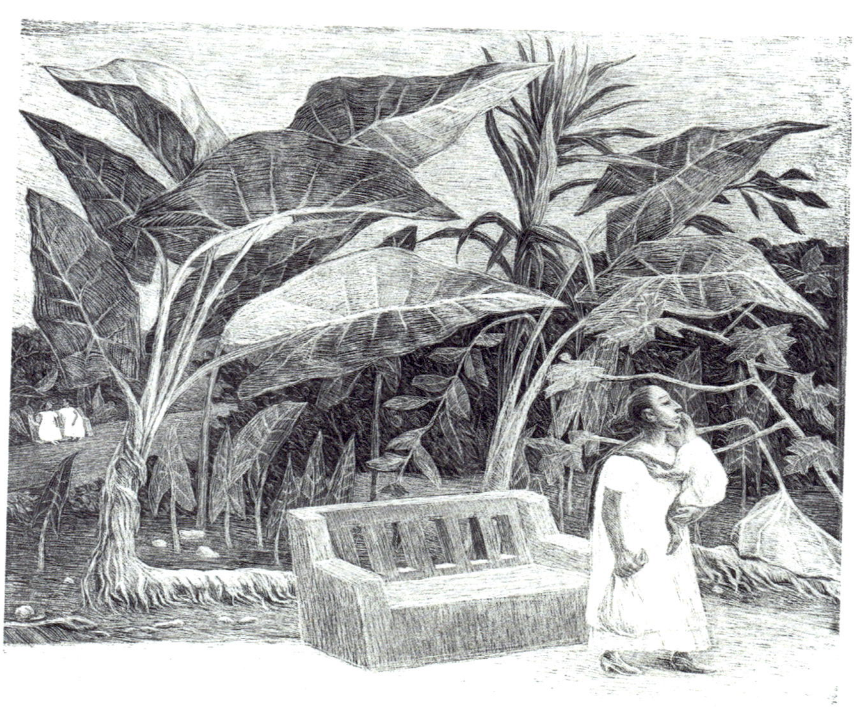

Fig. 7.8 Alfredo Zalce, *Garden of Hecelchacán*, from the series 'Estampas de Yucatán', 1945, published 1946. Lithograph.

During the same period, an array of younger artists from other countries inspired by the egalitarian ideals of the TGP and Mexican public art made pilgrimages to the workshop. They took part in a guest artist programme that offered tutelage and collaboration, and some even made Mexico their permanent home. Among them was Mariana Yampolsky (1925–2002), who was still a teenager when she arrived on pure speculation, without speaking a word of Spanish. She had been inspired by a lecture given at the Art Institute of Chicago by artists Max Kahn (1902–2005) and Eleanor Coen (1916–2010), who extolled the virtues of their own visit. As the child of Russian Jewish refugees, Yampolsky was particularly enamoured with the group's antifascist activism, and was welcomed warmly, eventually becoming the group's first official female member.

Today, Yampolsky is best-known as an influential photographer who spent her life capturing the realities of rural Mexican life in exquisite detail. However, she maintained a parallel printing practice and was active in the TGP for over 15 years. She began by working on collaborative posters with Zalce and O'Higgins, before embarking on close to 60 portfolio projects, many of which were concerned with educational reform and the global peace movement.

Elizabeth Catlett (1915–2012) was equally enthused by the ethos of the workshop, and her career was ultimately defined by it. She travelled to the TGP in 1946 with her then-husband, Charles White (1918–1979). By that time, both were already acclaimed artists and educators concerned with amplifying and elevating Black voices. It was here that Catlett produced what would become one of her greatest bodies of work: 'The Black Woman' (1946–7). This series of 15 linocuts presented well-known civil rights figures, including Sojourner Truth and Harriet Tubman (fig. 7.9), alongside images of everyday workers and scenes of violence and segregation. Catlett's impetus for the project was to produce a series focused on the realities and invisible labour of Black women's lives, as well as the exceptional and heroic actions of well-known figures. Ultimately, she wanted to present these individuals as 'beautiful, dignified, strong people'.[11]

The emphatic simplicity of Catlett's relief work was evidently inspired by other workshop members such as Méndez, and she also recalled owing a debt to Kollwitz.[12] By contrast, her lithographs share a greater affinity with the stylised modernist curves of her

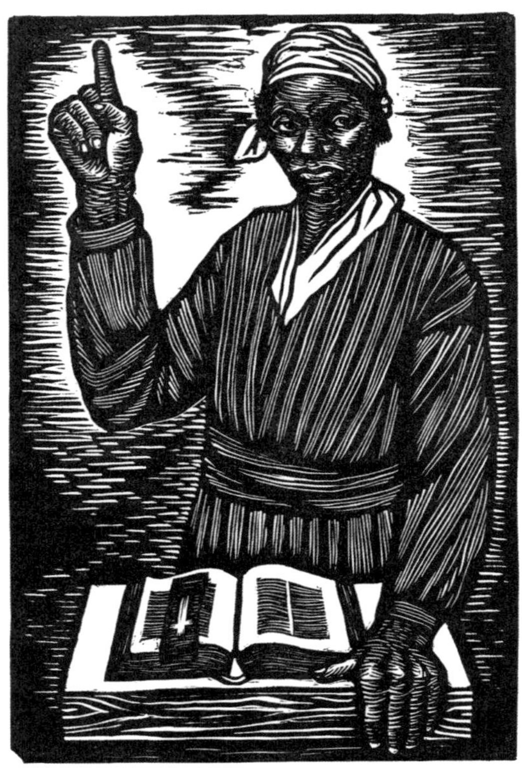

Fig. 7.9 Elizabeth Catlett, *In Harriet Tubman I Helped
Hundreds to Freedom*, from the series 'The Negro Woman',
1946–7 (re-titled 'The Black Woman', 1989), printed by
Robert Blackburn, 1989. Linocut.

sculpture, as seen in *Mother and Child* (fig. 7.10). Regardless of her
chosen medium, she maintained a steadfast dedication to relaying
the experiences of Black women with care and respect.

Catlett and White were among a cohort of African American
artists who found the TGP to be a far more sympathetic and supportive environment than that endured back home. With its focus on
indigenous rights and social reform, this cooperative was in natural
allegiance with the civil rights struggle. The long history of explicitly
political art and figurative realism within Mexico proved the perfect
environment in which to articulate their cause and expand upon its
visual language. This relationship is clear in an excerpt from Catlett's
1975 essay for *The Black Scholar*:

                                        THE STORY OF PRINTMAKING

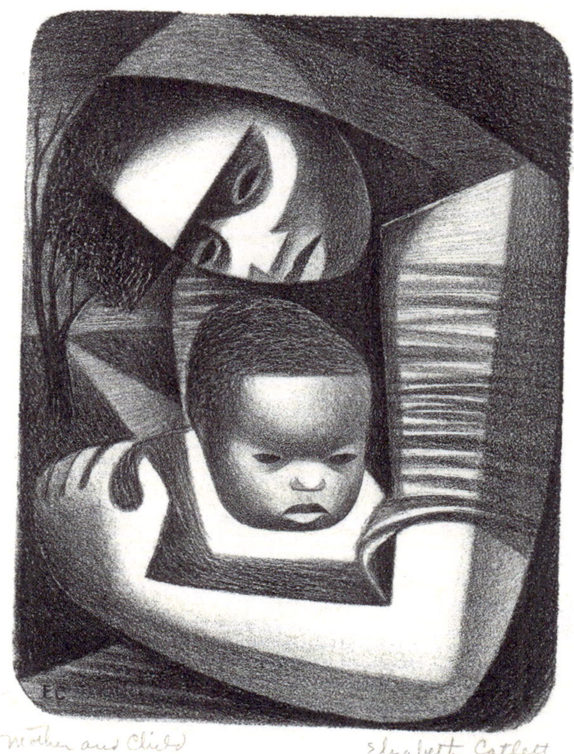

Fig. 7.10 Elizabeth Catlett, *Mother and Child*,
1944. Lithograph.

Our struggle is not for black culture but black liberation. We should analyze the role of our artistic production in these terms. A work of art might be spiritual, emotional or intellectually rewarding especially in the realm of the real/ordinary/popular. It does not need revolution as its subject in order to be revolutionary.[13]

As these guest artists explored novel modes of expression, they moved beyond familiar subjects and took inspiration from their new compatriots. Boston-born John Wilson (1922–2015), for example, spent six years making prints that not only engaged with the oppression and violence of the Jim Crow South, but also with the multifaceted experiences of the Mexican working class. Similarly, Margaret Taylor Goss Burroughs (1915–2010) spent a year creating work that aligned with her radical activism back in Chicago, once again evoking motifs that spoke specifically to indigenous heritage and civil rights.

Once more women joined the ranks of the TGP, its visual output shifted considerably. Fanny Rabel (1922–2008) and María Luisa Martín (1927–1982), who were born in Poland and Spain, respectively, had resettled in Mexico after fleeing European conflicts. Both enjoyed a rich art education in their adopted capital, as did the established Mexican artist Celia Calderón de la Barca (1921–1969). She was already a celebrated muralist and teacher by the time she joined the workshop, and soon became a senior member of the group. Together, these artists honed multifaceted female representation that moved beyond tropes of domesticity or passivity. This is particularly evident in Calderón's personification of Mexico in works such as *The Oil Is Ours* (1954) and *The Country Will Not Accept Foreign Bases* (1960), where a benevolent and powerful matriarch protects her people.

As the 1960s drew on, membership of the TGP fractured along the lines of political discord. Whereas once the group had managed to come together for the greater good, collective promise now gave way to in-fighting and questions of authorship. Once founding members such as O'Higgins and Méndez broke away, many removed their blocks and plates from the archive. Siqueiros's own militant politics had increasingly left him at odds with many of his peers. The TGP had originally welcomed him back after a period of exile and imprisonment, following his failed plot to assassinate Leon Trotsky in 1940. His co-conspirators were fellow members Luis Arenal and José Sánchez (active 1945–85). Some have said that the attack was even planned in the printing room.

Despite this gradual demise, the legacy of the TGP as an exemplar of socialist enterprise has influenced and inspired generations of subsequent printmakers. One final account speaks to the nigh-on fanatical dedication of some of these workshop members, not only in terms of politics, but also with regard to the tangible realities of running a printing workshop. Sánchez – the same young man who had aligned himself with Siqueiros and his assassination plot – became the cooperative's most valued and experienced lithographer, with a work ethic that knew no bounds. In 1948, Méndez recalled a hideous accident that would have ended the career of most printers:

José Sánchez, our lithographer, lost his right arm in an accident at the press where he worked during the day. Fortunately, however, this worker has shown exemplary mettle. . . . When the machine severed his arm at the elbow, he didn't pass out. With his left hand, he held his arm, which was hanging from some tendon, and while the owner of the press, who was behind him, ran off to hide in his office like a rat, and another worker fainted and others didn't know what to do, he very calmly set about giving himself some first aid, asking one of his workmates to tie his arm to staunch the bleeding, and in that way he remained fully conscious until the operation. Pablo [O'Higgins] and I see him nearly every day, and at the TGP we're planning the best way to help him.[14]

This vivid account could easily have been published in one of Posada's sensational broadsheets, with its perfect marriage of disaster, cowardice and heroism. Sánchez's own note, sent to O'Higgins from hospital, was less colourful: 'Pablo, I send you greetings and inform you that having suffered an accident, I am in bed at the Italian Sanatorium. . . . If something crops up with regard to work, come and see me and warn the boys.'[15]

This matter-of-fact account displays an extreme commitment to the needs of the group at the expense of the individual. A sense of collective responsibility also led members to rally and raise the money towards Sánchez's prosthetic, and his remarkable resolve soon saw him return to work with the assistance of his wife María Luisa Plata. He learned to pull the press and write with his left hand, and went on to establish his own independent lithography enterprise, undeterred by his injury. It seems that, even in the darkest of times, the resilient spirit of the People's Graphic Workshop could endure.

CHAPTER 8

PRINT GOES POP

AMERICAN LITHOGRAPHY AND THE RISE OF THE SCREENPRINT

I am not interested in production, but in [the] revelation of things
– Tatyana Grosman, undated notebook

COMIC-STRIP BLASTS and Campbell's soup cans, glossy advertising slogans and celebrity snapshots: these are the images that come to mind when conjuring the world of American Pop Art. By the late 1960s, artists had collapsed the boundaries between 'high' and 'low' culture by reappropriating and elevating the visuals of everyday life and embracing the aesthetics of advertising and enterprise. This new impetus rewrote the rules of how art should be produced, as well as the veneration afforded to a unique object.

The relationship between mass production and commercial graphic traditions made lithography the perfect medium for this fresh vanguard. However, it was not through the well-trodden path of industrialised printing that it truly made its mark. Instead, its creative potential was completely reimagined through a constellation of printmaking workshops that emerged in the 1950s. These ventures were founded by an array of independent figures who were committed to an intimate and ongoing collaboration between artists and master printers, to produce original works. Their influence instigated a lithography renaissance in the USA, which ultimately shaped both the landscape of print and the Pop Art movement as a whole.

The shift began in New York in 1947, when a gifted printmaker named Robert Blackburn (1920–2003) set up a workshop in a Chelsea loft. He was the son of Jamaican immigrants, who grew up surrounded by the intense creative and intellectual pulse of the Harlem Renaissance, where a new form of African American modernity and Black cultural identity was being forged. By the time he was a teenager he was already reaping the rewards of a rigorous artistic education, thanks to introductions from his uncle, who was a painter-decorator. He joined classes at the Harlem Arts Workshop with the pre-eminent painter Charles Alston (1907–1977); studied with the acclaimed sculptor Augusta Savage (1892–1962) at the Uptown Art Laboratory; trained in lithography with the accomplished printmaker Riva Helfond (1910–2002); and furthered his skills at the influential Art Students League under the watchful eye of Will Barnet (1911–2012), who became a lifelong friend.

This vibrant community-driven education informed the establishment of the Robert Blackburn Printmaking Workshop (RBPMW). With no admittance interviews or portfolio reviews, and fees that were subsidised or waived entirely for those in need, the workshop became a haven for people who had suffered discrimination at other studios, or else felt their work was misunderstood. They hailed from across the five New York boroughs, but also from China, Peru, Ethiopia and Puerto Rico, eager to learn from a master printer whose patience knew no bounds, but whose standards were notoriously high. Juan Sánchez (b. 1954), a key figure in the Nuyorican cultural movement (established by those of Puerto Rican heritage), joined the workshop in 1984 thanks to one of its many fellowships. He described this open door policy as a 'United Nations of Printmaking . . . This was a whole 'nother universe on West 17th Street.'[1]

While the RBPMW shared many of the egalitarian principles of the Taller de Gráfica Popular (see p. 165) and worked with some of its members – including Elizabeth Catlett and Charles White – its founder was not concerned with ascribing any particular aesthetic or political allegiance. He also resisted any strict adherence to a single technique, despite his own specialisation in lithography. He installed an etching press following a brief stint working at Atelier 17, shortly after its founder Stanley William Hayter's return to Paris (it was here that Blackburn befriended Krishna Reddy, who taught him the wonders of viscosity printing; see also p. 154). His members were welcome to create whatever they wished, whether it be the representational protest art of the civil rights struggle, or pure abstraction. In fact, Blackburn's own work gradually moved towards the latter, as he dived deeper into the possibilities of complex multicoloured lithographs and eventually experimental woodcuts.

The transition can be seen in one of his early acclaimed works, *Girl in Red* (fig. 8.1), a remarkably complex print replete with bold, Cubist inflections. Blackburn used ten different colours rendered on separate stones, and employed a range of devices including litho crayons, tusche, and scraping techniques to build depth and tone. Diverse impressions show how he often varied his inking, switching up pigment intensities and even reworking entire areas to add shadow or details.

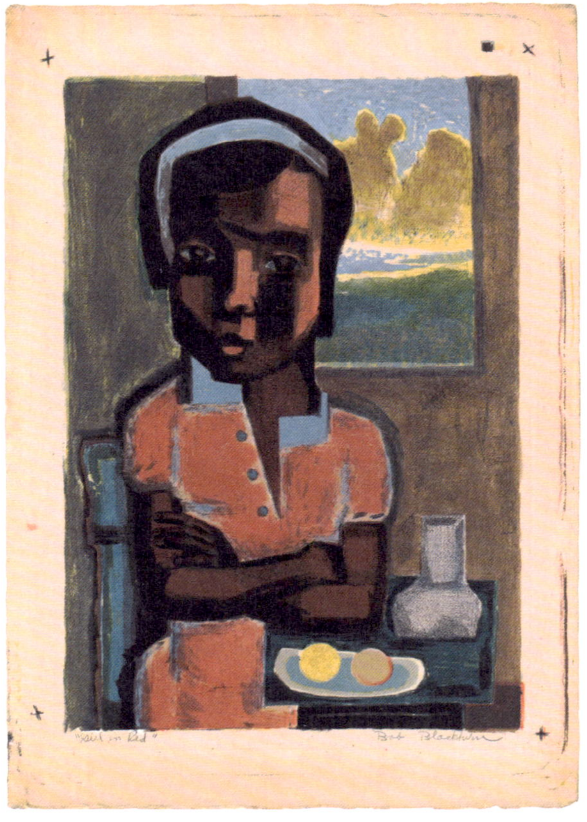

Fig. 8.1 Robert Blackburn, *Girl in Red*, 1950. Lithograph.

THE STORY OF PRINTMAKING

The evolution of this fluid, experimental attitude is evident in later, more abstract works. Iterations of *Heavy Forms* (1958–61; fig. 8.2), for example, were printed with at least 20 variations, including reorientating the entire composition and alternating the sequence of colour layers. There are spatters, cross-hatching, scrapes and pencil marks, all of which are imbued with an entirely different sensibility when rendered in hues ranging from verdant green to popsicle pink.[2]

When making his own work, Blackburn rarely produced numbered editions. His prints were more akin to a close-knit genealogy, filled with subtle variations and similarities born from a fascination with process. This personal practice demanded exceptional skill, and set him apart not only as an exemplary technical professional who could produce meticulous multiples on behalf of other artists, but also as a visionary in his own right.

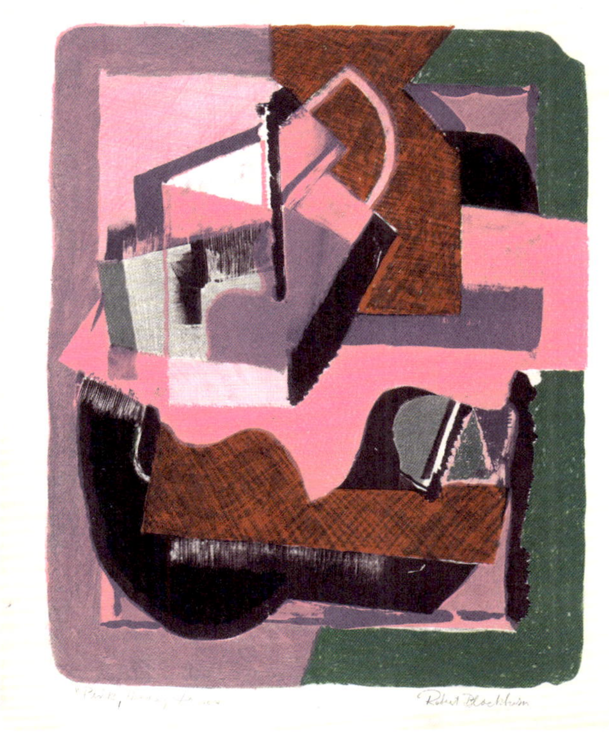

Fig. 8.2 Robert Blackburn, *Heavy Forms (Pink)*, 1958. Lithograph.

Blackburn's unwavering dedication to the workshop and the livelihood of its members ultimately overshadowed his own artistic practice. If he was not standing over the presses, advising, tutoring and demonstrating, he was seeking out opportunities for his extended print family, finding them further employment and scholarships, or else paths to visas and exhibition invitations. He was also preoccupied with trying to make ends meet. If supplies were low he would set off on his bicycle, returning with a glass jug of nitric acid balanced in its basket.[3] He also cajoled members into helping him transport portable presses in a borrowed van, so that he could offer free classes to local school children in situ. Multiple jobs at other studios, as well as paid teaching positions, were essential for keeping the workshop afloat. In fact, due to a sojourn in Europe on an artist fellowship, Blackburn was sure he would have to close his doors for good. Much to his surprise, loyal members pulled together to keep the studio going in his absence.

Blackburn's legacy is integral to the story of American printmaking, not least because his workshop remains in operation as part of the Elizabeth Foundation for the Arts. The roster of artists includes acclaimed individuals such as Faith Ringgold (1930–2024), Kay WalkingStick (b. 1935) and Romare Bearden (1911–1988). Blackburn also strove to promote programmes abroad, not least at the Asilah Workshop in Morocco, which he co-founded with fellow artists Camille Billops (1933–2019) and Jim Hatch (1928–2020) in the late 1970s. He was committed to his cause right up until his death in 2003, and upheld the values of openness and accessibility that helped give so many artists a foothold in the world of printmaking and beyond. As he noted, 'There's nothing [you] can do alone. You have to have support, no matter where you come from.'[4]

* * *

Only a few years after the RBPMW was founded, another more commercially minded but equally radical workshop opened on Madison Avenue. Margaret Lowengrund (1902–1957) announced the opening of her nascent enterprise, tantalisingly named The Contemporaries, on a notice she posted with the New York Public Library Art Division. The advertisement was split into two columns, with the first describing a gallery focused on prints: 'Work in graphics is a creative impetus to artists in other fields when the means is made available. Exhibiting all fine arts media side by side extends the scope of contemporary art.' The second told of: 'A workshop for artists, professional or student. We offer instruction in lithography, etching and all related printing techniques at moderate rates. Special attention given to beginners. Editions printed for professionals.'[5]

This marriage of technical education, commercial printing and a gallery set a fresh precedent for the functions of a print workshop, and removed the barriers delineating where work was conceived, produced and sold. Lowengrund also wished to dispel the entrenched hierarchies she had encountered in her arts education at the Philadelphia School of Design for Women, and to embrace the more collegiate approach she had enjoyed at the Art Students League (the very same school Blackburn had attended).

Lowengrund was not only an artist and professional printer, but also a curator and dealer. She put together impressive exhibitions combining works on paper with sculpture and painting, to encourage an appreciation of print amid the wider arts and to persuade a newly affluent, post-war middle class to buy art for their homes. In selecting 'The Contemporaries' as a name, she also made a conscious break from the European 'modernity' that still held dominance in the USA, even as she aligned herself with the teachings of groups such as the Bauhaus, with its complete fusion of the arts.

The Contemporaries welcomed all kinds of artists into its remit. Abstract artists such as Alice Trumbull Mason (1904–1971) and Stuart Davis (1892–1964) produced works alongside sculptors David Smith (1906–1965) and Peter Lipman-Wulf (1905–1993). Lowengrund was also very receptive to Japanese artists and the *sōsaku hanga* movement (these 'creative prints', which emerged in the wake of the Second World War, were expressive woodcuts conceived, carved and printed by a single artist). The calligrapher and painter Saburō Hasegawa (1906–1957) was particularly celebrated. He entered the workshop by chance while preparing for an exhibition at another gallery, and was invited to try his hand at lithography. The resulting four prints – including the joyous *Iroha* (Alphabet) from 1954 (fig. 8.3) – are stunning examples of the expansive nature of the medium's possibilities, thanks to the varied tools and processes that can be applied to the stone.

Lowengrund's directorship was cut short by her untimely death at only 55 years old. Fortunately, her legacy was protected by the workshop's

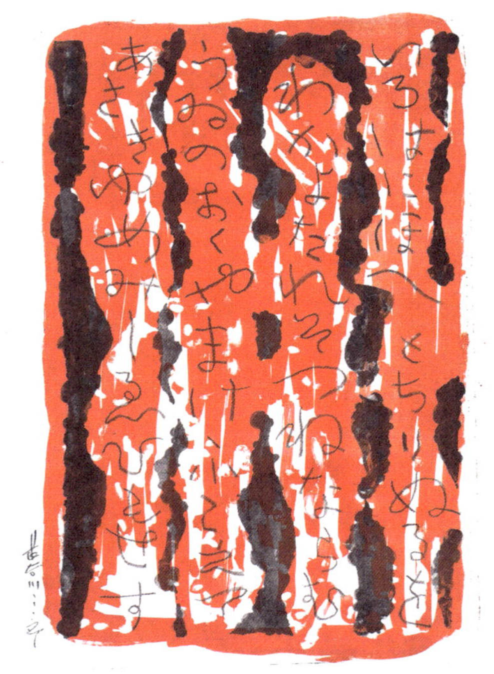

Fig. 8.3 Saburō Hasegawa, *Iroha* (Alphabet),
1954. Lithograph.

integration into the Pratt Institute in Brooklyn, where her unique blend of education, craft and commerce continues to thrive. Much like Blackburn, her commitment to enlivening the possibilities of printmaking was brought on through her equal devotion to fostering community.

* * *

Unlike her two immediate predecessors, Tatyana Grosman (1904–1982) was not a professional printmaker. However, this did not stop her from founding a groundbreaking and influential studio on Long Island: Universal Limited Art Editions (ULAE). Grosman began her life far away from the USA, and her early years were marred by tragedy and the imminent threat of war. She fled her hometown in Siberia after Tsar Nicholas II was murdered only streets away, and spent an itinerant childhood in Japan, Germany and France. After marrying a poor, divorced artist named Maurice Grosman and decamping to Paris, she suffered the death of her daughter and her father's suicide.

　　　　　　　　　　　　　　THE STORY OF PRINTMAKING

In 1940 the couple escaped the impending Nazi invasion by a matter of days, making the dangerous crossing over the Pyrenees on foot. When approached by officials they were saved not by any official document but by a certificate issued to Maurice by the Louvre, permitting him to make copies of a Diego Velázquez painting. The confusion that arose granted them safe passage, and they were soon embarking on a long voyage to begin a new life in Manhattan. Tatyana Grosman had an analogy for this fortuitous fate, writing in an autobiographical note: 'I was dreaming about bears as a child, about escaping on my sled from the wolves. Always there was a danger. And then comes a miracle and I am saved, like a Siberian fairytale.'[6]

This fortune continued when, following a move to Long Island for Maurice's health, Grosman discovered two large lithographic stones embedded in her front lawn. A kindly neighbour informed her of their intended use, and offered her their old lithography press for free, minus a $15 delivery fee. Despite knowing absolutely nothing about printmaking, Grosman was determined to make use of the technology and became set on the idea of creating lavishly produced books that were the result of collaborations between visual artists and poets, as well as limited-edition prints. She had seen such publications in Paris, and knew her strengths lay in bringing people together.

The ULAE name was born in 1957 and Grosman soon set about looking for a technical expert who 'knew how to work on stones'.[7] Her quest led her to none other than Blackburn, who resisted at first, as he wished to focus on his own workshop. However, Grosman's unabating enthusiasm proved persuasive, and what was meant to be a few brief months of work soon turned into years.

Blackburn thus helmed the press for ULAE's first project, a book called *Stones* (1957–60; fig. 8.4), conceived by Larry Rivers (1923–2002) and the poet Frank O'Hara (1926–1966), who at that time were both close friends and lovers. The experimental project was based on a call-and-response between text and image, as well as comprising an ode to the limestone slabs themselves. At Grosman's suggestion, the curved edges were inked to make their entire shape visible, something that would have been anathema to standard technical professionals.

Among the subsequent roster were many of the greatest names of the Abstract Expressionist era and the incoming American Pop Art scene, including Jasper Johns, Buckminster Fuller (1895–1983),

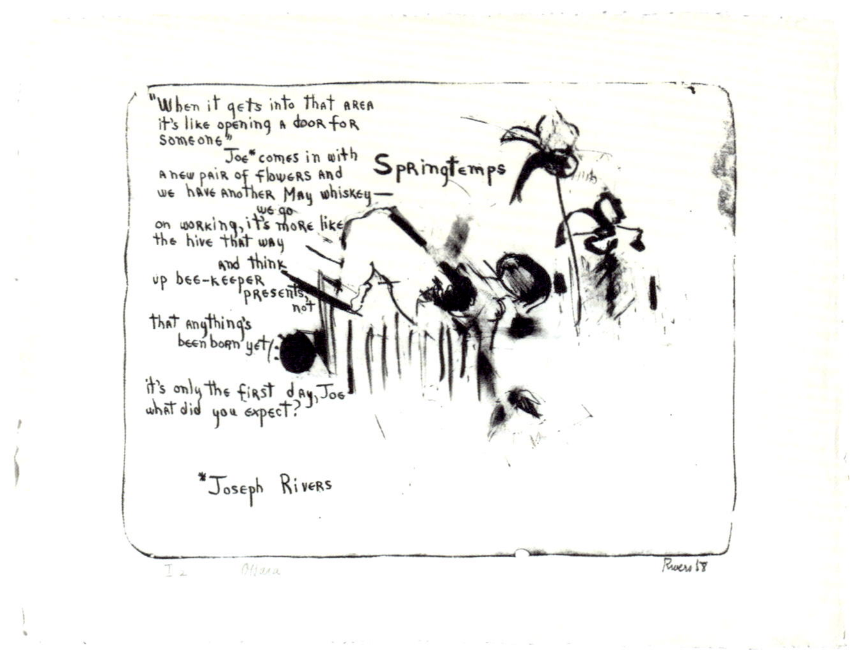

Fig. 8.4 Larry Rivers, *Springtemps*, from the book *Stones*, text by Frank O'Hara, 1958. Published by Universal Limited Art Editions, 1960. Lithograph.

Marisol Escobar (1930–2016), Robert Motherwell and Helen Frankenthaler (1928–2011). Many originally shared the belief that lithography was outmoded, yet they found themselves persuaded by an unrelenting Grosman. Once convinced, every possible dispensation was made. There were no fixed hours at the studio, and many artists preferred to work way into the night. Friends and animals were welcome, and food was always prepared. Fuller, for one, was fed his preferred diet of steak, spinach and Jell-O.

Such freedom and unwavering support were embraced by Robert Rauschenberg (1925–2008), another artist who resisted Grosman's overtures at first. He initially declared that the second half of the twentieth century was 'no time to start writing on rocks',[8] yet ULAE eventually set him on an entirely new path of printmaking, which had a profound effect on his wider practice. Among his most celebrated works was *Accident* (fig. 8.5). This seemingly abstract composition was the result of a broken stone that had given way under the pressure of the press. When Blackburn showed the devastating

                    THE STORY OF PRINTMAKING

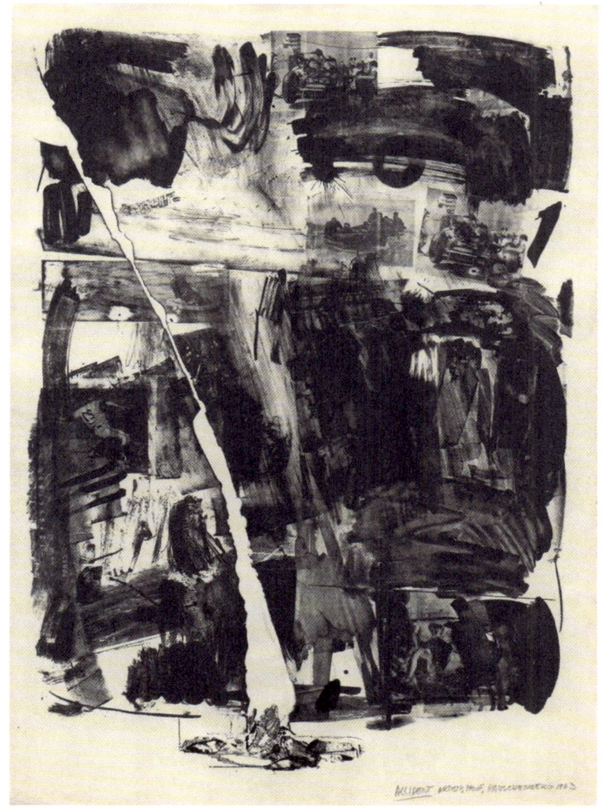

Fig. 8.5 Robert Rauschenberg, *Accident*, 1963. Printed by Robert Blackburn and published by Universal Limited Art Editions. Lithograph.

fractures to Rauschenberg, the artist asked if it was possible to print the haemorrhaged surface anyway.

The resulting edition was heralded as a groundbreaking moment in the critical understanding of print process, and won Rauschenberg first prize at the prestigious Ljubljana Biennale of Graphic Arts in 1963. The same accolade was not afforded to Blackburn, even though the work was only possible through his extensive technical knowledge. As Phil Sanders (b. 1976), who worked at both ULAE and RBPMW as a master printer and studio director, explained, 'Most printers of this era would not have even entertained the question [of whether it could be printed] and most artists would not have asked.'[9]

This exchange goes some way to explaining the dynamic in the ULAE studio. Grosman believed in the genius of the artist above all else, but she also had faith in her position as a director (she is described as such in the frontispiece for *Stones*), though she relied on the expertise of her printers to facilitate and execute this vision. Blackburn even used some of his own prints to educate many of the artists and assistant printers on site, enlightening them as to the unending possibilities of multicoloured lithography.

Bill Goldston (b. 1943), who joined the studio in 1969 (and would become its director in 1982), recalled Grosman's passion for artistic integrity, which sometimes manifested as outbursts if she felt that her printers had overstepped. On one occasion, after he introduced Jasper Johns to an offset lithographic press, the artist was overjoyed with the results. The feeling was not shared by Grosman, who considered the process too automated: 'Tanya [as she was known to those close to her] was furious and accused me of trying to destroy everything she had created. But, once she saw how happy Jasper was, she had to admit it was a good idea.'[10]

Grosman's obsession with fine quality meant she paid meticulous attention to papers, inks and minute adaptations, with seemingly no regard for time or cost. Her quest to produce prints that were truly works of art in their own right set a precedent for highly sought-after limited editions, which came with the distinct ULAE 'chop'. This embossed mark is found in the margin of a print, to assure authenticity. Its history dates back to the red seals prevalent in *nishiki-e* prints, but it became a mainstay for twentieth-century studios looking to differentiate their work from other imprints, or else inferior copyists. For Grosman, printmaking was far removed from the idea of copying or even interpreting an existing work. Her goal was to introduce an entirely new facet to an artist's practice. As she explained: 'I am not interested in production, but in [the] revelation of things, in the creation of art. Every print has his "reason d'etre" [*sic*].'[11]

As a result, ULAE expanded the thinking of what exactly a lithographic print could be. Fuller embraced the possibilities of his beloved geodesic dome by producing three-dimensional 'books' that formed an equilateral triangle. These 'Tetrascrolls' were a technical feat beyond the imagining of most studios, and reached approximately 9 metres long. In an even bolder move towards what might be termed a 'lithographic object', Rauschenberg printed segments of plexiglass with newspaper and magazine clippings, utilising innovations that

   THE STORY OF PRINTMAKING

could transfer photographs to the stone. *Shades* (1964) consisted of plastic slices that could be reordered in six million permutations within an aluminium frame featuring five slots. The piece was backlit by a lightbulb and could well be described as a sculpture, but it was only made possible through the printmaking imagination.

The studio went on to specialise in other techniques, embracing both intaglio and woodblock, the latter of which facilitated Frankenthaler's earliest experiments with abstract reliefs. Although the artist had already made lithographs that embraced the loose gestures of her paintings (thanks to Grosman's idea that the stones should be placed in a row on the floor, so that Frankenthaler could employ the broad movements used to paint on canvas), she became fascinated by the relatively unyielding qualities of wood and its long printing history. She went on to create some of the most striking and innovative relief prints of the late twentieth century, incorporating an astonishing fluidity achieved through unorthodox approaches towards applying and diluting inks. Although she worked with a number of master printers, her early grapples with this new form of creative struggle occurred at ULAE, as is evident in her account of the creation of *Savage Breeze* (fig. 8.6), which was executed with Goldston and fellow printer, Juda Rosenberg. Frankenthaler recalled:

> *Savage Breeze* went dead like a lead balloon. So after many tries, I finally said, let's scratch it. I was almost exasperated. I couldn't get the light I desired. I knew the drawing was right. I knew the scale was right. Then I thought – why don't we whitewash the paper first and then print the other colors I'd mixed over it. We did. And it glowed.[12]

The innovation and dedication of invited artists and the ULAE workforce continued under Grosman's watchful eye until her death in 1982, and still lives on today. The cottage that she shared with Maurice – where so much of the early work took place – stands as a testament to her legacy, bolstered by the factory-like proportions of its enterprise that operates just down the road. Her figure looms large in an enormous portrait that hangs above one of the main printing rooms, like a caring and perhaps slightly overbearing mother. Rauschenberg's own ode to the founding director comes in the form

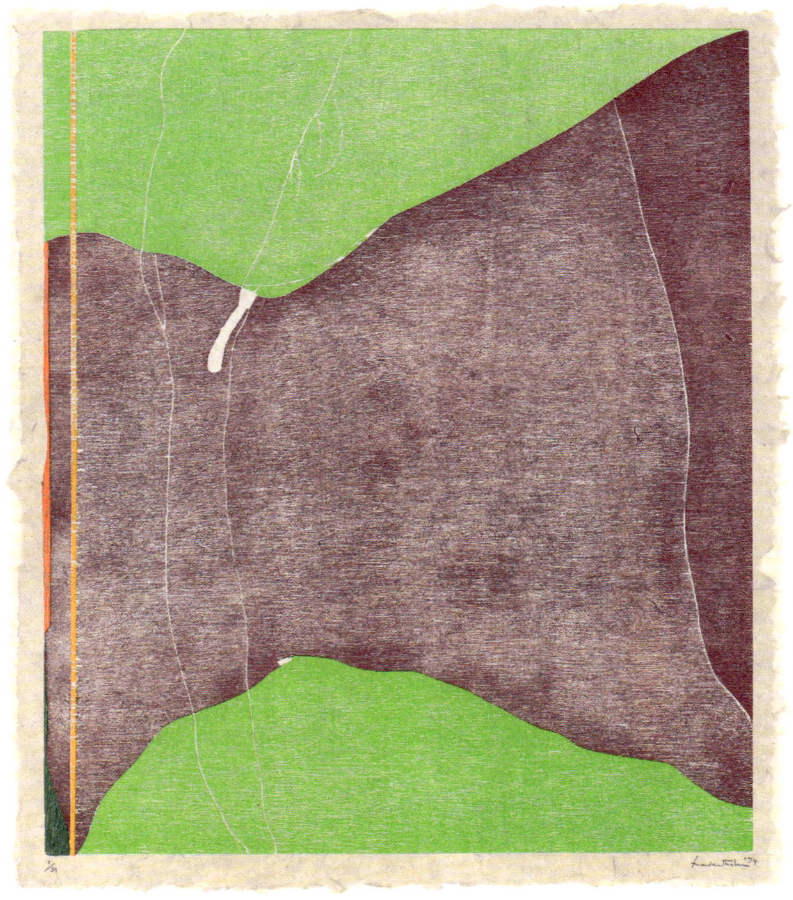

Fig. 8.6 Helen Frankenthaler, *Savage Breeze*, 1974. Printed by Bill Goldston and Juda Rosenberg, published by Universal Limited Art Editions. Woodcut.

of a 1974 lithographic portrait dubbed *Tanya*, made to commemorate ULAE's fifteenth anniversary. An even more remarkable ode to the friendships forged in the workshop can be found in a very specific item given to Goldston upon Rauschenberg's death. A small, dark bottle inscribed with 'RR' holds the late artist's ashes, and has been kept in his friend's pocket every day since. That way, Goldston said, 'I can always carry Bob with me.'[13]

* * *

                    THE STORY OF PRINTMAKING

The strong bonds fostered at the printing press were soon replicated across a burgeoning network of studios that developed on the West Coast in the 1960s. As something of an outlier, Kathan Brown (1935–2025) founded Crown Point Press in San Francisco, with a steadfast dedication to intaglio. She had become frustrated by the need to travel to Europe in order to gain technical expertise, and was committed to reviving these techniques in the style of Hayter's atelier. On learning about a dismantled etching press in a lodging house in Edinburgh, Scotland, she travelled two-and-a-half months by freighter to bring it back home and set up her studio.

Although the small-scale nature of etching might seem at odds with the prevailing aesthetics of the day, there were plenty of artists who were enamoured, including figurative painters Richard Diebenkorn (1922–1993) and Wayne Thiebaud (1920–2021). Subsequent conceptual interest in intaglio came from Minimalist artists including Sol LeWitt (1928–2007), Brice Marden (1938–2023) and John Cage (1912–1992), and Crown Point has been attributed with reviving a broad and sustained appreciation of etching among contemporary artists.

Beyond this example, lithography remained a dominant force throughout the 1960s. This was thanks in no small part to June Wayne (1918–2011), a printmaker and entrepreneur of grand proportions who persuaded the Ford Foundation to award her a $3 million grant to set up the Tamarind Lithography Workshop. This non-profit organisation was founded in 1960 in Los Angeles (and later moved to the University of New Mexico, where – as the Tamarind Institute – it is still based today), with an expressed educational remit that followed in Lowengrund's footsteps. It should come as no surprise that Wayne had printed at her predecessor's New York shop, and valued her as 'rare and wonderful, full of courage, and vision'.[14]

As well as promoting the lithography technique and producing exceptional collaborative editions, the goal at Tamarind was to train a new generation of master printers, who could in turn proliferate their knowledge throughout the country. Wayne believed that only a handful of people were needed to create a full lithography revival and to prevent this remarkable medium from '[dying] in its youth without having been asked to reveal its untapped powers for new esthetic expression'.[15]

The seminal technical manual, *The Tamarind Book of Lithography: Art & Techniques* (1971), is still considered something of a printer's bible, and covers such exhaustive subjects as grinding the stone, reconditioning leather rollers and the 'psychological difficulties in making color lithographs', as well as offering comprehensive guidance on how to set up and finance a workshop. This volume (and its 2008 follow-up, *Tamarind Techniques*) adorns the shelves of countless contemporary studios, putting paid to Wayne's original concern that 'this book's content may be nearly as bizarre in twenty years as alchemy is today'.[16]

Sure enough, Tamarind's programme spawned a whole host of printers who went on to set up their own ventures. Among them were Jean Milant (1943–2024) and Jack Lemon (b. 1936), who set up Cirrus Editions in Los Angeles and Landfall Press in Chicago, respectively. Donn Steward (1921–1985), meanwhile, was employed at ULAE as an expert in both lithography and etching.

Among the most ambitious alumni was Kenneth Tyler (b. 1931), co-founder of Gemini G.E.L. (and his later eponymous business Tyler Graphics Ltd), which became a standard bearer for Pop Art prints seeking bold and groundbreaking production. This was where Ellsworth Kelly (1923–2015) conceived colourful geometric forms; Ed Ruscha experimented with crisp lines of text; and Roy Lichtenstein (1923–1997) returned the painted motifs that he had lifted from comic books back to the printed domain.

Tyler had already opened a modest shop by the time he met his business partners. Former art student Sidney B. Felsen (1924–2024) and Stanley Grinstein (1927–2014) – whose forklift business had come in handy with artists needing to transport large works – recognised his talents immediately. Together, they launched Gemini as a business that could not only build on the popularity of lithography, but also harness the expertise of the aerospace and film industries to inform all kinds of print innovations. Much like ULAE, they went about reimagining the parameters of a work on paper, but pushed the envelope even further, fabricating fully three-dimensional objects and eventually producing original sculpture.

Although Gemini was hardly unique in its approach to mastering a whole breadth of processes, it was something of a trailblazer when it came to combining techniques to produce a single work. This was thanks in no small part to Rauschenberg, who had embarked on a completely reinvigorated practice since his first venture at ULAE. His wholehearted embrace of collaborative sensibility was recalled by Tyler himself:

Rauschenberg is absolutely a master. I've talked with printers who've worked with Picasso, Miró, you name them – but their collaboration was very simple compared with Rauschenberg's. Work with him and you get his life, spirit, energy: he's the only two-way street in the art world.[17]

The artist turned to the studio to help him on his quest to create the largest hand-pulled print ever produced at the time. The resulting *Booster* (fig. 8.7) is a technical feat on an impressive scale, measuring

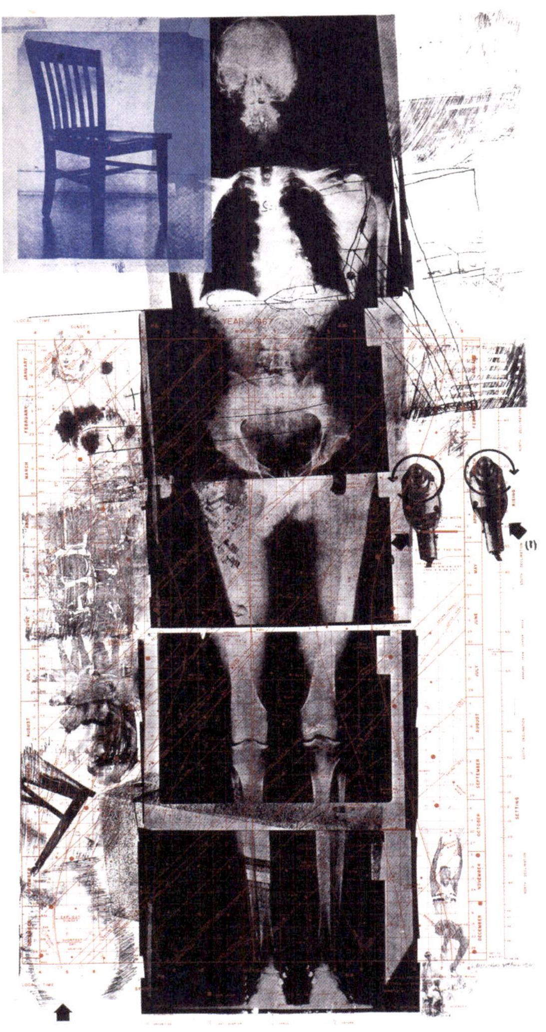

Fig. 8.7 Robert Rauschenberg, *Booster*, 1967. Printed by Kenneth Tyler and published by Gemini G.E.L. Lithograph and silkscreen.

just under two metres in height. The composition consists of an array of photographic imagery and newspaper clippings, but it is dominated by X-rays of Rauschenberg's own body. Other gestural components include drawings that reference the work of the artist Cy Twombly (1928–2011; Rauschenberg's former partner), thus solidifying a surprisingly autobiographical work that alluded to recent personal struggles.

The entire montage was overprinted with a series of planetary maps that charted the artist's interest in both space travel and the prophetic qualities of astrology. To achieve this delicate red layer of celestial calculations, the Gemini printers did not return to the limestone. Instead, they employed a more novel technique that held a similar history in industrialised production: the screenprint.

* * *

Much like woodcuts, the rich history of screenprints dates back to ancient China, where the technique was used not to produce works on paper but to achieve complex patterns destined for elaborate textiles. As the name might suggest, screenprinting is based on the simple principle of pushing ink through a fine mesh screen. Early iterations were made from woven human hair or silk, hence the alternative terms 'silk screen' and (the rather more archaic) 'serigraph', which stems from the Latin word for 'silk' and the Greek for 'draw'. Nowadays, more cost-effective and robust nylon and polyester meshes have been developed, with a selection of densities available according to the desires of the printer. The varying grades function like the resolution of a digital image: the higher the mesh count, the more detailed and precise the outcome, making it ideal for photographic imagery and fine typography.

This mesh is stretched taut over a thick wooden or aluminium frame, like the skin of a drum. Although the tension is receptive to even pressure, the procedure remains delicate. Many printers will be familiar with the frustration of ruining a newly purchased screen, by perforating it with a misplaced scalpel or fumbling hand.

Creating an image can range from a simple to an extremely complex endeavour. The basic principle lies in producing a stencil that renders select areas of the mesh impenetrable to ink. There are many ways to go about this process: hand-cut shapes formed from paper or masking film can be placed on the reverse of the screen, thus producing crisp blocks. Images can also be painted directly onto the mesh with an opaque resist, allowing for more spontaneous and gestural mark-making. More detailed imagery can be reproduced by using a photo-sensitive emulsion in conjunction with a positive transparency. If this method is being used, the screen is evenly coated with a thin layer of emulsion using a specialist scoop. Once the screen has dried, it is placed on an exposure unit, with the transparency laid out on top, vacuum-sealed to obstruct any adulterating external light, and exposed to a concentrated blast of ultra-violet rays. The areas shielded from the UV remain soft, while the surrounding emulsion hardens. These soft, unexposed areas can be washed away with water, and the result is a spectral imprint of what will soon appear on paper.

Once dry, the screen is ready to be inked. Unlike the presses discussed thus far, a screenprinting bed does not rely on a mangle or stamping method. Instead, it consists of a hinged frame to which the screen is affixed, so that it can be lowered onto the desired surface, not unlike closing the lid of a box. Before anything can be printed, however, a thick but narrow strip of ink is applied to the top of the screen, while the frame is still elevated. The pigment is then pulled down in an even layer across the entire stencil, with the aid of a squeegee. The preparatory pull is known as 'flooding', and it effectively wets the screen to prevent any unfortunate sticking or areas of poor adhesion. Finally, a piece of paper can be placed on the base of the printing bed. An industrial press will feature hundreds of tiny holes in the print bed, and it will utilise a suction vacuum to hold the paper steady, but more basic set-ups use a flat wooden board to good effect. Once the frame is closed down onto the paper, the ink can be pulled across the screen once more. The pressure from the squeegee forces the ink through the mesh and onto the paper. When the frame is released, the image reveals itself.

To produce an accurate and even impression takes considerable skill. One must determine the correct amount of ink, but also the exact angle of the squeegee, the speed of the pull, and the amount of force required. Press too hard and you might experience smears or an overspill of pigment. Press too lightly and the design will be patchy or undefined. Seasoned printmakers will develop considerable muscle memory, but they will also listen out for an exacting sound, like that of a squeaking windscreen wiper.

As with many other printing techniques, the possibility for multiple colour overlays demands the accurate registration of a number of separate layers. However, the precision achievable with screenprinting makes it particularly favourable to those looking to reimagine complex and colourful imagery, as well as bold, minimal motifs. Although the process had been utilised within the WPA (see p. 153) as a cheap form of art production, which rivalled lithography as the commercial printing technique of choice, it was not until the mid-century that it emerged as a creative force. With its relative lack of specialist equipment, it became a natural favourite for grass-roots publishers and counterculture collectives, as well as for artists enamoured with a process that embodied popular and egalitarian methods of mass communication.

What followed was a screenprinting surge in the American Pop Art movement and its counterpart in the UK, both of which were defined by a resolute graphic impulse. Kelpra Studio – one of the most celebrated British enterprises to emerge during this period – was set up by Chris Prater (1924–1996) and Rose Prater (d. 1982) around their kitchen table in north London. They went on to produce editions for Eduardo Paolozzi (1924–2005), Peter Blake (b. 1932) and Richard Hamilton, and capitalised on the distinct blend of photomontage and eye-popping colour that defined these artists' oeuvres.

* * *

The one name that is truly synonymous with the screenprint is Andy Warhol (1928–1987). The ultimate celebrity artist began utilising the process in the early 1960s, not as a form of print per se, but as a shortcut to replicate his appropriated imagery on canvas. His obsession with the aesthetics of consumer culture was seeded while he was a student at Carnegie Institute of Technology in Pittsburgh, where a degree in pictorial design and a subsequent early career in commercial illustration exposed him to the allure of attention-grabbing advertising, not to mention the high-contrast qualities of mass reproduction.

With the aid of a team of printers and assistants at The Factory (his famed Manhattan studio, which doubled as a hedonistic party venue and ad hoc performance space), canvases were laid out and printed on the floor. This rather DIY approach speaks to the contradictions inherent in Warhol's work. He often alluded to his wish for complete detachment and mechanised process, even refraining

   THE STORY OF PRINTMAKING

from touching his artwork entirely. Yet he also collaborated closely with his friends and associates, including Gerard Malanga (b. 1943), Rupert Jasen Smith (1953–1989) and David Whitney (1939–2005). The latter directed Warhol's burgeoning publishing business, wittily titled 'Factory Additions', which featured portfolios that emulated the 'painted' prints for which he was so well known. Early series included 'Marilyn Monroe' (1967), 'Campbell's Soup I' and 'Campbell's Soup II' (1968–9) and 'Flowers' (1970; fig. 8.8), which were produced in a limited edition of 250. To create these works on paper he worked with established studios such as Aetna Silkscreen Products and Salvatore Silkscreen Co., which had prospered amid a buoyant market for expertly executed, eye-catching editions. Within these portfolios Warhol produced identical images in a range of different colour combinations, thus investigating ideas of surface appearance and perception, including the illusionary elements of fame.

The artist's signature approach to using overexposed, pre-existing imagery also lay at the crux of the age-old question concerning creative authorship. He was at the centre of multiple lawsuits regarding copyright infringement, including the use of Patricia Caulfield's (1932–2023) flower images, which were originally published in *Modern Photography* magazine. Warhol's transgressive approach to production also further complicated the idea of highly prized limited editions, which were usually assiduously proofed and prepared by the printer, before being signed off by the artist. Traditionally, this final pass is marked with 'AP', meaning 'artist proof', and serves as a blueprint by which the rest of a uniform print run is produced. All previous proofs, adorned with their various corrections and alterations, might be archived, but they were certainly not usually destined for sale.

Warhol manipulated this process to its fullest. He not only produced entirely unique variations that were either classified as standalone pieces or grouped within editioned portfolios, but he also reconstituted the value of the trial proof. During a period in the 1980s that was dominated by portraits of celebrities and historical figures, he gathered the many colour and compositional experiments that had been tested on paper before the ultimate work was produced on canvas. These pieces were ostensibly one-offs, and the artist presented them as distinct artworks, many of which were embedded with a delicate sheen of diamond dust.[18]

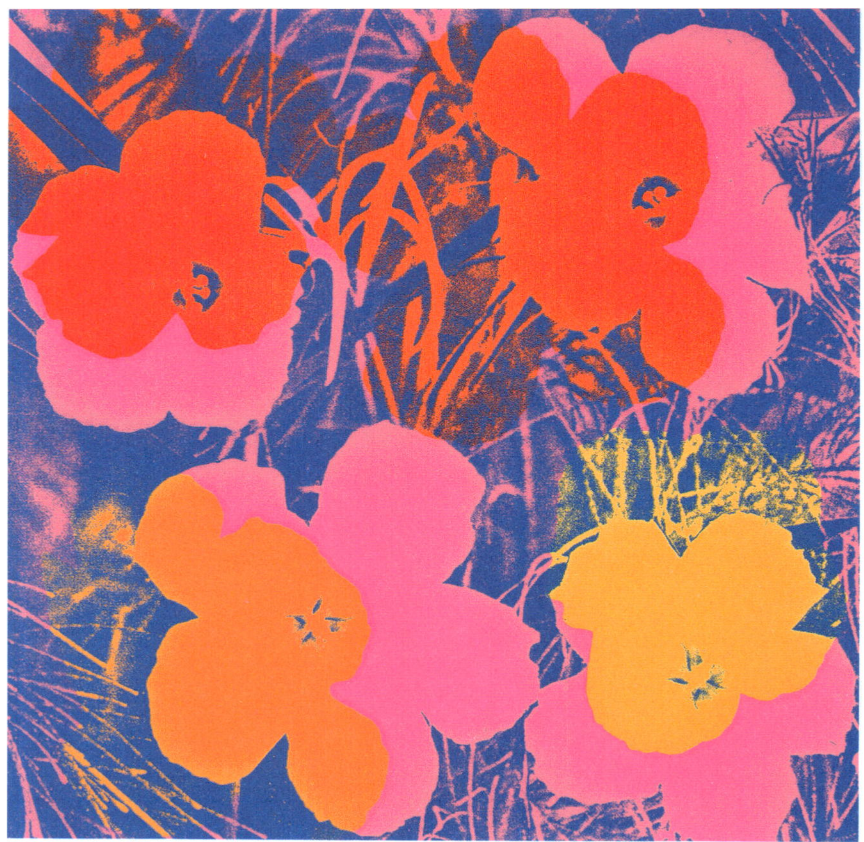

Fig. 8.8 Andy Warhol, *Flowers*, 1970. Printed by Aetna Silkscreen Products, Inc., and Du-Art Displays, and published by Factory Additions. Screenprint.

The accuracy of screenprinting led to an evolution among Pop artists, who began to treat text as allegorical image. Once again, this development was deeply informed by the language of advertising and a playful appropriation of well-known slogans and logos. The most enduring image is surely Robert Indiana's *LOVE*, which was first printed as a MoMA Christmas card, in 1965 (fig. 8.9). Its closely honed letterforms and high-octane palette have appeared as both paintings and sculptures, but they hold a particular resonance as a widely disseminated print. The work has appeared on everything from coffee cups to postage stamps, and has been interpreted as an antiwar protest, a denouncement of corporate power, and a spiritual assignation.

　　　　　　　　　　　THE STORY OF PRINTMAKING

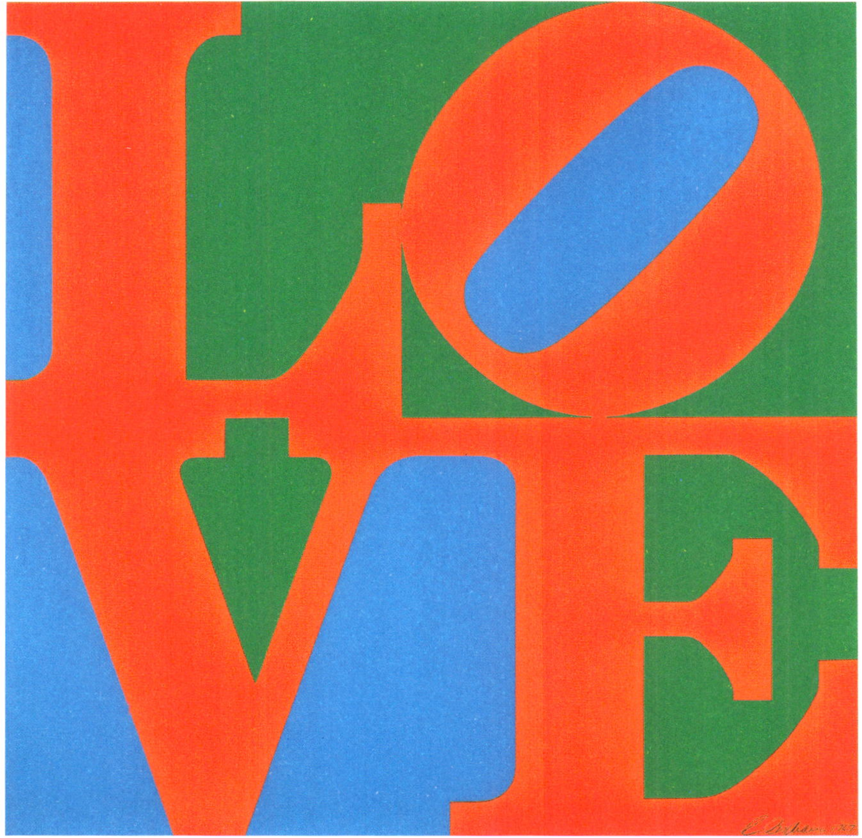

Fig. 8.9 Robert Indiana, *LOVE*, 1967. Printed by Sirocco Screenprinters and
published by Multiples, Inc. Screenprint.

A wholly unexpected figure to emerge within this context is the
Los Angeles artist Corita Kent (1918–1986), otherwise known as the
'Pop Art nun' Sister Mary Corita. She joined the Immaculate Heart
of Mary in Hollywood aged 18, in 1936. This progressive Catholic
order ran its own college, and she soon took on a faculty position
in the art department, while embarking on concurrent studies at the
University of Southern California, where she learned to screenprint.
This became her steadfast technique, and she soon brought her
expertise back into the classroom. In her list of ten rules for a great
working environment, she included: 'Nothing is a mistake. There's
no win and no fail. There's only make.'[19]

As part of her teaching duties she embraced the wealth of exhibitions on offer in the city, by taking students on weekly field trips. One such encounter was with an early show of Warhol paintings depicting Campbell's soup cans.[20] These canvases mimicked the effects of a screenprint and appeared as a grid of subtly distinct multiples. The show sent Kent on a new path of discovery, away from the figurative convention of devotional art and into the iconoclastic realm of textual appropriation. Her 1964 print *The Juiciest Tomato of All* functions as a cheeky response to the Warhol works, by invoking the advertising jingle of another food purveyor, Del Monte. Rather than using literal depictions, Kent creates layers of meaning through dynamic treatment of text and a selective use of colour. Bold, sleek uppercase letters are inscribed with more diminutive handwritten script, which rather shockingly declares that 'Mary Mother is the juiciest tomato of them all'. Although such a suggestion scandalised some of her religious peers, this print set a precedent for Kent's very particular amalgamation of joyous spirituality and popular vernacular language.

Kent took many of her letterforms directly from magazine advertising, cutting out pages from titles such as *Life*, *Vogue* and even *Playboy*, in the Pop Art tradition of reappropriation. To produce her prints she projected these cutouts, often scaling or warping their appearance before tracing them onto paper. The resulting letters were then used as stencils that could be layered on various screens. In some of her works, such as the technically brilliant diptych *(give the gang) the clue is in the signs* (fig. 8.10) and *(our best) reality proves very little* (1966), she experiments with complex text alignments that border on abstraction. She also wrote directly onto the mesh with varnish, thus producing stopped-out longhand that appeared white, even when overprinted with various colourful shapes. The text itself fuses secular and spiritual prose by combining an advertisement for Canada Beverages with the writings of a radical Jesuit priest.[21]

Kent's canny abilities with wordplay managed to fulfil her duty of spreading the gospel while engaging with the most pressing political issues of the day. Her prints are montaged with the rhetoric of supermarket advertising, song lyrics, poetry and protest speeches, including those decrying the violence of the Vietnam War and the assassination of political figures such as John F. Kennedy and Martin

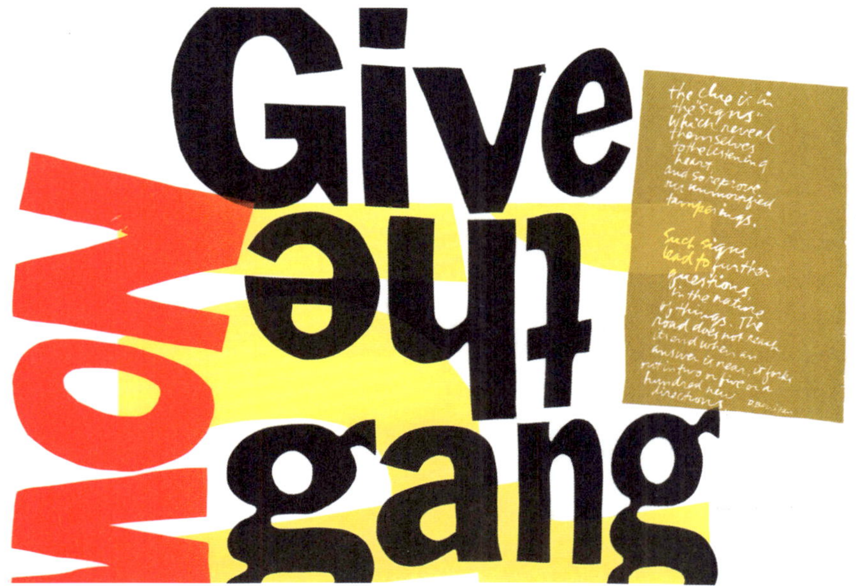

Fig. 8.10 Corita Kent, *(give the gang) the clue is in the signs*, 1966. Screenprint.

Luther King Jr. Hers was a language ripe with symbolism which sought the good in the everyday, whether that be appreciating the lyrics of a Beatles song, or perceiving a slice of Wonder Bread as the Eucharist. Perhaps more than any other Pop artist, Kent revealed the complexities of modern American life, with its inherent celebration of individualism, belief in a higher power, and unending worship at the altar of consumerism.

CHAPTER 9

THE REACH OF RORKE'S DRIFT

SOUTH AFRICAN PRINTS AND THE STRUGGLE AGAINST APARTHEID

I don't attempt to convey the simplicity of representation. I am interested in a more complex and layered process.

— Nhlanhla Xaba, 1998

IN 1881, THE French engraver Léopold Flameng (1831–1911) was commissioned to produce a copy of an academic military painting, for Britain's Fine Art Society. Titled *The Defence of Rorke's Drift, 22 January 1879* (1880), it lionised a key conflict in the Anglo-Zulu war which took place in what is now the South African province of KwaZulu-Natal. Invading British soldiers successfully defeated Zulu forces at the rural outpost that gives the work its name, and were heralded as heroes back home. This propaganda scene was deemed the perfect subject with which to disseminate the ideals of empire through print and cement a mythology that overlooked the crushing defeat in neighbouring Isandlwana, which had occurred only hours before.

A century later, Rorke's Drift was synonymous with far more than bloody conflict. Thanks to an unlikely educational venture it played a significant role in the development of a rich contemporary printmaking culture, which became a vital tool in the struggle against apartheid. The transformation began in 1963, when artists Ulla and Peder Gowenius (a married couple from Stockholm) set up an arts and crafts centre with assistance from the Swedish Evangelical Lutheran

Church. Its express purpose was to develop formal creative education for Black South Africans. At this time, the National Party's oppressive racist policies strictly segregated every element of society, including schooling. Following the Bantu Education Act of 1953, facilities, funding and governance were separated by race, with art studies directly serving discriminatory ideology. A Eurocentric 'fine arts' curriculum including painting and sculpture was reserved for white students, whereas crafts associated with manual labour, including needlework and woodworking, were mandated for those who were Black.

The Gowenius project – officially named the Evangelical Lutheran Church Art and Craft Centre, but more commonly referred to simply as 'Rorke's Drift' – aimed to do away with such restrictions and offer opportunities for open-ended creativity and quality training, thereby providing a possible path to financial enterprise. What began as occupational therapy at a hospital in neighbouring Ceza soon blossomed into a hub for all kinds of practice, including painting, ceramics, weaving and printed textiles. This new school offered room and board, and introduced a certificate in fine arts studies that would have been impossible to obtain elsewhere. Students were encouraged to engage with as many different mediums as possible and to find their own path, but the relative scarcity of resources meant that concessions had to be made. Teachers might find themselves fixing roofs or digging septic tanks, or collecting discarded linoleum floor tiles to be used for relief block carving. This particular form of ingenuity sparked a long-held association between linocut and a prevailing Rorke's Drift style.

Among the earliest and most influential students was Azaria Mbatha (1941–2018), who first came into contact with the Goweniuses while hospitalised for depression. Although he did not seem immediately enamoured by linocut, he was amazed by the printed result and its apparent likeness to *amabhaxa*. These highly decorative wooden slats were well-sought craft items in the area, and featured intricately carved surfaces that were blackened by burning.[1]

Mbatha's significance as both a printmaker and educator is widely recognised. His continual engagement with religious themes, and what he envisaged as an 'Africanised' version of the Bible, dealt with the injustices of South African society through imagery that could avoid censorship and speak to a broad public. He sought to reconcile

Christian theology with Zulu values and heritage, and employed linear narrative structures that were well suited to the monochrome formalism that linocut could offer. In works such as *Nebuchadnezzar and Old Testament Stories* (fig. 9.1) and *The Revelation of St John* (1965), the compositions are split into distinct thirds that keep pace among vibrant, textured vignettes, akin to a comic book or ancient frieze. They were celebrated as contemporary parables of South African life soon after they were printed, and impressions were collected by MoMA and the South African National Gallery, marking a level of institutional recognition that was rare for a Black African artist at the time.

Following a scholarship to study in Stockholm, Mbatha made a permanent move to Sweden, but not before undertaking a vital year of teaching at Rorke's Drift. As a former student and the first South African educator on site, he set the precedent for a younger cohort of printmakers who grappled with the graphic properties of linoleum to develop their own distinct language. Among them were Sokhaya Charles Nkosi (b. 1949), Daniel Sefudi Rakgoathe (1937–2004) and the Namibia-born John Ndevasia Muafangejo

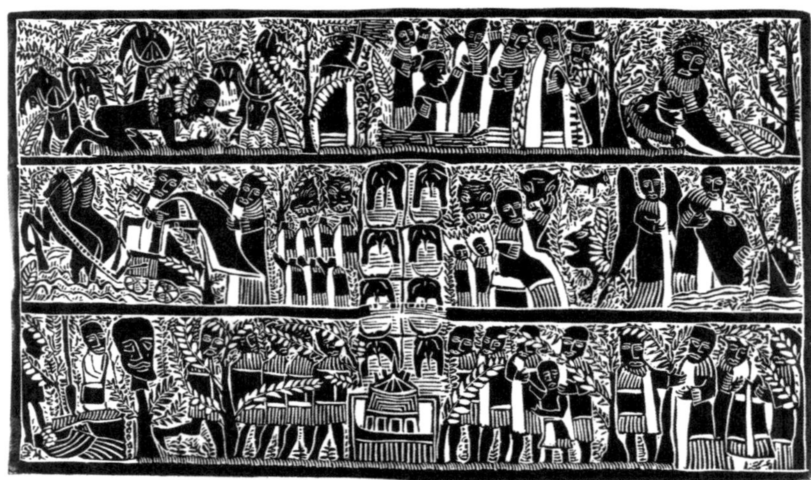

Fig. 9.1 Azaria Mbatha, *Nebuchadnezzar and Old Testament Stories*, 1965. Linocut.

  THE STORY OF PRINTMAKING

(1943–1987), all of whom developed expressive cutting styles that owe a debt to Mbatha's practice, particularly in their engagement with spiritual themes.

Nkosi was exceptionally astute when it came to rendering more traumatic interpretations of Christian scripture. He was closely affiliated with the Black Consciousness Movement, which emerged in the mid-1960s as a political and philosophical resistance organisation that instilled pride in Black identity. In his series 'Black Crucifixion', both the physical and psychological brutalities of apartheid are conveyed through deeply gouged formations and surface scratches.

Rakgcathe was more concerned with the metaphysical elements of life. His sinewy incisions often have a celestial underpinning, as demonstrated in the 1973 print *Moon Bride and Sun Bridegroom* (fig. 9.2), with its rings of curvaceous ripples. He often found himself at odds with the evangelical premise of Rorke's Drift, even if that sentiment was broadly ignored by teaching staff (Peder Gowenius was technically a missionary, but this was more of an administrative consideration). Despite the underlying idealism and a wish to

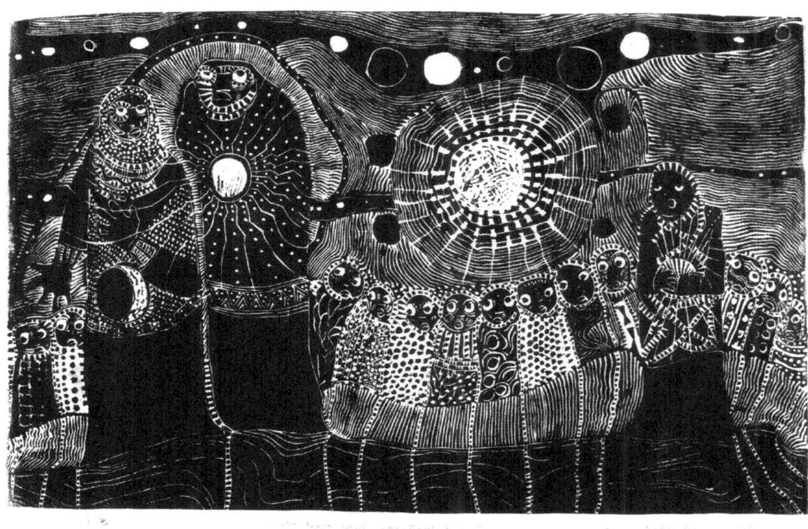

Fig. 9.2 Daniel Sefudi Rakgoathe, *Moon Bride and Sun Bridegroom*, 1973. Linocut.

abstain from promoting 'western' art practice, the inherent colonial nature of the project garnered some criticism. While Rakgoathe was sympathetic to the teaching staff's wish to learn from their students, his close friend and peer Cyprian Mpho Shilakoe (1946–1972), who became well-known for his aquatint etchings before his unexpected death in a car crash, felt somewhat differently: 'Sure I appreciated all they've done, but too often their Light overshadowed our Light. They cut us off – did not teach us of the Kingdom of Benin, of glorious masks, of our beautiful ancestors.'[2]

This statement points to the inequities of power within any apartheid-era institution, as well as the importance of establishing a teaching system that is both made for and run by Black artists. The strong directive at Rorke's Drift was not without flaws, but it did foster an extraordinary network of artist-educators who actively shaped the path of South African art.

* * *

While the presence of Rorke's Drift was felt within the wider arts ecosystem, its rural location set it physically apart from community workshops and creative enterprises that developed among more urban centres. Many were broad organisations that embraced printmaking as one mere facet, a few of which predated the Lutheran project. The African Art Centre, for example, opened in the city of Durban in 1959. It focused on textile and sculptural crafts, as well as prints, and created much-needed opportunities to sell work. It also established a biennial called 'Art: South Africa Today', which was eventually able to present awards to outstanding contributors, including Mbatha. In fact, it was through founder Jo Thorpe (1921–1995) that the artist's linocuts first entered the MoMA collection.

The Polly Street Art Centre in Johannesburg followed a more traditional studio model. It was formalised in 1952 thanks to the appointment of Cecil Skotnes (1926–2009), a London-born white South African, as the ambiguously named Cultural Recreation Officer. The programme originally focused on broad artistic endeavours, including music, but within five years there was a renewed attention on the visual arts, such as painting, drawing and sculpture. By presenting itself as a recreational enterprise, it avoided the limitations placed on official forms of education, in a model that inspired the Goweniuses prior to the founding of their school.

The challenges faced at Polly Street were nevertheless enormous. To begin with, Skotnes asked fellow artists to volunteer to share their expertise, and relied on donations and gifted materials to keep classes going. Curfews placed on the Black populace meant that classes had to end promptly, so that attendees could return to the surrounding townships. Increasingly hostile segregation also forced the centre to move several times, first to Jubilee Street and then to Mofolo Park in Soweto, where an increasing number of Black teachers were able to function, and eventually take over the operation.

Rakgoathe was one such artist. He joined the staff to teach all forms of visual art (and was eventually promoted to Cultural Officer in 1975), but he was quick to introduce printmaking to the curriculum, particularly relief. As with his experience at Rorke's Drift, he preferred to demonstrate techniques and let students find their own way through the process. He encouraged the use of imagination but also studying from life, as well as warning against any concerted effort towards a particular style. In fact, he only made his own prints after hours, so that he might not unduly influence his pupils, explaining that everyone eventually finds their own language: 'People use the same words . . . but their pronunciation is different.'[3]

From the late 1970s onward, branches of printmaking practice began to spread out across artist networks like a broad family tree. Muafangejo returned to the Namibian missionary school he had attended before Rorke's Drift to teach linocut, woodcut and etching. Durant Sihlali (1935–2004), who had studied under Skotnes at Polly Street and is best-known as a painter, worked at the Ntokozweni Community Centre in Soweto, teaching painting and printmaking to teenagers and adults alike. This work coincided with his appointment as the head of the Federated Union of Black Artists (FUBA), which in turn led to the establishment of the African Institute of Art at Funda (also in Soweto), complete with a programme headed by Nkosi.

Dumisani Mabaso (1955–2013), another Rorke's Drift alumnus, founded the Sguzu Printmakers' Workshop with a press he had acquired from the centre after his training. This made his space something of an exception when it came to the meagre supply of printing equipment readily available. In fact, established printers would often offer to demonstrate and share their expertise with others in exchange for time on their presses. Otherwise, the obvious alternative was to specialise in relief methods that could be printed by hand.

Despite his experience in etching, Sihlali favoured lino and wood-cut expressly because they involved materials that his students could replicate elsewhere. An embrace of found materials also led to the introduction of collography, a technique that involves building up a plate by glueing textured materials such as cardboard, textiles and string onto its surface, which can also be incised or torn. This extremely versatile and inexpensive technique first gained popularity in the mid-twentieth century, but has often been regarded as an experimental or even amateur method because the plates degrade so quickly. Nevertheless, the exceptional tactility that comes with creating a plate adds to its inherently expressive nature, and the technique can feel far less daunting than other processes that demand specialist materials and knowledge.

Practical necessity was also of paramount concern among activist organisations that turned to screenprinting as a utilitarian political tool. The Community Arts Project (CAP) in Cape Town, which counted Skotnes among its teaching cohort, became a powerful centre for activism throughout the 1980s, thanks to the decision to build a dedicated screenprinting workshop. This provided facilities to manufacture posters, banners, stickers and T-shirts, and was used by organisations that aligned with the African National Congress (ANC). These included the Medu Art Ensemble, which was based over the border in Botswana, and known for its powerful anti-apartheid iconography, and the United Democratic Front, a federation of community groups including trade unions and student bodies.

CAP became a standard-bearer for the notion of the 'cultural worker', whereby artists produce work as a political weapon to directly aid the liberation of oppressed people. It was followed by other initiatives in Johannesburg, such as the Screen Training Project, with its directive to teach screenprinting skills to political activists, and the Congress of South African Trade Unions (COSATU), which acquired its own press to produce reams of paper-based materials. This highly political framework followed many of the principles of Mexican organisations discussed in chapter 7, particularly an initial dedication to collective working and anonymity.

Such operations came with considerable risk. Workshops were often subjected to police raids, arrests and deadly violence. COSATU was bombed by police in 1987, destroying all its apparatus. Two years previously, the South African Defence Force had raided the Medu headquarters and the homes of its members, killing twelve people. These extreme threats often resulted in the closure or disbandment of programmes, which might have been short-lived but nevertheless had a huge impact on the visual imprint of resistance among everyday people.

* * *

With the dawn of the 1990s came the dismantling of apartheid law and the onset of the first democratic election, which declared Nelson Mandela president in 1994. With the ANC's vision for a new South Africa came a mandate to broaden the scope of facilities and opportunities afforded to Black artists, particularly access to equipment and expertise. The new administration also allowed organisations that had previously operated under strict educational or recreational parameters to embrace the multiplicity of printmaking and the various forms of expression it could afford, including a wider interest in intaglio and lithography. The impulse to produce explicitly political imagery also developed into a more multifaceted field of self-reflective practice. However, a dedication to social justice and accessible community education remained integral to almost all of the spaces that developed during this period.

Artist Proof Studio (APS) is among the most significant and far-reaching initiatives. This non-profit in Johannesburg is committed to fostering collaborative practice and educational outreach for a host of emerging and established artists, coupled with facilitating technical excellence within the field. It was founded by Kim Berman (b. 1960) and Nhlanhla Xaba (1960–2003) – another Rorke's Drift student and former teacher at FUBA – in 1991, with the aid of an etching press that Berman had acquired while training in Boston.

With an original membership that included Nkosi and other former Rorke classmates such as Daniel Gordon Gabashane (1949–2014), the group embraced the principles of *ubuntu*,[4] a philosophical concept that embodies humanity towards others. In doing so, the studio attempted to deconstruct the deeply entrenched racist power systems that had been instilled during apartheid. As Berman noted, 'Teaching at the fledgling APS became far more challenging than simply imparting technique. It was a process of mutual learning and exposure to our different experiences of both life and art.'⁵

Moreover, these printmaker founders wished to impart their own sizeable knowledge, and to mentor practices beyond the realms of didactic or purely representational art – a tradition that still held true, particularly with regard to the appreciation and critical reception of Black artists. For Xaba, this was something he sought in his own work, both formally and conceptually, explaining that: 'I attempt to convey – not the simplicity of representation – but a more complex and layered process.'⁶

To fund the studio, part-time sessions for wealthier, white artists were introduced. This strategy made it possible to buy materials for less advantaged members, and to support a programme of internships and training aimed at employment as professional printers and independent practitioners. This professionalisation was possible thanks to an increase in nascent publishing businesses and commercial galleries, which not only took advantage of a growing international recognition for South African prints, but also the relative free trade that emerged following the lifting of apartheid-era global sanctions.

Xaba died in a devastating fire that destroyed the original studio in 2003, but his legacy as a painter and printmaker lived on. His students and fellow artists dug remnants of prints from the ashes, and produced enormous collages that commemorated not only his life's work but also the future vision of APS. This included continual outreach that brought the creative possibilities of print to all kinds of settings, such as the 1993 and 1994 editions of the Johannesburg 'Arts Alive' street festival, where spontaneous collaborative works were made using a steamroller. A more internationally minded print exchange, dubbed 'Volatile Alliances', was initiated in 1995 as part of the first Johannesburg Biennale. It featured representatives of art centres from across ten different countries, inviting them to make limited editions that engaged with the complexities of race and class.

Other contributions to activist print portfolios demonstrate an ongoing commitment to dispelling misinformation and stigma surrounding HIV/Aids. 'Break the Silence!' (2000–01) was organised by the human rights organisation Artists for Humanity, and the portfolio was sold as a collection to museums and institutions as well as being exhibited at Durban Art Gallery. Most significantly, the works were reproduced as posters and enormous billboards, which were pasted throughout rural and urban areas greatly affected by the epidemic. In so doing, the prints reached the widest possible public, and took their message directly to the streets, in what can be seen as a radical evolution of the political portfolios discussed in previous chapters.

Xaba's contribution to this compendium consisted of a woodcut (and possible collograph elements) titled *AIDS Exodus*, which holds biblical allusions. The collaged effect of multiple blocks and the tactile imprint of various textiles demonstrate the artist's remarkable compositional skills. The print's palette is rather subdued when compared to the complex multicoloured impressions that the artist produced elsewhere across reduction linocut, etching and lithography. Berman used similarly earthy hues in her mixed intaglio piece (fig. 9.3), which is formed like a brickwork grid, covered in violent

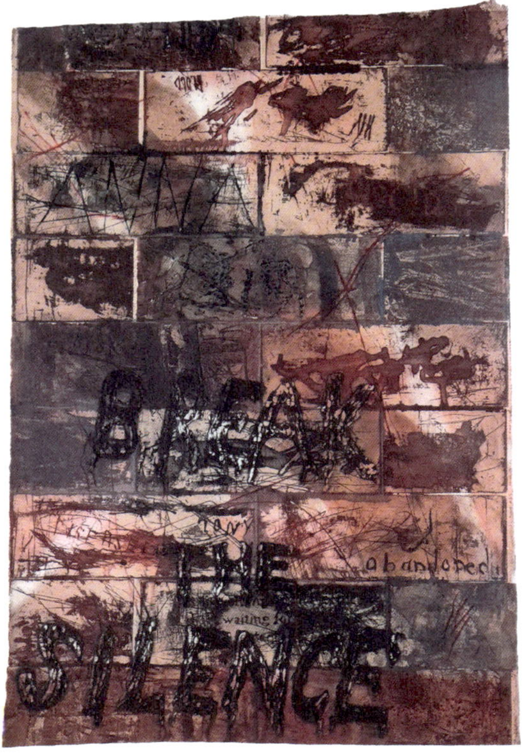

Fig. 9.3 Kim Berman, *Break the Silence* from the 'Break the Silence!' portfolio, 2001. Mixed intaglio.

scratches. She borrows the title of the series by emblazoning it across her surface in thick, impasto letterforms that hold an inherent sense of urgency.

Although APS has embraced everything from tomato boxes to plastic sheets in the quest for accessibility and experimentation, it has a reputation as one of the best professional studios in the country. Thanks to the groundbreaking expertise offered on site, long-standing relationships have been fostered with leading artists from South Africa and beyond, who have in turn supported the studio in various ways. One of its biggest homegrown supporters is William Kentridge (b. 1955), who is internationally renowned for his prolific output across all kinds of media. He not only works across drawing, sculpture, printmaking, theatre and film, but also combines them in complex assemblages that defy easy categorisation. As the child of anti-apartheid lawyers, he originally studied politics, before embarking on supplementary training at the Johannesburg Art Foundation, where he was introduced to printmaking.

* * *

Some of the most ambitious works that Kentridge has produced with APS push the limits of scale and technical possibilities, thanks to the enormous presses which the studio now operates. Take, for example, *Walking Man* (fig. 9.4). This enormous linocut measures roughly 2.5 metres in height, and was produced from a single large panel of linoleum flooring. Working at the studio with master printer Osiah Masekoameng (b. 1965), Kentridge managed to translate the tension between the gestural, inky brushwork and delicate background textures that typify his drawings, and to reimagine them on a grand scale.

This foreboding depiction of a human-tree hybrid is beyond human proportions. The man appears to be in perpetual motion, thanks not only to his trudging gait, but also to the closely cut line work that surrounds him like noisy static. The dark, graphic flatness of the body is punctured by the stitched detailing of his clothing, which dissipates amid a ruptured trunk emanating from his neck. In this tense interplay between positive and negative space, the eye can be tricked into seeing the tangled mass of branches as something entirely different. For a moment, it is as if devastating cracks have formed against an open sky, assuredly foretelling imminent disaster.

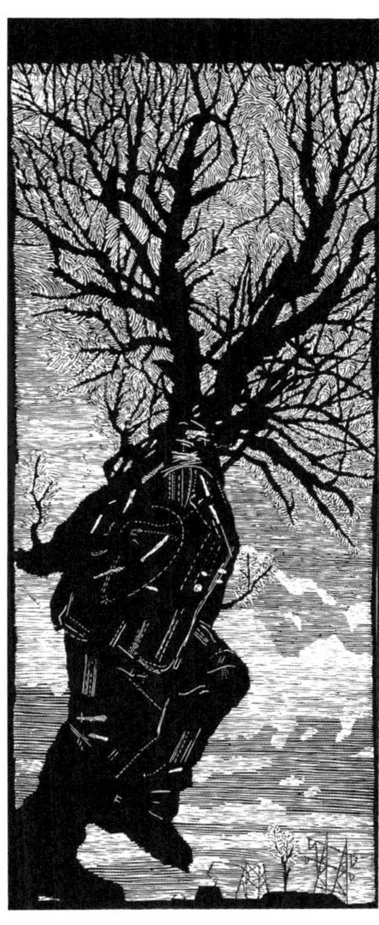

Fig. 9.4 William Kentridge, *Walking Man*, 2000. Printed by Osiah Masekoameng and published by David Krut Fine Art. Linocut.

This technically accomplished work can be read as an analogy for anti-apartheid marchers and uprooted communities, while the idea of procession – an ongoing concern for the artist – relates to constructs of power, forced movement and protest. Kentridge rarely focuses on linocut, despite its established associations with South African art-making, but he has turned to woodblock for other monumental experiments in relief. Among them was the public art project *Triumph and Laments* (2016), which took the form of a gigantic frieze installed along the banks of the River Tiber in Rome, and relating to the city's historical refugee population.

The final outcome of this series consisted of an innovative form of negative stencilling, achieved with the aid of a jet washer used to blast away decades of embedded grime from the stone walls along the riverside. The designs themselves, however, were born from a years-long collaboration with the David Krut Workshop, another important printing and publishing studio based in Johannesburg, which has worked with the artist for decades. With the aid of a team of 18 people, including master printer Jillian Ross (b. 1978), interpretations of Kentridge's drawings were constructed from 170 individual sheets and 66 woodblocks, which were brought together like a complex mosaic. This creative evolution, first from charcoal to ink, then to woodblock, and finally to Mylar stencils and large-scale urban installation, speaks to the multifaceted nature of Kentridge's practice.

When it comes to smaller-scale expression, the artist prefers intaglio due to its proximity to the immediacy of drawing. In fact, he has used the technique to build on broader print histories and intertwine them with the injustices experienced closer to home. In his early series 'Industry and Idleness' (1986), for example, he aligns the corruption of his home city with Hogarth's moral story of the same title, but highlights the failings of this rigid tale of righteousness amid the systemic oppression of apartheid. Kentridge's version does away with the exacting lines of engraving, and creates a messier truth through frenetic etching and aquatint. His scenes chronicle the experiences of an exploitative businessman who prospers, while a diligent worker is caught in an endless cycle of deprivation.[7]

Kentridge printed these works with The Caversham Press in rural KwaZulu-Natal. Unlike Rorke's Drift, this outpost was a private studio housed in a decommissioned Methodist church, and focused on providing expertise and resources on a more domestic scale. It was founded by Malcolm Christian (b. 1950) in 1985, making it one of the earliest comprehensive professional facilities in the country. Having trained in England and taught at various South African universities, Christian was inspired to set up a print-focused countryside retreat where artists could lose themselves in the techniques. During its decades-long tenure (it closed in 2024), the studio welcomed individuals including Kentridge, Robert Hodgins (1920–2010), Deborah Bell (b. 1957) and Lionel Davis (b. 1936), and excelled in forms of collaborative production akin to premises established by the earlier American initiatives discussed in chapter 8.

Another significant enterprise was established by Mark Attwood (b. 1966), a master printer who trained at the Tamarind Institute before founding a dedicated lithography studio, known as The Artists' Press, in 1991. Its first iteration formed part of a Johannesburg studio cooperative called The Bag Factory, which was established by artist and activist David Koloane (1938–2019) and British philanthropist Robert Loder (1934–2017). Their goal was to build a distinct artist community on a dedicated site, which included excellent technical facilities. Attwood embarked on his venture with a salvaged offset press and a focus on highly experimental lithographs, priding himself on creating 'hand-pulled' impressions as opposed to using semi-automated, large-scale machines to produce work in high volume and on considerable scale. His command of a medium still relatively unexplored among contemporary artists bore collaborations with an array of Bag Factory members, including Koloane, Mmakgabo Helen Sebidi (b. 1943), Penny Siopis (b. 1953) and Sam Nhlengethwa (b. 1955).

The Artists' Press relocated to Mpumalanga province in 2003 and has continued to offer artist residencies similar to those formerly offered by The Caversham Press, albeit with a renewed focus on ecologically conscious practices, including self-sustaining farming, generating renewable energy, and limiting the use of carcinogenic printing materials. Along with other studio founders mentioned thus far, Attwood has played a significant role in establishing a rich contemporary printmaking culture in South Africa, which extends far beyond the prevailing association with relief works alone.

A vibrant testament to these multiple histories comes from a suite of lithographs made at The Artists' Press by Nhlengethwa, who is widely celebrated for his mixed-media paintings detailing contemporary urban life. In 'Tributes' (2008–14), however, he abandons direct depictions of people in favour of imagined interiors that are designed as homages to artists who have inspired and influenced him. These wonderfully articulate prints are populated with an array of chic, modern items of furniture and objects that function as a portrait of each individual, alongside immensely detailed copies of their work.

In these joyful fictitious living rooms, Nhlengethwa places contemporaries such as Kentridge (fig. 9.5), Skotnes and Koloane alongside international figures such as Henri Matisse and Jean-Michel

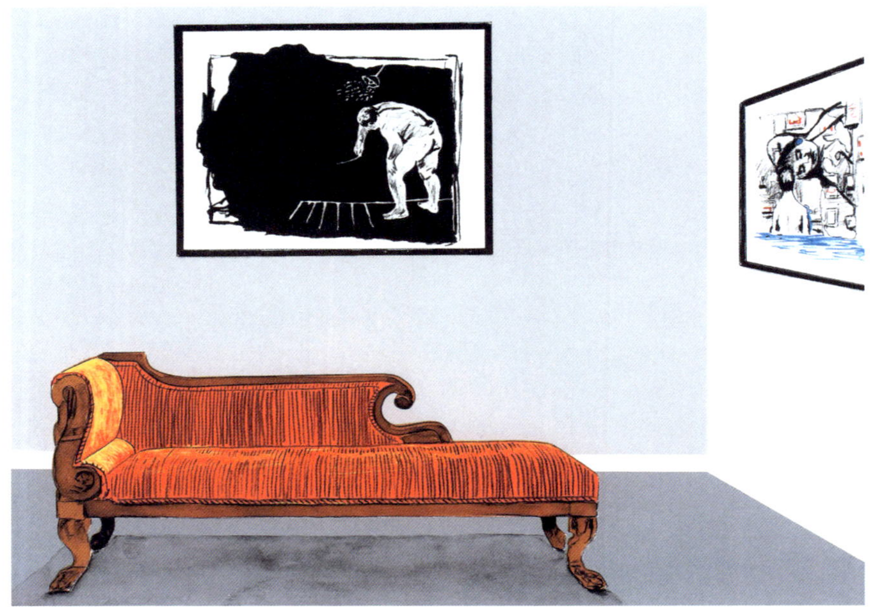

Fig. 9.5 Sam Nhlengethwa, *Tribute to Kentridge*, from the series 'Tributes', 2008–14. Published by The Artists' Press. Lithograph.

Basquiat. In doing so, he not only builds an intricate picture of his own inspirations and the trappings of cosmopolitan South African life, but also harnesses the expressive, representational and reproductive qualities of the lithograph. His combination of gestural daubs, tightly wrought scribbles and graphic lines demonstrates the versatility of the medium, as well as the expert collaboration between printer and artist.[8]

Thirty years before, while still a student at Rorke's Drift, Nhlengethwa had produced a screenprint depicting his experiences at the centre. The cruder execution belies a younger artist finding his style, and represents industrious artistic endeavour against a rural backdrop, complete with cattle and the outlines of a missionary church. It is a world away from the inner-city scenes he would go on to produce, but the seeds of what would become a truly distinct and commanding aesthetic are already evident. Even without invoking the relief imprint that was so closely associated with the school, it is clear that the institution's teachings have left their impressions, and its legacy ultimately lives on.

　　　　　THE STORY OF PRINTMAKING

CHAPTER 10

As Seen on Screen

Expanded Possibilities in the Digital Age

[It's] in the printmaking that new things are invented
— Julie Mehretu, 2021

IN 1989, WHILE working at the European Organisation of Nuclear Research (better known as CERN), British computer scientist Tim Berners-Lee introduced colleagues to his proposal for an information-sharing platform that would connect scientists across the world. To begin with, this 'World Wide Web' was restricted to powerful NeXT computers, which only select academics had access to. However, within the space of a year CERN intern Nicola Pellow had developed code that allowed the web browser to function on any system. The internet, as we know it, had been born.

The technological advancements of the new millennium are defined by this radical innovation, and its indelible impact has quite rightly been compared to that of the Gutenberg press. Just as printed pages spread at an unprecedented rate during the fifteenth century, so communication is now possible in a manner that was previously unfathomable. In fact, within less than two decades, vast swathes of the global population have gone from using a desktop machine attached to a screeching dial-up modem, to owning a handheld device that has more than 100,000 times the processing power of the computers that facilitated the moon landing.

The question of how printmaking fits within this latest evolution of the Information Age has manifold answers. Digital developments have impacted every area of society, and few will be unaware of the impact that the online world (and a new vanguard of artificial intelligence) has had on the way we consume and understand images. The drastic decline in everyday printed materials has been one of the greatest cultural shifts of the twenty-first century, and many specialist studios and educational facilities have suffered and even shuttered due to the impact of a less tangible world of visual media.

However, the accelerated pace of technological innovation has also offered new possibilities for print, which is by its very nature in a process of constant evolution. In fact, as early as the 1950s, printmakers were using mainframe computational devices such as plotters to produce images on conventional presses. That being said, it was not until the 1990s that truly accessible digital programmes came to the fore. Advanced image processors, computerised plate-making systems and creative software have all contributed to the shift, as has 3-D printing innovation that bridges the gap between two-dimensional objects and sculpture.

These advancements are ostensibly cutting-edge tools that can either supplant or supplement existing printmaking techniques, while opportunities to combine multiple processes have certainly been aided by digital intervention. Take, for example, Ellen Gallagher's (b. 1965) ambitious 60-piece portfolio 'DeLuxe' (figs 10.1, 10.1a).

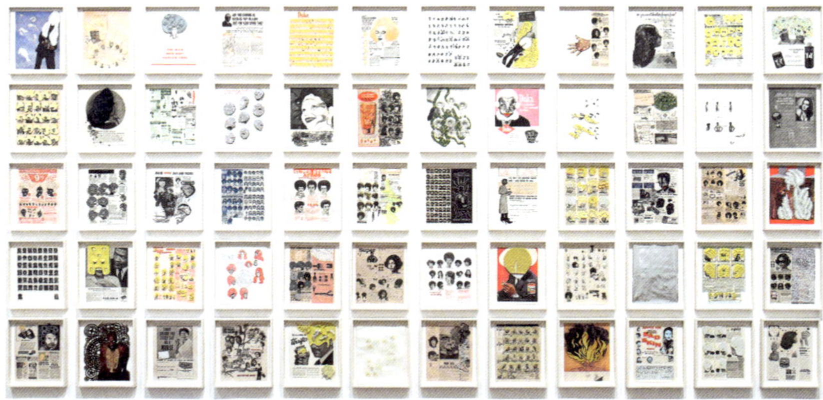

Fig. 10.1 Ellen Gallagher, 'DeLuxe' portfolio, 2004–5. Grid of 60 photogravures, etchings, aquatints and drypoints with lithography, screenprinting, chine collé and other mixed media.

                    THE STORY OF PRINTMAKING

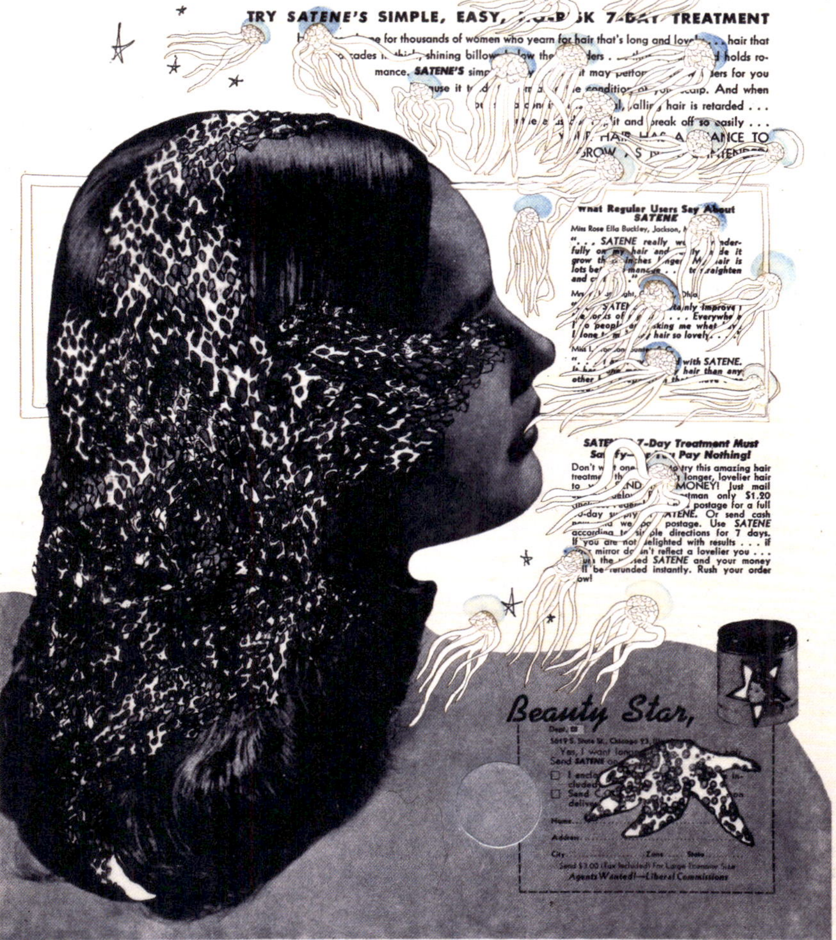

Fig. 10.1a Ellen Gallagher, *DeLuxe – Beauty Star*, 2004–5 (single panel detail of 'DeLuxe' portfolio)

This comprises a set of individually framed prints that are hung in a grid formation and feature beauty advertisements published in magazines aimed at African American audiences (such as *Ebony* and *Our World*), all of which date from the 1930s through to the 1970s. Gallagher transforms these depictions through exceptionally intricate layering, combining techniques including screenprinting, aquatint, drypoint and lithography, before manipulating further with materials as disparate as glitter, gold leaf, novelty 'googly eyes' and Plasticine. Through this onslaught of visual material, Gallagher transforms both the form and content of stereotypical depictions of Black women, engaging with the complexities of surface, and all the conceptual meaning it can hold.

Just under two decades before, April Greiman (b. 1948) was already exploring the creative possibilities of digital interfaces and their inter-pretation through print. The American artist and graphic designer views computer programming – and its many shortcomings – as an independent antagonist within her work. This is most evident in her groundbreaking lithograph *does it make sense?* (fig. 10.2), which came about after Greiman was invited to produce a special issue of *Design Quarterly*. Instead of the usual 32-page magazine, she set about creating a two-foot-by-six-foot print that began life as a video image, and was conceived entirely with cutting-edge Apple software. It was installed on the Macintosh 128K – the brand's first personal computer.

Using early graphics applications such as MacDraw and MacVision, Greiman tested the limits of the programmes' creative capacity and functionality, implementing lines of typeset text, creating freeform images and interpreting pre-existing imagery, including a composite of her own naked body and shots of swirling galaxies. Her account of the experiment speaks to the unpredictable nature of this new electronic interface:

> This may all sound straightforward, but in practice it was a hair-raising adventure. MacDraw is like an intelligent, friendly, flexible assistant – until you ask it to do one too many things. Then, without warning, it can become wildly irrational, losing whole sections of an image or creating mysterious artefacts on screen.[1]

Constructing the digital imagery was only half the battle. The resulting document was so big that when Greiman sent the file to print, the job took all night. She used a LaserWriter (Apple's first laser printer, released in 1985) to create her proofs, in order to perfect her design before it was sent to a commercial studio to be printed via offset lithography. After one trial, she discovered that half of her body was missing from the printout, and in fact the entire imprint of her figure had disappeared from the screen. These glitches demonstrate the fallibility of electronic interfaces, which can produce unexpected outcomes that are not dissimilar to those that occur when dipping a plate in an acid bath or fine-tuning the pressure on a press. Included in the final proof is the text 'made in space by April Greiman', which speaks not only to futuristic possibilities, but also to a strange digital netherworld where all kinds of mistranslations can occur.

Although *does it make sense?* has often been referred to as a poster, Greiman views it as an experimental form of hybrid imagery, which spans video, computer graphics and print. She has revisited the project, first as an early, adaptive internet experiment in which users could manipulate visuals through key words and other forms of digital input, and more recently as an augmented reality object. Working with Isovist (an open access technology aimed at advancing spatial architecture in both the real world and the digital realm), she developed *alt<DQ, Does It Make Sense?* (2024), an updated version of the original lithograph, in which implied space becomes a reality. With the aid of a tablet or smart phone, the two-dimensional image becomes animated in three-dimensional space, and users can interact with various graphic elements. These in turn serve as portals to the wealth of ever-changing information on the internet, effectively creating an image that constantly evolves in time and space.

While Greiman continues to reimagine print through vanguard technologies, other artists have returned their digital imagery to a truly analogue state. The German artist Christiane Baumgartner (b. 1967) reinterprets her digital video stills as large woodcuts, which she painstakingly hand-carves and prints, to accentuate the horizontal strips of static one might encounter through a monitor. By reproducing these images through such a historical technique, she raises questions concerning the fleeting nature of her source material. For example, in *Nordlicht* (2018) and *Pink Moon* (fig. 10.3) spectral lens flares and transient light sources are rendered solid by graphic lines of positive and negative space. In something of a full circle moment, it was while studying printmaking at the Royal College of Art (RCA) in London that Baumgartner first became interested in making video works, and it was only later that she found a natural synergy between the two.

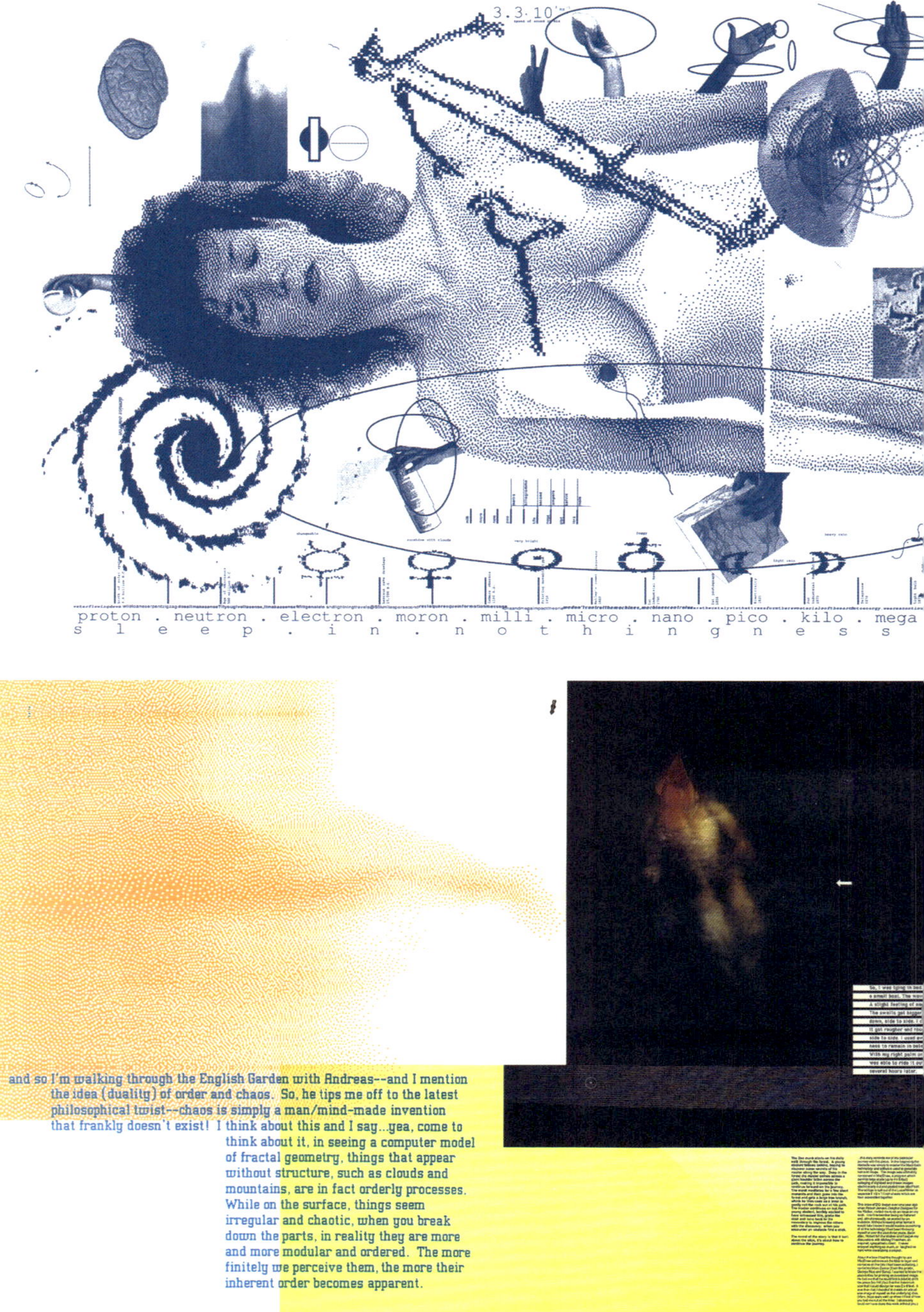

Fig. 10.2 April Greiman, *does it make sense?*, 1986.

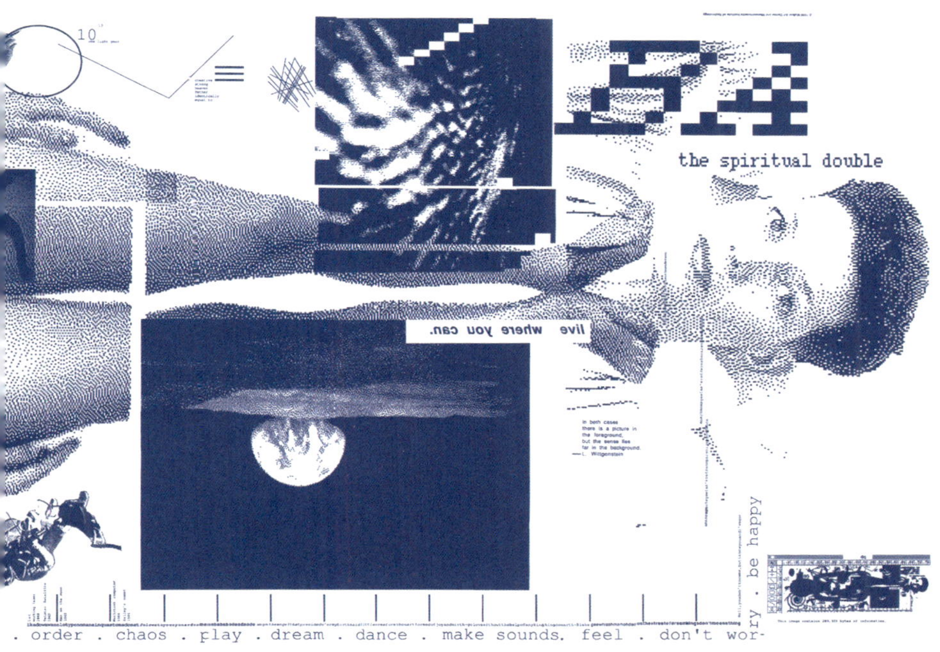

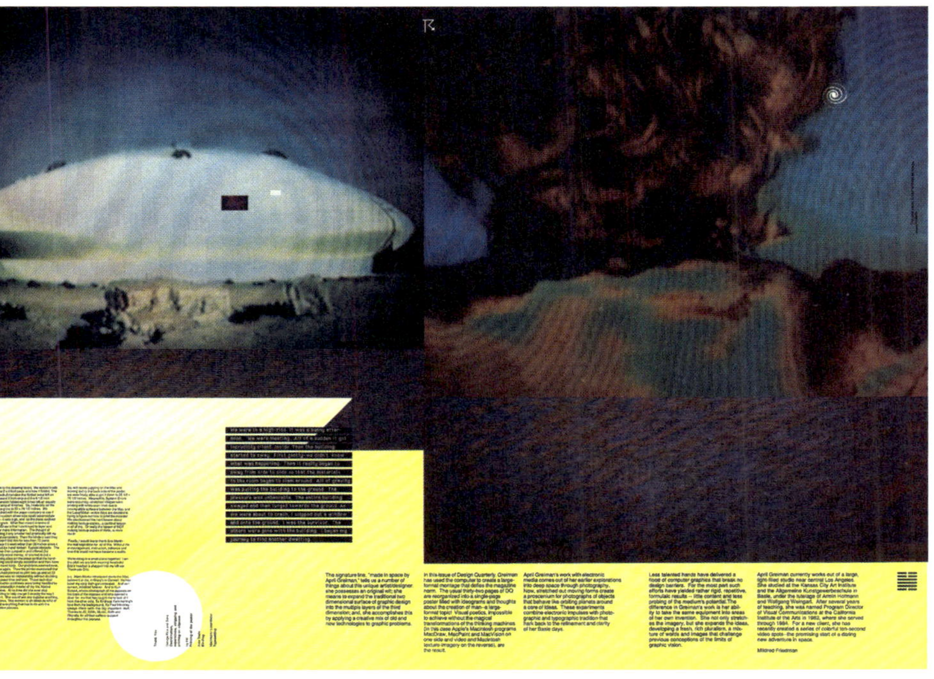

Produced as a fold-out issue of *Design Quarterly*, no. 133. Offset lithograph.

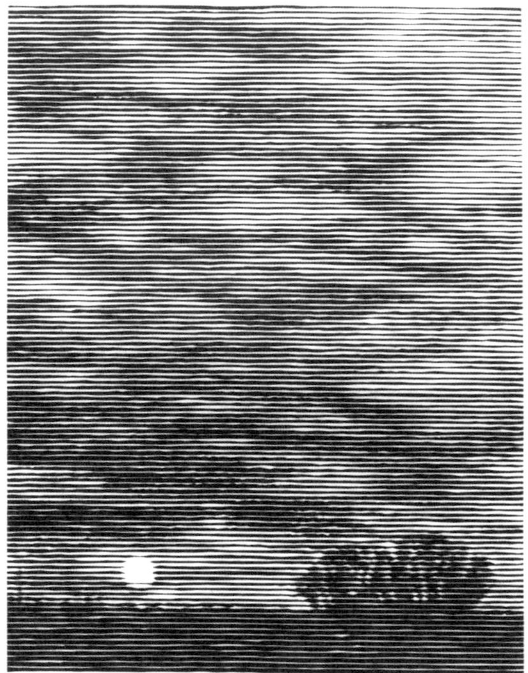

Fig. 10.3 Christiane Baumgartner, *Pink Moon* (detail), 2019. Woodcut.

Sin Wai Kin (b. 1991), another RCA graduate, took a similarly expansive reading of printmaking during their studies. They used the prism of print culture and all of its troubling digital constructs – from highly edited fashion advertising to social media filters – to question and disassemble constructs of gender. Although they are usually described as a performance and multimedia artist who works within the field of drag, their practice involves more material associations with print techniques. Before removing the heavy makeup used to create characters inspired by Hollywood actresses, Cantonese opera heroines and K-Pop celebrities, Sin presses their face into a wet wipe, thus creating a unique imprint that serves as a commemorative record of that persona (fig. 10.4). This action effectively produces a monotype.

This technique has a history dating back to the mid-fifteenth century, and bridges the gap between drawing and printmaking. It is

   THE STORY OF PRINTMAKING

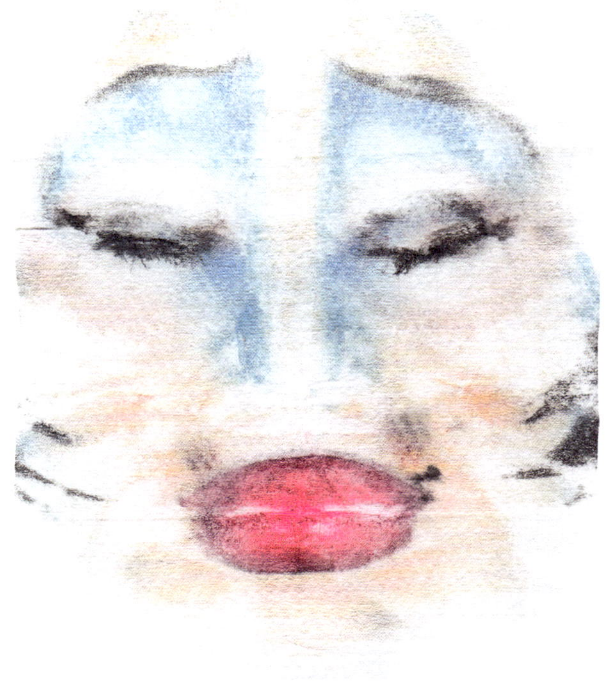

Fig. 10.4 Sin Wai Kin, *You have not been given the words to describe how multiple yourselves are*, 2019. Face wipe monotype.

based on the principle that a single image is being created, through a process of impression; this varies slightly from a monoprint, which alludes to a unique image produced through reprintable elements, such as woodblocks or elements of a plate. Producing a monotype might involve painting onto a plate with ink or watercolour, before running it through a press to transfer a single image to paper. Alternatively, ink can be rolled onto a sheet of Perspex, before a piece of paper is delicately placed on top. Marks are then made on the reverse with a pencil, or even rubbed with fingers, to create a spontaneous sketch.

* * *

Another invention to have a profound impact on printmaking culture in the digital age is the giclée. The term was first coined by printmaker Jack Duganne (1942–2020) around 1991, derived from the French word *gicler*, meaning 'to spray'. It is a process whereby an inkjet printer reads a digital file and disseminates an extremely accurate reproduction via a fine mist of high-quality pigments. These inks are often referred to as 'archival', in an allusion to their colourfastness and stability. Unlike more analogue printing methods, giclée can follow an on-demand method, whereby one print or one hundred prints can be produced at any given moment.

Although the opinion that giclée offers nothing more than quality reproduction is valid in some instances, it is merely a variation on the age-old argument that has plagued prints for centuries. Just as deeply experimental and expressive works have been produced across intaglio, screenprinting, lithography and relief, so too have artists and printmakers engaged in the capabilities of creating something truly original through this digital method.

The market for prints has gained a new lease of life, thanks in no small part to the beautifully accurate, richly tonal reproductions that are possible with giclée – as well as their relatively low price. In fact, it is not only the digital nature of the production, but also the buying and selling of works themselves, that has contributed to this change. The birth of online platforms has allowed for transparency, easy navigation and bespoke computer analysis, not to mention global reach. All of these elements suit a younger cohort of collectors best described as 'digital natives', who want to own art made available at a realistic price point. Many have seen giclée as a gateway to a greater appreciation and understanding of other printmaking techniques, as well as the nuances of editions and collaborative works. Selling techniques borrowed from fashion brands – including scheduled limited-edition 'drops', whereby a product is only available on a certain platform and at a certain time – have also been used by auction sites and individual artists, creating a rarefied market in line with Hogarth's strategies (see pp. 81–2). Whereas he invited prospective clients to his studio (among other sales tactics), multimedia marketing is now commonplace, including behind-the-scenes videos that demonstrate exactly how a work is produced.

Avant Arte is one online auction platform that has developed a successful model utilising plenty of these characteristics. The company employs the expertise of Make–Ready, a major screenprinting and digital studio based in North London. Harnessing both technological innovations and the ingenuity one would expect from expert printers, they have worked with everything from glow-in-the-dark inks to gold foiling and die-cutting to produce works that push the possibilities of a printed edition. This includes an ongoing collaboration with the African American artist Mickalene Thomas (b. 1971), known for her elaborate portrait paintings encrusted in rhinestones and glitter. To reinterpret her works on canvas, Make–Ready have developed various processes that incorporate metallic inks and hand-applied glitters, the latter of which are used to dramatic effect in *Portrait of Maya #10* (2024). A photographic image of the model's bare chest is laid on top of the drawn image of her body, while a shimmering layer of glitter articulates her Afro hair and bright red lips.

This edition was sold in support of the Broad Museum in Los Angeles. As is evident through various examples in this book, print sales have long been tied to philanthropic endeavours and social justice causes. However, both online models and digital printing have quickened the response as well as the pace, thanks to relatively rapid production times and potential for flexible output. Artists and printmakers need not do more than transmit a file to be produced in aid of emergency fundraisers responding to climate disasters, international conflicts and other devastating events. This model was particularly evident during the Covid-19 pandemic, when limits on human contact forced so many people to live life through their screens.

The relatively accessible print market has grown steadily in recent times, as have the upper echelons of the printmaking trade. In fact, since the 2010s, prints by renowned artists have reached unprecedented prices at auction. In 2022, Picasso's *The Frugal Repast* (see fig. 6.9) sold for a world-record-breaking £6 million at auction, while other household names including Warhol, Munch and Basquiat have all broken the million-pound ceiling this side of the millennium.

This flourishing trade still experiences all of the pitfalls that characterise the wider printmaking environment. A lack of technical understanding, as well as the complexities of limited editions, artist proofs and later impressions, all add to an oftentimes opaque and misunderstood industry. The value ascribed to a work remains volatile in regard to the fickle mentality of the wider art market, and an obsession with categorisation does much to denigrate the vital role that print plays within so many facets of creativity. This is perhaps best signified by variations in the prices achieved by

Warhol works. While complete sets of his editioned print portfolios have reached over £1 million at auction, they are vastly outstripped by his individual screenprinted paintings. In 2022, *Shot Sage Blue Marilyn* (1964) sold for £158 million, making it the most expensive twentieth-century artwork ever to hit the auction block.

* * *

The schisms surrounding the delineation of an artistic object, whether it be in terms of creation or dissemination, are intrinsic to one of the most recognisable prints of the twenty-first century. Shepard Fairey's (b. 1970) *Hope* (fig. 10.5) became an official symbol of Barack Obama's first presidential campaign, following its widespread popularity both in the USA and internationally. The success of this

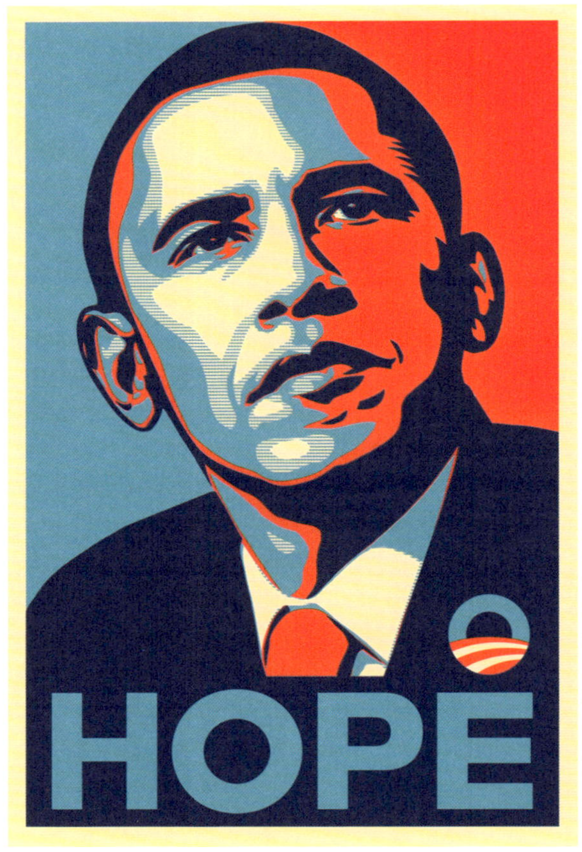

Fig. 10.5 Shepard Fairey, *Hope*, 2008. Offset lithograph.

 THE STORY OF PRINTMAKING

political poster lies not only in Fairey's succinct command of graphic iconography – which marries both street art aesthetics and historical propaganda – but also in the work's multidimensional proliferation through printed paste-ups, downloadable JPEGs, and the fractal lens of social media.

As someone who has studied fine art and remains fully embedded in skate and graffiti culture, Fairey has cited influences as varied as Robert Rauschenberg (see p. 184), the Russian artist-designer Alexander Rodchenko (1891–1956) and DIY punk zines. Fairey also considers screenprinting to be the cornerstone of his practice, and turned to the technique's visual lexicon to produce the original concept for his seminal work. Using Rubylith (a red ultra-violet masking film usually utilised for stencilling), he conceived of four layers of flat colour, which together formed his own interpretation of an Associated Press photograph taken by Mannie Garcia.[2] This highly stylised blue-and-red portrait was then composited digitally, before being disseminated as a poster across Los Angeles.

The text in Fairey's original version did not state 'hope' but, rather, 'progress'. The slogan was updated after the Obama team raised concerns that the sentiment appeared too closely associated with Socialist Realism. In an unlikely turn for a street artist, Fairey had sought official permission following the popularity of the first print run, for fear that his graffiti-related criminal offences might harm the presidential campaign. This revised iteration became an icon of American optimism, appearing as 300,000 posters (both screenprints and offset lithographs), numerous stickers, T-shirts, a website download, and even a trio of large-scale collages, which Fairey denotes as 'unique painted variations'.[3] The fact that these pieces were produced after the original poster is yet another example of how the concept of print functioning only as a facsimile is both reductive and vastly overstated.

The enduring success of the Obama poster is quite rightly associated with the rise of progressive US politics during the first decade of the 2000s, but it also marks a distinct shift in the way prints have been both fabricated and consumed. The thrill of having a real encounter with Fairey's creation out on the streets was documented online, just as the compressed digital image was proliferated. This strange slippage between the physical and the online world has continued to grow, as onscreen existence becomes an increasingly dominant reality.

Fairey's *Hope* is not the only print to gain specific sociopolitical relevance in recent times. Paula Rego (1935–2022) was a pre-eminent painter and printmaker based in London, who was known for her disquieting interpretations of folk tales and story books, which often embody a crackling eroticism and dangerous sense of gendered power play. Rego helped to shape the discourse around reproductive rights in her native Portugal, with her 'Abortion' series. These works were first produced as paintings and pastels in 1998, before she reimagined them as a suite of eight etchings between 1999 and 2000 (fig. 10.6). She made these works after the first referendum to legalise terminations in her home country failed by a narrow margin. The series expressed the physical suffering and emotional distress so many women go through when forced to turn to illegal procedures, and they built on Rego's personal history as well as accounts from others.

In the run-up to a second referendum in 2007, several of Rego's etchings appeared in Portuguese newspapers. These astute, visceral

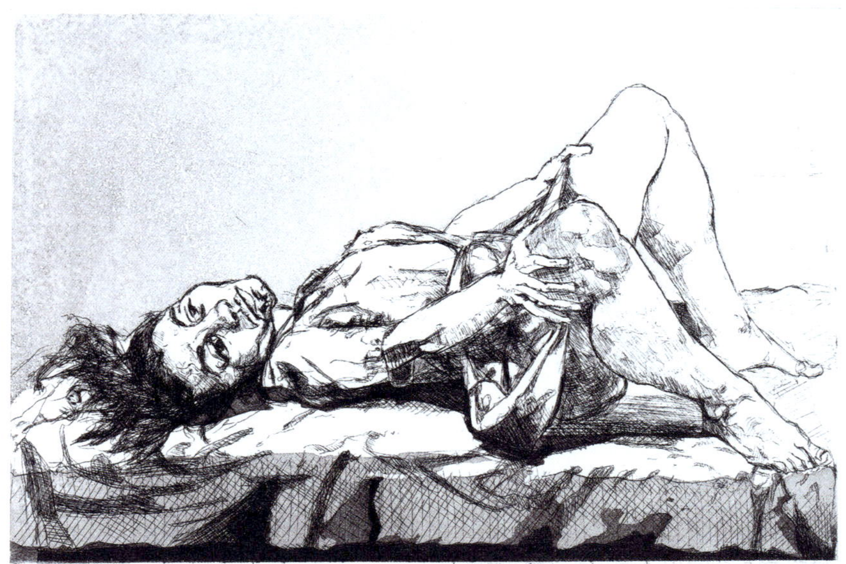

Fig. 10.6 Paula Rego, *Untitled 1*, from the series 'Abortion', 1999. Etching.

and deeply intimate images were a far cry from the ideological rhetoric usually employed. Their influence brought the debate back to women's experiences, and have been recognised as helping to shape the shift in public opinion. The series gained new relevance and visibility in 2022, when the USA's Supreme Court overturned the constitutional right to abortion that had been established by the Roe v. Wade ruling in 1973. Both the Metropolitan Museum of Art and the Museum of Modern Art in New York acquired editions of the series in 2023.

There is no doubt that Rego's etchings achieved something that would have been impossible through photography – the preferred visual medium of any newspaper. Her depictions portrayed profoundly private moments that could be subject to all manner of ethical questions if documented directly (as such, they might easily have been censored), but they also crystallised a visceral understanding of a traumatic bodily experience through her particular artistry. The same can be said of Tracey Emin (b. 1963), who turned to monoprints to produce diaristic interpretations of her own suffering. While her text-based blankets and video works speak to a more public reckoning, these diminutive, scratched and smudged imprints are more intimate. In *Terribly Wrong* (1997), Emin recalls a traumatic abortion that had lasting health implications. It is an urgent image, which shows a foreshortened, naked body, coupled with emphatic lines of text that once again speak to a palpable sense of anguish.

Both of these examples attest to the material connections so often felt when encountering works of print, even in – and perhaps because of – an increasingly digital age. The hunger for tactility, a meditative pace and a sense of permanence is something many printmakers continue to strive for in their engagement with process, and their sentiment is encoded within each subsequent impression. In a world dominated by digital screens and an increasing sense of remove, the material nature of a printed image still holds a very particular resonance, whether it is carved from a block, forged from acid, or embedded with UV inks. As is evident from the many stories shared throughout this book, prints can take on so many guises and serve so many different purposes, but they are ultimately concerned with driving an understanding of the world around us.

In 2018, the Ethiopian American artist Julie Mehretu (b. 1970) produced a series of glorious colour aquatints in collaboration with Gemini G.E.L., titled 'Six Bardos' (fig. 10.7). She worked with a team of etchers headed by Case Hudson (b. 1968) to create her expressive, extraordinarily complex prints. Each of these large-scale compositions employs *à la poupée* to articulate gestural lines reminiscent of both graffiti spray cans and Abstract Expressionist canvases, as opposed to working with distinct layers born from separate plates. Mehretu, whose works on canvas explore themes including 'psychogeography'[4] and social unrest, has described printmaking as integral to her practice, particularly in developing a sense of intuitive process. For her, '[it's] in the printmaking that new things are invented'.[5]

For 'Six Bardos', conceiving the images on a single plane was both a technical exercise and a conceptual act. The works were inspired by a trip to none other than the Mogao Grottos, the site of spiritual pilgrimage where our ancient story of print began (see p. 7). For Mehretu, convening with the Buddhist cycle of death and rebirth,

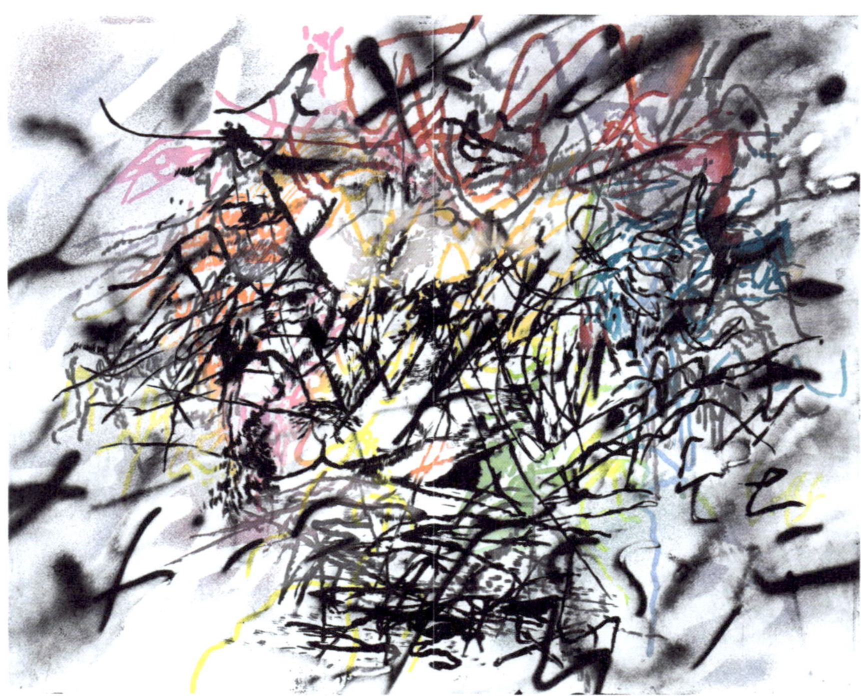

Fig. 10.7 Julie Mehretu, *Transmutation*, from the series 'Six Bardos', 2018. Aquatint.

                                        THE STORY OF PRINTMAKING

as well as a sense of interconnected life force, was a catalyst for this latest series. These principles can also serve as an analogy for the many interconnected histories of printmaking culture, which might fade and dissipate, only to emerge again once more. With each and every impression, the narratives of our world are being written. What comes next is yet to be inscribed.

GLOSSARY

Aquatint A tonal etching process that produces a painterly effect, achieved by dusting a plate with acid-resistant rosin and fusing with heat. Produces a fine dotted surface that can be re-bitten to produce darker layers.

Artist proof An impression retained by the artist, which is not included in the official numbered edition. Usually labelled 'AP'.

Baren A disk-shaped pad produced from coiled cord and covered in a sheath of bamboo. Used to print reliefs by hand, particularly in traditional Japanese woodblock.

Burin A steel cutting stylus used in engraving, featuring a wedge-shaped point and a toadstool-shaped pommel, allowing a carver to exert considerable pressure.

Burr A soft, velvety line produced in drypoint. The effect results from the textured edges that surround each groove, which hold on to excess amounts of ink.

Chop mark A distinct embossed mark found in the margin of a print, identifying the workshop where it was printed. Often viewed as a mark of authenticity and quality.

Collography A technique that uses everyday materials, such as cardboard, textiles and string, to create a relief plate.

Drypoint An intaglio process whereby a needle is used to incise the plate surface. Due to the fragile, shallow lines the plate can degrade quickly. Features a characteristic soft line known as a 'burr'. Often used in conjunction with etching.

Edition Refers to a designated number of multiples produced in a print run, which are usually signed and numbered. The term can refer to the entire group, or to a single impression within that group.

Engraving The oldest intaglio process derived from metalwork. Marks are inscribed onto a plate using a burin or other carving tool, creating recesses that are then filled with ink and transferred onto paper.

Etching An intaglio process which employs acid to eat away at areas of the plate not protected by resistant varnish or 'ground', thus producing deep grooves that can be inked and printed. More expressive and less laborious than engraving.

Giclée From the French *gicler*, meaning 'to spray'. A process whereby an inkjet printer accurately reproduces a digital file by spraying a fine mist of high-quality pigments.

Graver A tool used in wood engraving, similar to a burin.

Hard ground An acid-resistant layer used to prepare etching plates, traditionally made from bitumen and wax. It is left to harden before a needle is used to draw on top and disturb the surface, thus exposing the metal below.

Impression A single print that has been produced on paper, through any printmaking technique.

Intaglio From the Italian *intagliare*, meaning 'to engrave'. The general term given to a range of printing processes which inscribe into the surface of a plate to create a positive line.

Letterpress A form of relief printing whereby individual characters are cast from metal and bound together to produce moveable blocks of type. Popularised by Gutenberg and his relief press, which was perfected by 1440. Earlier forms of relief text printing date back to Korea in the 12th century.

Linocut A form of relief printing which is carved from blocks of linoleum. Unlike woodblock, it features no grain and is often considered easier to manipulate.

Lithography A chemical printing process named from the Greek for 'stone scribing', based on the principle that oil and water do not mix. First patented by Alois Senefelder *c.*1799. An image is embedded into a limestone surface using a range of greasy materials, then fixed using solvents.

Mezzotint An intaglio process, meaning 'half-tone' in Italian. First developed around 1660 in Germany, but popularised in Britain in the mid-17th century. Consists entirely of tonal qualities, as opposed to line, and is defined by drawing light out of darkness. The teeth (i.e., crevices) of the textured plate are gradually burnished using specialist tools, creating smooth areas that will not hold on to ink, therefore producing light areas.

Monoprint A technique that produces a unique image by utilising reprintable elements, such as woodblocks or elements of an existing plate.

Monotype A technique dating back to the mid-15th century, which produces a unique print that cannot be replicated. This might involve brushing ink or paint directly onto a plate before running it through a press, or drawing onto the back of a piece of paper which has been pressed directly onto an inked surface.

Mordant A solution used to etch intaglio plates, which is usually acidic.

Offset lithography A mechanised lithography process whereby a design is imprinted onto a rubber cylinder instead of a stone slab, thus speeding up production. First developed in the early 1800s, gaining popularity by the second half of the 19th century.

 GLOSSARY

Plate A piece of metal (usually copper) or other material used to produce intaglio prints by way of inscribing its surface.

Press A machine used to produce a print. A relief press utilises a stamping motion; an intaglio press uses two rollers, akin to a mangle; a lithographic press features a scraper bar that is pulled across the stone (i.e., limestone printing surface) with considerable force.

Relief A printing process that consists of carving away negative space from a block, so that the image stands proud from the surface. Most commonly associated with woodcut and linocut.

Rocker A tool used in mezzotint to prepare the rough surface of the plate. It features a curved steel plate that is rocked back and forth across the surface, creating cuts at carefully calculated angles.

Rosin A fine acid-resistant powder traditionally formed from concentrated pine tree sap, used to produce aquatint grain by means of fusing the particles to the plate surface through exposure to heat.

Roulette A specialist scraper used predominantly in mezzotint. It features a textured cylinder that is used to gradually burnish areas of the plate to create mid-tones and areas of light.

Scraper A stiff squeegee that forms part of a lithography printing press. The pressure is set using a screw-and-wheel mechanism before the bar is lowered by means of a lever, so it can be pulled across the surface of the paper and stone, exerting considerable pressure.

Screenprint A technique based on the simple principle of pushing ink through a fine mesh screen. It has historically been used to transfer designs to paper and textiles by means of stencils, which mask areas of negative space. Sometimes referred to as 'silk screen' or 'serigraph'.

Screenprinting bed The machine used to create screenprints. It consists of a table that often features a suction vacuum to keep the paper in place, and a hinged frame that is used to affix the screen.

Serigraph See *Screenprint*

Soft ground An acid-resistant layer used to prepare etching plates, which features a solution containing fat, so that it remains sticky and does not harden like hard ground. Creates a more delicate and receptive surface that can replicate various textures, such as pencil and pastel crayon.

State An impression taken at various stages while building a final printed image, usually representing the layering of various techniques as they are added.

Stop-out An acid-resistant varnish used in etching to mask areas of a plate, thus protecting them from subsequent exposure in the acid bath. It can be used to create variations in tone, or to maintain areas of negative space.

Sugar-lift A form of aquatint in which a sugar, soap and ink solution is painted directly onto a clean plate, creating marks that are closely aligned with the fluidity of a painter's brush.

Trial proof An impression taken during the printing process that may be modified or perfected to determine the final outcome. Often marked 'TP' and not included in the final edition.

Tusche A greasy liquid used in lithography to produce painterly marks, including tones akin to watercolour as well as inky lines.

Wood engraving A relief printing technique that involves cutting into the end grain of a piece of hard wood, using a steel rod known as a graver. Allows for extremely fine lines, often incorporating the natural pattern of the grain.

Woodblock/woodcut Perhaps the oldest printing technique in the world. The process consists of carving away negative space from a block of wood, leaving the desired design standing proud from the surface in relief, ready to be inked.

Notes

1. Gods, Empresses and Ancient Scrolls: Print's Origins in Asia

1 Aurel Stein's accounts of his travels are available to view online (accessed 2 June 2025). See Stein, *Serindia: Detailed Report of Explorations in Central Asia and Westernmost China* (1921).

2 The *Mahāpratisāra Bodhisattva* with text of 'Da Sui qiu tuoluoni' was engraved by Wang Wenzhao in 980. It now resides in the British Museum. See Spee, *The Printed Image in China: From the 8th to the 21st Centuries* (2010), p. 68.

3 As quoted in Rong Xinjiang, 'Ye Changchi: Pioneer of Dunhuang Studies', *IDP News: Newsletter of the International Dunhuang Project*, no. 7 (1997), p. 4.

4 For a detailed analysis of Wu's links to printing, see Barrett, *The Woman Who Discovered Printing* (2008).

5 For more on these rubbings, see Wood and Barnard, *The Diamond Sutra: The Story of the World's Earliest Dated Printed Book* (2010), pp. 68–9.

6 See Peter Kornicki, 'Empress Shōtoku as a Sponsor of Printing', in Hildegard Diemberger, Franz-Karl Ehrhard and Peter Kornicki (eds), *Tibetan Printing: Comparison, Continuities and Change* (Leiden: Brill, 2016), pp. 45–50.

7 For more on the construction of the miniature pagodas, as well as Shōtoku's life and rule, see Mimi Hall Yiengpruksawan, 'One Millionth of a Buddha: The "Hyakumantō Darani [*sic*]" in the Scheide Library', *The Princeton University Library Chronicle* 48, no. 3 (1987), pp. 224–38.

8 For more on rituals and symbolism, see Lust, *Chinese Popular Prints* (1996).

9 As translated in Ellen Johnston Laing, *Divine Rule and Earthly Bliss: Popular Chinese Prints. The Collection of Gerd and Lottie Wallenstein* (Berlin: Nicolaische Verlag Beuermann, 2010), p. 13.

10 More details can be found in Po Sung-nien and David Johnson, *Domesticated Deities and Auspicious Emblems: The Iconography of Everyday Life in Village China. Popular Prints and Papercuts from the Collection of Po Sung-nien* (Berkeley, CA: Chinese Popular Culture Project, 1992).

2. *Renaissance Revelations: The Advent of Engraving and Artistic Celebrity*

1 For a dynamic history, see Google Arts & Culture, *The Invention of Movable Metal Type: Goryeo Technology and Wisdom*, n.d. (accessed 2 June 2025).

2 For more on the Islamic history of paper-making, see Jonathan M. Bloom, *Paper before Print: The History and Impact of Paper in the Islamic World* (New Haven, CT: Yale University Press, 2001).

3 See 'How a Gutenberg Printing Press Works', published on YouTube by Sabrina Huyett, 2014 (accessed 19 June 2025).

4 See Hellinga, *Caxton in Focus: The Beginning of Printing in England* (1982), pp. 54–5.

5 This translation was described in the 2021 Linbury Lecture with art historian Joseph Koerner, held at the National Gallery in London, and available online (accessed 2 June 2025).

6 See Wouk and Spinks (eds), *Albrecht Dürer's Material World* (2023).

7 For more on humoral theory, see Jill Burke, *How to Be a Renaissance Woman: The Untold History of Beauty and Female Creativity* (London: Wellcome Collection, 2023), p. 22.

8 As quoted in William M. Ivins Jr, 'Notes on Three Dürer Woodblocks', *Metropolitan Museum Studies* 2, no. 1 (1929), p. 102.

9 For more on this subject, see Landau and Parshall, *The Renaissance Print: 1470–1550* (1994), pp. 110–13.

10 See Suzanne Boorsch and Nadine M. Orenstein, 'The Print in the North: The Age of Albrecht Dürer and Lucas van Leyden', *The Metropolitan Museum of Art Bulletin* 54, no. 4 (1997), pp. 1, 13–60.

11 For Dürer's letters, see *Memoirs of Journeys to Venice and the Low Countries by Albrecht Dürer*, trans. Rudolf Tombo (Auckland: The Floating Press, 2010).

12 For an extensive study of Dürer's copyright claims, see Peter J. Karol, 'Albrecht Dürer's Enforcement Actions: A Trademark Origin Story', *Vanderbilt Journal of Entertainment and Technology Law* 25, no. 3 (2023), pp. 421–82.

13 See colophon of Dürer, *The Life of the Virgin* (1511).

14 Manet reimagined the grouping of the three classical deities as a modern picnic featuring a startlingly nude woman and fully clothed male companions. For more on the comparison, see Lisa Pon, *Raphael, Dürer, and Marcantonio Raimondi: Copying and the Italian Renaissance Print* (New Haven, CT, and London: Yale University Press, 2004), p. 2.

15 See Landau and Parshall, *The Renaissance Print* (1994), p. 112.

16 Ibid., p. 113.

17 See '1/2 The Durer [*sic*] Rhinoceros – Masterpieces of the British Museum', published on YouTube by Art Documentaries, 2014 (accessed 5 April 2024).

18 The Meissen statue was designed by Johann Gottlieb Kirchner in 1731. For more about the print's legacy, see Gijs van der Ham, *Clara the Rhinoceros: Wonder, Beast, Sensation*, exh. cat., Rijksmuseum, Amsterdam (Rotterdam: nai010, 2022).

3. Etching the Artist's Line: Creativity, Commerce and Chiaroscuro

1 For more on the origins and development of etching, see Jenkins, Orenstein, Spira et al., *The Renaissance of Etching* (2019).
2 As quoted in Michael Limberger, ' "The greatest marketplace in the world": The Role of Antwerp in the Economic and Financial Network of the Habsburg Empire', in Ludolf Pelizaeus (ed.), *Les Villes des Habsbourg du XVᵉ au XIXᵉ siècle : communication, art et pouvoir dans les réseaux urbains*, Studia Habsburgica, vol. 2 (Reims: Épure, 2021), pp. 47–8.
3 For an excellent study of Aux Quatre Vents's influence, see Van Grieken, Luijten and Van Der Stock (eds), *Hieronymus Cock: The Renaissance in Print* (2013).
4 For more on the particulars of the building, see Petra Maclot, 'An Imaginary Visit to The Four Winds, the House and Shop of Hieronymus Cock and Volcxken Diericx', *Simiolus: Netherlands Quarterly for the History of Art* 39, no. 3 (2017), pp. 161–70.
5 For a history of the Liefrinck dynasty, see Friedrich Wilhelm Heinrich Hollstein, comp. Jeroen Luyckx, ed. Huigen Leeflang, *The New Hollstein Dutch & Flemish Etchings, Engravings and Woodcuts, 1450–1700*, 'The Liefrinck Dynasty' vols I and II (Ouderkerk aan den IJssel: Sound & Vision, 2021).
6 This subject is discussed in Arthur J. DiFuria, 'Towards an Understanding of Mayken Verhulst and Volcxken Diericx', *Women Artists and Patrons in the Netherlands, 1500–1700*, ed. Elizabeth Sutton, published on www.academia.edu, 2019 (accessed 14 March 2024).
7 Dr Jeanine De Landtsheer conducted the Dutch translation from Latin on which the English version is based, as seen in Van Grieken, Luijten and Van Der Stock (eds), *Hieronymus Cock* (2013), p. 82.
8 Lia Markey offers a great overview of female printmakers in 'The Female Printmaker and the Culture of the Reproductive Print Workshop', in Rebecca Zorach and Elizabeth Rodini, *Paper Museums: The Reproductive Print in Europe, 1500–1800*, exh. cat. (Chicago, IL: Smart Museum of Art, University of Chicago, 2005), pp. 51–73. For a more recent overview, see Andaleeb Badiee Banta, Alexa Greist and Theresa Kutasz Christensen (eds), *Making Her Mark: A History of Women Artists in Europe, 1400–1800*, exh. cat., Baltimore Museum of Art; Art Gallery of Ontario (Fredericton, New Brunswick: Goose Lane Editions, 2023).
9 See frontispiece and title page, Van Schurman, *The Learned Maid; or, Whether a Maid may be a Scholar? A Logick Exercise* (London: John Redmayne, 1659).
10 As quoted in Evelyn Lincoln, 'Making a Good Impression: Diana Mantuana's Printmaking Career', *Renaissance Quarterly* 50, no. 4 (1997), p. 1105.
11 As quoted in Evelyn Lincoln, 'Printing and Visual Culture in Italy, 1470–1575', PhD thesis, University of California, Berkeley, CA, 1994, p. 183.
12 A brilliant survey of the printmaker's life and work can be found in Leeflang and Luijten, *Hendrick Goltzius (1558–1617): Drawings, Prints and Paintings* (2003).

13 King Louis XIV of France, in alliance with England, Cologne and Münster, attacked the Dutch Republic in 1672, causing a short-term political and economic crisis.

14 The complete inventory was drawn up on 14 July 1656 by the commissioners of the Desolate Boedelkamer. The original document is in the Amsterdam City Archives and is available online (accessed 2 June 2025).

15 See Erik Hinterding, *Rembrandt Etchings from the Frits Lugt Collection*, 2 vols (Bussum: Thoth; Paris: Fondation Custodia, 2008).

16 See Simon Schama, *Rembrandt's Eyes* (Toronto: Random House Canada, 1999), p. 395.

17 According to the Städel Museum online catalogue, *Rembrandt in Amsterdam: Creativity and Competition*, 2021–2 (accessed 2 June 2025).

4. Satire and Shadows: Mezzotint and Aquatint in Britain and Beyond

1 As quoted in Wax, *The Mezzotint: History and Technique* (1990), p. 17.

2 Ibid., p. 15.

3 See Hogarth, *The Analysis of Beauty* [1753] (2015); quote on pp. 160–61.

4 Figure published in Moira Goff, 'Early History of the English Newspaper', 17th and 18th Century Burney Newspapers Collection (British Library, 2007).

5 As quoted in Faramerz Dabhoiwala, 'The Appropriation of Hogarth's Progresses', *Huntington Library Quarterly* 75, no. 4 (2012), p. 577.

6 See Mark Hallett, 'The Original: Hogarth's *A Harlot's Progress*, 1732', Paul Mellon Centre for Studies in British Art lecture, 24 May 2021.

7 See Ersy Contogouris and Béatrice Denis, 'Hannah Humphrey, London's Leading Caricature Printseller', *ABO: Interactive Journal for Women in the Arts, 1640–1830* 12, no. 2 (2022): Article 1.

8 To view the process in action, see 'Michael Phillips Demonstrates William Blake's Printing Process', published online by the British Library (accessed 2 June 2025).

9 See Bindman, *William Blake: The Complete Illuminated Books* (2000), p. 9.

10 See Martin Myrone and Amy Concannon (eds), *William Blake*, exh. cat., Tate Britain, London (Princeton, NJ: Princeton University Press, 2019); quote on p. 58.

11 See Richard Garnett, *William Blake, Painter and Poet* (London: Seeley and Co.; New York: Macmillan and Co., 1895); quote on p. 20.

12 See 'Gustave Doré', *The Aldine Press* 2, no. 4 (1869), p. 1.

13 See Jerrold and Doré, *London: A Pilgrimage* [1872] (2005).

14 See McDonald et al., *Goya's Graphic Imagination* (2021), p. 104.

15 As quoted in Janis A. Tomlinson, *Goya: Images of Women*, exh. cat., Museo Nacional del Prado, Madrid; National Gallery of Art, Washington, DC (New Haven, CT, and London: National Gallery of Art, in association with Yale University Press, 2002), p. 257.

16 References are found in collection catalogues at The Art Institute of
Chicago, and in McDonald et al., *Goya's Graphic Imagination* (2021),
p. 115.

5. *Japan's Floating World:* Ukiyo-e *and the Parisian Poster Boom*

1 For more on the development of the colour print, see Illing, *The Art of
Japanese Prints* (1980), pp. 39–49.
2 This specific genre was suppressed as part of Meiji modernisation, which
included the introduction of European moral standards. For more, see
Timothy Clark et al. (eds), *Shunga: Sex and Pleasure in Japanese Art*,
exh. cat. (London: British Museum Press, 2013).
3 To understand more on this particular title, see Marks, *Japanese Woodblock Prints* (2021), p. 425.
4 For more details, see John T. Carpenter et al., *The Tale of Genji: A
Japanese Classic Illuminated*, exh. cat. (New York: The Metropolitan
Museum of Art, 2019).
5 For more on this, see Trede and Bichler, *Hiroshige: One Hundred Famous Views of Edo* (2015), p. 15.
6 This incident is retold in Baatsch, *Hokusai: A Life in Drawing* (2016),
p. 11.
7 Both quotes as translated by Ryōko Matsuba in Hokusai, *Mad about
Painting* (2023), pp. 37 and 95.
8 For more, see Julie Nelson Davis, 'Hokusai and Ōi: Art Runs in
the Family', British Museum blog, 18 June 2017 (accessed 2 June
2025).
9 For more, see Yasuyo Ohtsuka, 'Sisters from the Shadows – Katsushika
Ōi', British Museum Asian and African studies blog, 5 July 2021 (accessed 2 June 2025).
10 As translated by Ryōko Matsuba in Hokusai, *Mad about Painting*
(2023), p. 31.
11 For more on Burty's influence, see Ives, *The Great Wave: The Influence
of Japanese Woodcuts on French Prints* (1974), p. 20.
12 As quoted in Trede and Bichler, *Hiroshige* (2015), p. 27.
13 Karin Breuer, *Japanesque: The Japanese Print in the Era of Impressionism*, exh. cat. (San Francisco, CA, and New York: Fine Arts Museums
of San Francisco, in association with Prestel, 2010), p. 67.
14 A full archive of Van Gogh's Japanese prints is available via the Van
Gogh Museum's website (accessed 2 June 2025).
15 As translated in Mark Roskill (ed.), *The Letters of Vincent van Gogh*
(London: Flamingo, 2000), p. 290.
16 As quoted in the Library of Congress records accompanying the archive
collection file of Mary Cassatt's *The Fitting* (1891).
17 See Rosen and Pinsky, *Mary Cassatt: Prints and Drawings from the
Artist's Studio* (2000), pp. 15–16
18 According to the German Patent and Trade Mark Office.
19 See Chapin, *Posters of Paris: Toulouse-Lautrec and his Contemporaries*
(2012).

6. *Artistic Impulse: Expressionism, Surrealism and Psychological Process*

1 As quoted in Hilla Rebay (ed.), *Concerning the Spiritual in Art by Wassily Kandinsky* (New York: Solomon R. Guggenheim Foundation, 1946), p. 80.

2 For more on how this print was created, see Prelinger and Robison, *Edvard Munch: Master Prints* (2010), pp. 68–70.

3 As quoted in Figura and Jelavich, *German Expressionism: The Graphic Impulse* (2011), p. 14.

4 As quoted in Carey and Griffiths, *The Print in Germany 1880–1933: The Age of Expressionism* (1984), p. 33.

5 See Tom Almeroth-Williams, 'Exposing a Nazi: The Exhibition Destroying a Myth', available via University of Cambridge website (accessed 2 June 2025).

6 For more on these years, see Hartley Whitford, *Käthe Kollwitz, 1867–1945: The Graphic Works*, exh. cat. (Cambridge: Kettle's Yard, 1981), pp. 7–11.

7 This specific translation of this widely quoted extract comes from the Käthe Kollwitz Museum Köln, and is published on its website (accessed 2 June 2025).

8 As quoted in Carey and Griffiths, *The Print in Germany 1880–1933* (1984), p. 61.

9 As quoted in Whitford, *Käthe Kollwitz*, p. 14.

10 Again, this specific translation of the letter comes from the Käthe Kollwitz Museum Köln, and is published on its website (accessed 2 June 2025).

11 For more analysis, see the website of the Museum of Modern Art, New York (MoMA) dedicated to its German Expressionist collection, which includes process videos, detailed descriptions, chronologies and essays (accessed 2 June 2025).

12 See Pat Gilmour, 'Picasso & his Printers', *The Print Collector's Newsletter* 18, no. 3 (1987), pp. 81–2.

13 As recalled in an interview with Norman Ackroyd at his home in London, March 2024.

14 As quoted in Stephen Coppel, *Picasso Prints: The Vollard Suite*, exh. cat. (London: British Museum Press, 2012), p. 23.

15 As quoted in Gilmour, 'Picasso & his Printers' (1987), p. 89.

16 The name stems from the studio address at 17, rue Campagne-Première.

17 Hayter, *New Ways of Gravure: A Practical Guide* (1949), p. 270.

18 For more on this subject, see Darwent, *Surrealists in New York: Atelier 17 and the Birth of Abstract Expressionism* (2023), and Weyl, *The Women of Atelier 17: Modernist Printmaking in Midcentury New York* (2019).

19 The Abstract Expressionists went on to use lithography as a deeply expressive form of mark-making.

20 As quoted in Joann Moser, 'The Impact of Stanley William Hayter on Post-War American Art', *Archives of American Art Journal* 18, no. 1 (1978), p. 2.

21 This was the first work that Hayter made in the USA, and it also features the screenprinting technique, which is discussed further in chapter 8.

7. *Resistance and Revolution: Mexican Metal Cuts and the Taller de Gráfica Popular*

1 Juárez fought against the foreign occupation of Emperor Maximilian (Archduke of Austria), and sought constitutional reforms to create a democratic federal republic. He was the elected president of Mexico from 1861 to 1872.

2 As translated and illustrated in Ron Tyler (ed.), *Posada's Mexico* (Washington, DC: Library of Congress, 1979), p. 51.

3 As translated in Julian Rothenstein (ed.), *José Guadalupe Posada: Mexican Popular Prints* (London: The Redstone Press, 1988), p. 21.

4 This process is discussed by Thomas Gretton in 'Posada and the "Popular": Commodities and Social Constructs in Mexico before the Revolution', in Buchloh and Harewood (eds), *From Posada to Isotype, from Kollwitz to Catlett: Exchanges of Political Print Culture. Germany–Mexico 1900–1968* (2022), pp. 54–71. See also Rachel Freeman's explanation in 'The Making of the Mexican Broadside Print: Technical Note', in Diana Miliotes, *José Guadalupe Posada and the Mexican Broadside*, exh. cat. (Chicago, IL: Art Institute of Chicago, 2006), pp. 37–40.

5 As quoted in Frank, *Posada's Broadsheets: Mexican Popular Imagery, 1890–1910* (1998), p. 230.

6 As quoted in Tyler (ed.), *Posada's Mexico* (1979), p. 49.

7 As quoted in Caplow, *Leopoldo Méndez: Revolutionary Art and the Mexican Print* (2007), p. 125.

8 For more on this print, see Adès and McClean, et al., *Revolution on Paper: Mexican Prints 1910–1960* (2009), p. 13.

9 For more on this, see Caplow, *Leopoldo Méndez* (2007), pp. 134–5.

10 Ibid., p. 163.

11 Excerpt from audio recording of Elizabeth Catlett, published in MoMA's 'Collection 1880s–1940s' audio guide (accessed 2 June 2025).

12 For more on this, see Nickels, *Persevere and Resist: The Strong Black Women of Elizabeth Catlett* (2021), p. 30.

13 Elizabeth Catlett, 'The Role of the Black Artist', *The Black Scholar* 6, no. 9 (1975), pp. 12–13.

14 As translated in Buchloh and Harewood (eds), *From Posada to Isotype, from Kollwitz to Catlett* (2022), p. 183.

15 Ibid.

8. *Print Goes Pop: American Lithography and the Rise of the Screenprint*

1 As quoted in an interview with Juan Sánchez, part of *The Only Thing That Lasts: An Oral History of Robert Blackburn's Printmaking Workshop* (2024), available at hauserwirthinstitute.org (accessed 20 June 2025).

2 Further details concerning process are discussed by conservation research fellow Basia Nosek in the Library of Congress lecture 'Finding Pictures: Purposeful Mastery – A Detailed Look into Robert

Blackburn's Early Color Lithographs', 16 November 2022 (accessed 2 June 2025).

3 For more on the Chelsea loft and Blackburn's legacy, see Deborah Cullen, 'Robert Blackburn (1920–2003): A Printmaker's Printmaker', *American Art* 17, no. 3 (2003), pp. 92–4.

4 Interview with Vincent Smith for the radio programme 'Dialogues with Contemporary Artists'. Part of the Camille Billops and James V. Hatch archives at Emory University, and available via the Robert Blackburn Printmaking Workshop website (accessed 2 June 2025).

5 A photograph of this card is published in Rosenblum and Weyl (eds), *A Model Workshop: Margaret Lowengrund and The Contemporaries* (2023), p. 13.

6 As quoted in Castleman, *Tatyana Grosman: A Scrapbook* (2008), p. 9.

7 Ibid., p. 66.

8 The origins of this statement vary, but it is published in a MoMA press release from 1963, as recorded on the Robert Rauschenberg Foundation website (accessed 2 June 2025).

9 Quoted from IFPDA Print Fair lecture, 'The Creative Spirit; Robert Blackburn & the Printmaking Workshop with Phil Sanders', 4 October 2022 (accessed 2 June 2025).

10 Bill Goldston recalled this incident during our conversation at ULAE studios on 1 November 2023.

11 As published by ULAE on Instagram (photograph of handwritten notebook page), 17 October 2024 (accessed 2 June 2025).

12 As quoted in exhibition wall text accompanying *Savage Breeze* (1974), in *Helen Frankenthaler Prints: The Romance of a New Medium* held at the Art Institute of Chicago in 2018.

13 Bill Goldston showed me this bottle and relayed this story during our conversation at ULAE on 1 November 2023.

14 As quoted in Rosenblum and Weyl (eds), *A Model Workshop* (2023), p. 17.

15 As quoted in Clinton Adams, 'An Informed Energy: Lithography and Tamarind', original article published 1997; revised version on the Tamarind Institute website (accessed 2 June 2025).

16 See Antreasian with Adams, *The Tamarind Book of Lithography: Art & Techniques* (1971); quotes on pp. 186 and 8.

17 See Ruth E. Fine, 'Writing on Rocks, Rubbing on Silk, Layering on Paper', in Walter Hopps and Susan Davidson, *Robert Rauschenberg: A Retrospective*, exh. cat. (New York: Guggenheim Museum Publications, 1997); quote on p. 381.

18 For more on this subject, see Jörg Schellmann, *Andy Warhol Unique* (Stuttgart: Hatje Cantz, 2014), and Feldman and Schellmann, *Andy Warhol Prints: A Catalogue Raisonné 1962–1987* (2003).

19 The original printed list is published on the Corita Art Center website (accessed 2 June 2025).

20 The exhibition was held at the Ferus Gallery in 1962.

21 The context of this print is discussed at length in Dackerman (ed.), *Corita Kent and the Language of Pop* (2015), p. 106.

9. *The Reach of Rorke's Drift: South African Prints and the Struggle against Apartheid*

1 See Miles, *Polly Street: The Story of an Art Centre* (2005), p. 36.
2 As quoted in Hobbs and Rankin, *Rorke's Drift: Empowering Prints. Twenty Years of Printmaking in South Africa* (2003), p. 78.
3 As quoted in Miles, *Polly Street* (2005), p. 8.
4 The term has roots in various languages and cultures, and is often associated with the Zulu phrase 'Umuntu ngumuntu ngabantu', or 'a person is a person through other persons'.
5 See Kim S. Berman, *Finding Voice: A Visual Arts Approach to Engaging Social Change* (Ann Arbor, MI: University of Michigan Press, 2017); quote on p. 22.
6 As quoted in Wilhelm van Rensburg, *Nhlanhla Xaba: What Everyone Knows*, exh. cat. (Johannesburg: Gallery AOP, 2012), p. 1.
7 This series is discussed in Stewart and Wilson, et al., *William Kentridge Prints* (2004), pp. 30–32.
8 Commentary on this series, with further remarks from master printers, is included in Tlhoaele (ed.), *Leeto: A Sam Nhlengethwa Print Retrospective* (2019), pp. 101–5.

10. *As Seen on Screen: Expanded Possibilities in the Digital Age*

1 See Greiman, *Hybrid Imagery: The Fusion of Technology and Graphic Design* (1990); quote on p. 67.
2 Much like Warhol, Fairey was subject to a lawsuit mounted by the Associated Press for copyright infringement, which was settled out of court in 2011. Fairey maintains that his image was in line with fair-use restrictions, and amounts to an original work of art.
3 The artist discussed the production and variations of *Hope* (2008) with Wendy Wick Reaves, Curator of Prints and Drawings at Smithsonian Institution's National Portrait Gallery, 7 July 2009 (accessed 10 January 2025).
4 Psychogeography analyses the effect of a geographical location on the emotions and behaviour of individuals.
5 See *Julie Mehretu: A Decade of Printmaking at Gemini G.E.L.*, press release, 2021 (accessed 2 June 2025).

SELECT BIBLIOGRAPHY

Acton, David, David Amram, and David Lehman, *The Stamp of Impulse: Abstract Expressionist Prints* (Worcester, MA: Worcester Art Museum, in association with Snoeck-Ducaju & Zoon, 2001)

Adès, Dawn, and Alison McClean, with the assistance of Laura Campbell, ed. Mark McDonald, *Revolution on Paper: Mexican Prints 1910–1960* (Austin, TX, and London: University of Texas Press, in co-operation with British Museum Press, 2009)

Antreasian, Garo Z., with Clinton Adams, *The Tamarind Book of Lithography: Art & Techniques* (Los Angeles, CA: Tamarind Lithography Workshop; New York: Harry N. Abrams, Inc., 1971)

Baatsch, Henri-Alexis, *Hokusai: A Life in Drawing* (London: Thames & Hudson, 2016)

Barrett, T. H., *The Woman Who Discovered Printing* (New Haven, CT: Yale University Press, 2008)

Bindman, David, *William Blake: The Complete Illuminated Books* (London: Thames & Hudson, produced with The William Blake Trust, 2000)

Black, Peter, and Désirée Moorhead (eds), *The Prints of Stanley William Hayter: A Complete Catalogue* (London: Phaidon Press, 1992)

Breuer, Karin, Ruth E. Fine, and Steven A. Nash, *Thirty-five Years at Crown Point Press: Making Prints, Doing Art*, exh. cat., National Gallery of Art, Washington, DC; Fine Arts Museums of San Francisco (Berkeley and Los Angeles, CA: University of California Press, in association with Fine Arts Museums of San Francisco, 1997)

Buchloh, Benjamin H. D., and Michelle N. Harewood (eds), *From Posada to Isotype, from Kollwitz to Catlett: Exchanges of Political Print Culture. Germany–Mexico 1900–1968*, exh. cat. (Madrid: Museo Nacional Centro de Arte Reina Sofía, 2022)

Caplow, Deborah, *Leopoldo Méndez: Revolutionary Art and the Mexican Print*, Joe R. and Teresa Lozano Long Series in Latin American and Latino Art and Culture (Austin, TX: University of Texas Press, 2007)

Carey, Frances, and Antony Griffiths, with David Paisey, *The Print in Germany 1880–1933: The Age of Expressionism* (London: British Museum Publications, 1984)

Castleman, Riva, *Tatyana Grosman: A Scrapbook* (Bay Shore, NY: Universal Limited Art Editions, 2008)

Chapin, Mary Weaver, *Posters of Paris: Toulouse-Lautrec and his Contemporaries*, exh. cat. (Milwaukee, WI: Milwaukee Art Museum; Munich; London and New York: DelMonico Books/Prestel, 2012)

Dackerman, Susan (ed.), *Corita Kent and the Language of Pop*, exh. cat. (Cambridge, MA: Harvard Art Museums, 2015)

Darwent, Charles, *Surrealists in New York: Atelier 17 and the Birth of Abstract Expressionism* (London and New York: Thames & Hudson, 2023)

Eisenstein, Elizabeth L., *The Printing Press as an Agent of Change: Communications and Cultural Transformations in Early-Modern Europe, Volumes I and II*, repr. combined paperback edn, (Cambridge: Cambridge University Press, 1997)

Essick, Robert N., *William Blake, Printmaker* (Princeton, NJ: Princeton University Press, 1980)

Feldman, Frayda, and Jörg Schellmann, *Andy Warhol Prints: A Catalogue Raisonné 1962–1987*, 4th edn rev. and expanded by Frayda Feldman and Claudia Defendi (New York: D.A.P./Ronald Feldman Fine Arts/Andy Warhol Foundation for the Visual Arts, 2003)

Figura, Starr, and Peter Jelavich, *German Expressionism: The Graphic Impulse*, exh. cat. (New York: Museum of Modern Art, 2011)

Fine, Ruth E., *Gemini G.E.L.: Art and Collaboration*, exh. cat., National Gallery of Art, Washington, DC (New York: Abbeville Press, 1984)

Frank, Patrick, *Posada's Broadsheets: Mexican Popular Imagery, 1890–1910* (Albuquerque, NM: University of New Mexico Press, 1998)

Goldman, Judith, *American Prints: Process & Proofs*, exh. cat., Whitney Museum of American Art, New York (New York: Harper & Row, 1981)

Greiman, April, *Hybrid Imagery: The Fusion of Technology and Graphic Design* (London: Architecture Design and Technology Press, 1990)

Griffiths, Antony, *Prints and Printmaking: An Introduction to the History and Techniques* (New York: Alfred A. Knopf, Inc., 1980)

Hayter, Stanley William, *New Ways of Gravure: A Practical Guide* (London: Routledge & Kegan Paul, 1949)

Hecker, Judith B., *Impressions from South Africa, 1965 to Now: Prints from the Museum of Modern Art*, exh. cat. (New York: Museum of Modern Art, 2011)

Hellinga, Lotte, *Caxton in Focus: The Beginning of Printing in England* (London: The British Library, 1982)

Hinterding, Erik, Ger Luijten, and Martin Royalton-Kisch, *Rembrandt the Printmaker* (London: British Museum Press, 2001)

Hobbs, Philippa, and Elizabeth Rankin, *Printmaking: In a Transforming South Africa* (Cape Town and Johannesburg: David Philip, 1997)

Hobbs, Philippa, and Elizabeth Rankin, *Rorke's Drift: Empowering Prints. Twenty Years of Printmaking in South Africa* (Cape Town: Double Storey Books, 2003)

Hogarth, William, *The Analysis of Beauty* [1753] (Mineola, NY: Dover Publications, Inc., 2015)

Hokusai, Katsushika, *Mad about Painting*, trans. Ryōko Matsuba, Ekphrasis Series (New York: David Zwirner Books, 2023)

Illing, Richard, *The Art of Japanese Prints* (London: Octopus, 1980)

Irvine, Gregory, *Japonisme and the Rise of the Modern Art Movement: The Arts of the Meiji Period. The Khalili Collection* (New York: Thames & Hudson, 2013)

Ives, Colta Feller, *The Great Wave: The Influence of Japanese Woodcuts on French Prints* (New York: The Metropolitan Museum of Art, 1974)

Jacklin, Elizabeth, *The Art of Print: Three Hundred Years of Printmaking* (London: Tate Publishing, 2021)

Jenkins, Catherine, Nadine M. Orenstein, Freyda Spira, et al., *The Renaissance of Etching*, exh. cat. (New York: The Metropolitan Museum of Art, 2019)

Jerrold, Blanchard, and Gustave Doré, *London: A Pilgrimage* [1872], Anthem Travel Classics (London and Boston, MA: Anthem Press, 2005)

Landau, David, and Peter Parshall, *The Renaissance Print: 1470–1550* (New Haven, CT, and London: Yale University Press, 1994)

Leeflang, Huigen, and Ger Luijten, *Hendrick Goltzius (1558–1617): Drawings, Prints and Paintings*, exh. cat., Rijksmuseum, Amsterdam; The Metropolitan Museum of Art, New York; Toledo Museum of Art, Ohio (Zwolle: Waanders Uitgevers, 2003)

Lust, John, *Chinese Popular Prints*, Handbook of Oriental Studies, Section 4 China, Vol. 11 (Leiden, New York and Cologne: Brill, 1996)

Marchesano, Louis (ed.), *Käthe Kollwitz: Prints, Process, Politics*, exh. cat., Getty Center (Los Angeles, CA: Getty Research Institute, 2020)

Marks, Andreas, *Japanese Woodblock Prints* (Cologne: Taschen, 2021)

Martin, Simon, and Louise Weller, *Hockney to Himid: 60 Years of British Printmaking* (Chichester: Pallant House Gallery, 2021)

McDonald, Mark P., et al., *Goya's Graphic Imagination* (New York: The Metropolitan Museum of Art, 2021)

Miles, Elza, *Polly Street: The Story of an Art Centre* (New York: Ampersand Foundation, 2005)

Miliotes, Diane, *What May Come: The Taller de Gráfica Popular and the Mexican Political Print*, exh. cat. (Chicago, IL: Art Institute of Chicago, 2014)

Nickels, Heather, *Persevere and Resist: The Strong Black Women of Elizabeth Catlett*, exh. cat., Memphis Brooks Museum of Art, Tennessee (London: Paul Holberton Publishing, 2021)

Prelinger, Elizabeth, and Andrew Robison, *Edvard Munch: Master Prints* (Munich: DelMonico Books/Prestel, 2010)

Rego, Paula, and Marina Warner, *Nursery Rhymes* (London: Thames & Hudson, 2019)

Rosen, Marc, and Susan Pinsky, *Mary Cassatt: Prints and Drawings from the Artist's Studio*, exh. cat., Adelson Galleries, Inc., New York; Meredith Long & Company, Houston (Princeton, NJ: Princeton University Press, 2000)

Rosenblum, Lauren, and Christina Weyl (eds), *A Model Workshop: Margaret Lowengrund and The Contemporaries*, exh. cat., Print Center, New York (Munich: Hirmer, 2023)

Sanders, Phil, *Prints and their Makers* (New York: Princeton Architectural Press, 2021)

Sparks, Esther, *Universal Limited Art Editions: A History and Catalogue. The First Twenty-five Years* (Chicago, IL: Art Institute of Chicago; New York: Abrams, 1989)

Spee, Clarissa von, *The Printed Image in China: From the 8th to the 21st Centuries*, exh. cat. (London: British Museum Press, 2010)

Stewart, Susan, and Kay Wilson, in collaboration with William Kentridge and Anne McIlleron, *William Kentridge Prints*, exh. cat. (Grinnell, IA: Faulconer Gallery, Grinnell College, 2004)

Tlhoaele, Boitumelo (ed.), *Leeto: A Sam Nhlengethwa Print Retrospective*, exh. cat., Wits Art Museum, Johannesburg (Johannesburg: Goodman Gallery, 2019)

Trede, Melanie, and Lorenz Bichler, *Hiroshige: One Hundred Famous Views of Edo* (Cologne: Taschen, 2015)

Van Grieken, Joris, Ger Luijten, and Jan Van Der Stock (eds), *Hieronymus Cock: The Renaissance in Print*, exh. cat., M – Museum Leuven; Institut Néerlandais, Paris (New Haven, CT, and London: Yale University Press, 2013)

Wax, Carol, *The Mezzotint: History and Technique* (New York: Abrams, 1990)

Weyl, Christina, *The Women of Atelier 17: Modernist Printmaking in Midcentury New York* (New Haven, CT: Yale University Press, 2019)

Wood, Frances, and Mark Barnard, *The Diamond Sutra: The Story of the World's Earliest Dated Printed Book* (London: The British Library, 2010)

Wouk, Edward H., and Jennifer Spinks (eds), *Albrecht Dürer's Material World* (Manchester: Manchester University Press, 2023)

PICTURE CREDITS

1.1   Pictures from History / Bridgeman Images
1.2   27.6 × 499.5 cm. British Library, London, UK. The British Library archive / Bridgeman Images
1.3   Pictures from History / Bridgeman Images
1.4   45 × 5.7 cm (left, scroll); 21.3 × 10.2 cm (right, pagoda). Courtesy the Metropolitan Museum of Art, New York. Gift of Benjamin Strong, 1930
1.5   61 × 27.5 cm. Courtesy the C.V. Starr East Asian Library, Columbia University
1.6   31.4 × 21.6 cm. © The Trustees of the British Museum. All rights reserved
2.1   40 × 28.8 cm. Courtesy the Cleveland Museum of Art, Ohio. Gift of The Print Club of Cleveland
2.2   Book 17.1 × 66.7 × 48.1 cm. Courtesy the Metropolitan Museum of Art, New York. Gift of Mrs. George Khuner, 1981
2.3   11.6 × 15.6 cm. Courtesy the Rijksmuseum, Amsterdam
2.4   24.5 × 18.6 cm. Courtesy the Cleveland Museum of Art, Ohio. Gift of Leonard C. Hanna Jr.
2.5   29.1 × 43.7 cm. Courtesy the Metropolitan Museum of Art, New York. Rogers Fund, 1919
2.6   48.2 × 34.6 cm. Courtesy the Rijksmuseum, Amsterdam
2.7   25.8 × 24 cm. Courtesy the Cleveland Museum of Art, Ohio. The Fanny Tewksbury King Collection
2.8   Book, 47.5 × 35.5 × 8.7 cm. Courtesy the Metropolitan Museum of Art, New York. Gift of J. Pierpont Morgan, 1923
2.9   23.8 × 30.1 cm. Courtesy the Cleveland Museum of Art, Ohio. John L. Severance Fund
3.1   15.5 × 22.3 cm. Courtesy the Metropolitan Museum of Art, New York. The Elisha Whittelsey Fund, 1951
3.2   7.5 × 11.4 cm. Courtesy the Rijksmuseum, Amsterdam
3.3   27 × 20 cm. Courtesy the Metropolitan Museum of Art, New York. The Elisha Whittelsey Fund, 1949
3.4   21.1 cm × 25.9 cm. Courtesy the Rijksmuseum, Amsterdam
3.5   Book. Courtesy the Folger Shakespeare Library
3.6   42 × 57.5 cm. Courtesy the Metropolitan Museum of Art, New York. The Elisha Whittelsey Fund, 1949
3.7   40.4 × 29.4 cm. Courtesy the Cleveland Museum of Art, Ohio. Severance and Greta Millikin Purchase Fund

3.8   24.9 × 30.9 cm. Courtesy the Rijksmuseum, Amsterdam
3.9   10.4 × 9.4 cm. Courtesy the Rijksmuseum, Amsterdam
3.10 16.3 × 11.7 cm. Courtesy the Rijksmuseum, Amsterdam
3.11 28 × 39.4 cm. Courtesy the Rijksmuseum, Amsterdam
3.12 Fourth state, 37.5 × 44 cm. Courtesy the Cleveland Museum of Art, Ohio. Bequest of Ralph King and purchase from the J. H. Wade Fund
4.1   41.9 × 27.5 cm. Courtesy the Rijksmuseum, Amsterdam
4.2   63.3 × 44.2 cm. Courtesy the Metropolitan Museum of Art. Lila Acheson Wallace Gift, in honour of George R. Goldner, 2015
4.3   15.7 × 13.8 cm. Courtesy the Metropolitan Museum of Art, New York. The Elisha Whittelsey Fund, 1956
4.4   Second state, 58.1 × 45.4 cm. Courtesy the Metropolitan Museum of Art, New York. Harris Brisbane Dick Fund, 1953
4.5   First state of four, 31.6 × 37.9 cm. Courtesy the Metropolitan Museum of Art, New York. Harris Brisbane Dick Fund, 1932
4.6   Third state of three, 35.7 × 41.2 cm. Courtesy the Metropolitan Museum of Art, New York. Gift of Sarah Lazarus, 1891
4.7   Third state of three, 38.4 × 32.2 cm. Courtesy the Metropolitan Museum of Art, New York. Harris Brisbane Dick Fund, 1932
4.8   Third state, 38.3 × 31.7 cm. Courtesy the Metropolitan Museum of Art, New York. Harris Brisbane Dick Fund, 1933
4.9   26 × 36.2 cm. Courtesy the New York Public Library
4.10 47.5 × 33.2 cm. Courtesy the Metropolitan Museum of Art, New York. The Elisha Whittelsey Fund, 1959
4.11 26.1 × 20.5 cm. Courtesy the New York Public Library
4.12 12.1 × 7.6 cm. Courtesy Yale Center for British Art, Paul Mellon Collection
4.13 23.2 × 16.8 cm. Courtesy Yale Center for British Art, Paul Mellon Collection
4.14 22.3 × 16.2 cm. Courtesy Yale Center for British Art, Paul Mellon Collection
4.15 24.7 × 19.7 cm. © The Trustees of the British Museum. All rights reserved
4.16 34 × 24.3 cm. Courtesy the Metropolitan Museum of Art, New York. The Elisha Whittelsey Fund, 2010
4.17 29.2 × 22 cm. Courtesy the Metropolitan Museum of Art, New York. The Elisha Whittelsey Fund, 1968
4.18 Plate 12, 29.5 × 21 cm. Courtesy the New York Public Library
4.19 Plate 43, 29.5 × 21 cm. Courtesy the New York Public Library
4.20 Plate 5, 15.2 × 20.7 cm. Courtesy the New York Public Library
4.21 Plate 37, 15.3 × 20.2 cm. Courtesy the New York Public Library
5.1   25.7 × 37.9 cm. Courtesy the Metropolitan Museum of Art, New York. Bequest of Mrs. H. O. Havemeyer, 1929
5.2   26 × 18.4 cm. Courtesy the Metropolitan Museum of Art, New York. Gift of Estate of Samuel Isham, 1914
5.3   36 × 23.5 cm. Courtesy the Rijksmuseum, Amsterdam
5.4   35.7 × 24 cm. Courtesy the Metropolitan Museum of Art, New York. Rogers Fund, 1919

5.5   33.2 × 22.1 cm. Courtesy the Metropolitan Museum of Art, New York. Rogers Fund, 1914

5.6   25.4 × 38.4 cm. Courtesy the Metropolitan Museum of Art, New York. Rogers Fund, 1936

5.7   37.5 × 26 cm. Courtesy the Metropolitan Museum of Art, New York, Bequest of Henry L. Phillips, 1939

5.8   Book. 25.5 × 18 cm. © The Trustees of the British Museum. All rights reserved

5.9   Second state of two, 44.7 × 32.2 cm. Courtesy the Metropolitan Museum of Art, New York. Anne and Carl Stern Fund, 1970

5.10 43.6 × 30.5 cm. Courtesy the New York Public Library

5.11 39.2 × 26.2 cm. Courtesy the Art Institute of Chicago. Clarence Buckingham Collection

5.12 43.6 × 30.3 cm. Courtesy the New York Public Library

5.13 123.2 × 87.6 cm. Digital image, the Museum of Modern Art, New York/Scala, Florence. 2025 © Photo Scala, Florence

5.14 80.8 × 60.8 cm. Courtesy the Metropolitan Museum of Art, New York. Bequest of Clifford A. Furst, 1958

5.15 77.4 × 57.8 cm. Courtesy Art Institute of Chicago. Purchased with funds provided by Dr. and Mrs. Martin Gecht

6.1   29.5 × 36 cm. The Museum of Fine Arts Budapest / Scala, Florence. 2025 © Photo Scala, Florence

6.2   64.2 × 87.6 cm. Photo: Munchmuseet / Halvor Bjørngård

6.3   40.5 × 47 cm. Photo: Munchmuseet / Halvor Bjørngård

6.4   Sheet 1, second state, 15.5 × 15.3 cm. © The Trustees of the British Museum. All rights reserved

6.5   Third state, 42 × 48 cm. Courtesy Städel Museum, Frankfurt am Main

6.6   Edition of 400, 34.3 × 40 cm. Gift of the Arnhold Family in memory of Sigrid Edwards. Digital image, the Museum of Modern Art, New York / Scala, Florence. 2025 © Photo Scala, Florence

6.7   Edition of 125, 32.3 × 29.7 cm. Digital image, the Museum of Modern Art, New York / Scala, Florence. 2025 © Photo Scala, Florence © Estate of George Grosz, Princeton, N.J. / DACS 2025

6.8   Edition of 70, 19.7 × 29 cm. Gift of Abby Aldrich Rockefeller. Digital image, the Museum of Modern Art, New York / Scala, Florence. 2025 © Photo Scala, Florence. © DACS 2025

6.9   46.4 × 37.8 cm. Harris Brisbane Dick Fund, 1923. Image © the Metropolitan Museum of Art / Art Resource / Scala, Florence. 2025 © Photo Scala, Florence. © Succession Picasso / DACS, London 2025

6.10 Sheet 97, 24.7 × 34.5 cm. Photo Scala, Florence / bpk, Bildagentur fuer Kunst, Kultur und Geschichte, Berlin. 2025 © Photo Scala, Florence. © Succession Picasso/DACS, London 2025

6.11 Edition of 50, 53 × 64 cm. Digital image, the Museum of Modern Art, New York / Scala, Florence. 2025 © Photo Scala, Florence. © Succession Picasso / DACS, London 2025

6.12 22.8 × 19.1 cm. Image © the Metropolitan Museum of Art / Art Resource / Scala, Florence. 2025 © Photo Scala, Florence. © ADAGP, Paris and DACS, London 2025

7.1   40.1 × 29.5 cm. Courtesy the Library of Congress
7.2   60 × 40.5 cm. Courtesy the Library of Congress
7.3   36 × 25.7 cm. Courtesy the New York Public Library
7.4   23.3 × 46.5 cm. Gift of Jean Charlot, 1930. Image © The Metropolitan Museum of Art / Art Resource / Scala, Florence. 2025 © Scala, Florence. © DACS 2025
7.5   35.5 × 79.3 cm. Print and Drawing Club Fund. The Art Institute of Chicago / Art Resource, NY / Scala, Florence. 2025 © Photo Scala, Florence. © DACS 2025
7.6   30.3 × 17.6 cm. The Art Institute of Chicago / Art Resource, NY / Scala, Florence. 2025 © Photo Scala, Florence. © DACS 2025
7.7   35.2 × 51.3 cm. William McCallin McKee Memorial Endowment. The Art Institute of Chicago / Art Resource, NY / Scala, Florence. 2025 © Photo Scala, Florence. © DACS 2025
7.8   38.5 × 44.5 cm. Image © The Metropolitan Museum of Art / Art Resource / Scala, Florence. 2025 © Photo Scala, Florence. © DACS 2025
7.9   23.2 × 17.9 cm. Purchase, with funds from the Print Committee. Digital image, Whitney Museum of American Art / Licensed by Scala. 2025 © Photo Scala, Florence. © Catlett Mora Family Trust / VAGA at ARS, NY and DACS, London 2025
7.10   19.7 × 14.6 cm. Gift of Reba and Dave Williams, 1999. Image © The Metropolitan Museum of Art / Art Resource / Scala, Florence. 2025 © Photo Scala, Florence. © Catlett Mora Family Trust / VAGA at ARS, NY and DACS, London 2025
8.1   46.3 × 32.3 cm. © The Trust for Robert Blackburn. Used with permission. Image courtesy Library of Congress, Prints & Photographs Division
8.2   49.8 × 40.2 cm. © The Trust for Robert Blackburn. Used with permission. Image courtesy Library of Congress, Prints & Photographs Division
8.3   47.7 × 31 cm. The Museum of Modern Art, New York / Scala, Florence. 2025 © Photo Scala, Florence. With permission from the estate of Saburō Hasegawa
8.4   48.3 × 59.1 cm. Gift of Mr. and Mrs. E. Powis Jones. Digital image, the Museum of Modern Art, New York / Scala, Florence. 2025 © Photo Scala, Florence. © Estate of Larry Rivers / VAGA at ARS, NY and DACS, London 2025
8.5   Edition of 29, 104.8 × 74.9 cm. © Robert Rauschenberg Foundation and Universal Limited Art Editions. Photographed by Ron Amstutz
8.6   Edition of 31, 80 × 69.2 cm. Digital image, The Museum of Modern Art, New York / Scala, Florence. 2025 © Photo Scala, Florence. © Helen Frankenthaler Foundation, Inc. / ARS, NY and DACS, London 2025
8.7   Edition of 38, 182.9 × 90.2 cm. © Robert Rauschenberg Foundation and Gemini G.E.L.
8.8   Edition of 250, 1 from a portfolio of 10, 91.8 × 91.6 cm. © 2025 The Andy Warhol Foundation for the Visual Arts, Inc. / Licensed by DACS, Artimage, London
8.9   86.3 × 86.3 cm. Digital image, The Museum of Modern Art, New York / Scala, Florence. 2025 © Photo Scala, Florence. © Morgan Art Foundation, Ltd. / Artists Rights Society (ARS), NY and DACS, London, 2025

8.10 52 × 74.93 cm. © ARS, NY and DACS, London 2025
9.1   Edition of 100, 32.3 × 54.9cm. Gift of African Art Center, Durban. Digital image, the Museum of Modern Art, New York / Scala, Florence. 2025 © Photo Scala, Florence. © Azaria Mbatha / DACS 2025
9.2   40 × 63.2 cm. Digital image, the Museum of Modern Art, New York / Scala, Florence. 2025 © Photo Scala, Florence
9.3   1 from portfolio of 31 prints, 59.5 × 40 cm. © and courtesy the artist
9.4   242.6 × 97.8 cm. © the artist, courtesy Goodman Gallery
9.5   57 × 76.5 cm. © the artist, courtesy Goodman Gallery
10.1 Grid of 60, photogravure, etching, aquatint and drypoints with lithography, screenprint, embossing, tattoo-machine engraving, laser cutting and chine collé; some with additions of Plasticine, paper collage, enamel, varnish, gouache, pencil, oil, polymer, watercolour, pomade, velvet, glitter, crystals, foil paper, gold leaf, toy eyeballs and imitation ice cubes. Each: 33 × 26.5 cm.; overall: 215.3 × 447 cm. © Ellen Gallagher. Courtesy the artist and Hauser & Wirth. Photo: Alex Delfanne
10.1a © Ellen Gallagher. Courtesy the artist and Hauser & Wirth. Photo: D. James Dee
10.2 68.9 × 193.4 cm. © April Greiman
10.3 From a set of 6 woodcuts, edition of 12, 48 × 38 cm. Courtesy of the artist and Cristea Roberts Gallery, London. © Christiane Baumgartner. Photo: Prudence Cummings
10.4 20.5 × 17 cm. Courtesy of the artist and Soft Opening, London
10.5 91.4 × 61.3 cm. Courtesy of Shepard Fairey / obeygiant.com
10.6 38 × 48 cm. Private collection © Paula Rego. All rights reserved 2025 / Bridgeman Images
10.7 128.3 × 156.2 cm. © Julie Mehretu. Photo © White Cube (Ollie Hammick)

burr 67, **232**
Burroughs, Margaret Taylor Goss
    173–4

Cai Lun 12
Calderón de la Barca, Celia 174
capriccio style 98
caricature magazines 85
Cassatt, Mary 104, 119, 121–3,
    123, *125*, 129
Cassirer, Paul 143
Catlett, Elizabeth 157, 171–3, *172*,
    173, 177
Caxton, William 28
Ceán Bermúdez, Juan Agustín 101
Charlot, Jean 163–4
Chaucer, Geoffrey 28
Chéret, Jules 128–9, *128*
chiaroscuro
    term 38–9
    woodcuts 38–40, *40*
Chièze, Jean 1
China *see also* Mogao Grottos
    ('Caves of a Thousand
    Buddhas')
    Buddhism in 13, 15
    door guardians 19, *21*, 23
    imperial seals 14
    International Dunhuang
    Project 12
    invention of paper 12, 26
    nien hua (New Year's pictures)
    19–23, *21*, *22*
    origins of printing 11, 12–15,
    19
    stove god 20, *22*, 23
    Wu Zetian's reign 13–14, 15
chine collé technique 139, 141
chop mark **232**
Christian, Malcolm 212
Clemente Orozco, José 161, 165,
    166
Cock, Hieronymous 5, 6, 51–4, *52*
    see also Diericx, Volcxken
Collaert I, Jan 6, 50, *50*
collography 206, 209, **232**
Confucianism 13, 14
Convent of San Jacopo di Ripoli,
    Florence 55

Corneliszoon van Haarlem,
    Cornelis 62, 63
Cort, Cornelius 53
Cranach the Elder, Lucas 33
Crommelynck, Aldo 151–2
Crown Point Press 189
Cruikshank, George 87
Cruikshank, Isaac Robert 87

Degas, Edgar 119, 122
Delâtre, Auguste 120, 145, 148
Die Blaue Reiter (The Blue Rider)
    133, 136, 138
Die Brücke (The Bridge) 132, 136,
    137, 138
Diericx, Volcxken
    Aux Quatre Vents printmaking
    business 5, 6, 51–5, *52*, 59
    copperplate 54
    partnership with Hendrick
    Goltzius 59–60
    professional standing 45, 54–5
digital age
    digital video stills 219–20
    hybrid imagery 218–19
    printmaking in 215–16, 225
    sociopolitical works 225–9
Dircx, Geertje 69
Dix, Otto 144, *145*
Doetecum, Johannes and Lucas van
    52, 53
Dōkyō 16–17
Doré, Gustave 93–4, *94*
drypoint **233**
    by Rembrandt 67–9, *67*, *68*
    technique 67
Duganne, Jack 223
Dürer, Agnes 37
Dürer, Albrecht
    artist copyright claims 36–8
    business acumen 36
    engravings 30, 31–2, 33
    etching 48
    in private collections 66, 101,
    133
    Renaissance thought 26, 34–5,
    36
    The Rhinoceros 43–4, *43*
    trademark 25, 26, 36, 37, 38

in Restoration England 75–6
technique 72–5
term 72
Miró, Joan 148, 152, 153, 156
Mogao Grottos ('Caves of a
    Thousand Buddhas')
  Buddhism 7–8, 13, 230
  Diamond Sutra 7, 9, *10*, 11, 12,
    17
  'Library Cave' 8–9, *9*, 11–12
Monet, Claude 119
monoprint **234**
monotypes 222–3, **234**
mordant 46, **234**
Morisot, Berthe 104, 119, 122
Morris, Gabriel 124–5
Muafangejo, John Ndevasia 202,
    205
Mucha, Alphonse 131
Munch, Edvard 134–5, *135*, 136,
    136, 225
Münter, Gabriele 133
Murasaki Shikibu 109–10

Nazism 166–9, *167*, 183
Nevelson, Louise 153, 154
Nhlengethwa, Sam 213–14, *214*
nishiki-e see ukiyo-e
Nkosi, Sokhaya Charles 202, 203,
    207
Nolde, Emil 137
Nuremberg, Germany 30, 33
Nuremberg Chronicle 28–9, *29*

offset lithography **234**
O'Hara, Frank 183
O'Higgins, Pablo 165, 169, 171,
    174, 175
Oldenburg, Claes 152
Ouyang Xun 13, *14*
Ovid 42–3, 56

paper 12, 26
Parasole, Geronima Cagnaccia 55
Parasole, Isabella (Elisabetta) 55,
    56
Parmigianino
  chiaroscuro woodcuts 38–9
  collaborations 38, 41, 49

etchings 48–9, *49*
  in private collections 101
Passe, Magdalena van de 56
Pelliot, Paul 11, 12
periodicals 85
Pether, William 76
photomechanical printing
    162–3
photo-relief etching process 161
Picasso, Pablo
  collaborations 151
  The Frugal Repast 145–6, *146*,
    148, 225
  linocuts 150, *151*
  printmaking 145, 146–7, 148,
    150
  social commentary 147–8
  'Vollard Suite' 147, 148–50, *149*
Piranesi, Giovanni Battista 98
Pirckheimer, Willibald 37
Pissarro, Camille 119
Pitt, William 84–5
plate **235**
Pleydenwurff, Wilhelm 29
political cartoons
  in London (18th century) 83–4,
    85
  satirical publishing industry
    86–8, *87*
  social satire 85–6, *86*
  speech bubbles 85–6, 100
Pollock, Jackson 153–4
Pop Art
  Andy Warhol 194–5, *196*, 198
  Corita Kent 197–9, *199*
  lithography 176
  printer-artist collaborations 176,
    190
  screenprints in 194–9
portraiture 75–6
Posada, José Guadalupe
  association with the Mexican
    Revolution 163
  calavera imagery 157, *159*,
    160–1, *160*, *161*, 166
  metal relief blocks 3, 161–2
  mexicanidad 157
  posthumous legacy 3, 163–4,
    165, 166, *167*

screenprints **235**
    of Andy Warhol 194–5, *196*
    Kelpra Studio 194
    political expression in South
        Africa 206
    in Pop Art 194–9
    technique 192–4
Senefelder, Alois 126
Shilakoe, Cyprian Mpho 204
Shōmu, Emperor 16
Shōtoku *see* Kōken/Shōtoku
    (Princess Abe)
Siegen, Ludwig von 72, *73*, 75
Sihlali, Durant 205, 206
Silk Roads 7, 14, 26
Sin Wai Kin 222–3, *223*
Siqueiros, David Alfaro 162, 164,
    164, 165, 174
Skotnes, Cecil 204, 205, 206, 213
Smith, John 76
soft ground **236**
South Africa *see also* Rorke's Drift
    African Arts Centre 204
    amabhaxa 201
    apartheid 200–1
    Artist Proof Studio (APS) 207–10
    The Artists' Press 213
    'Break the Silence!' portfolio
        208–10, *209*
    The Caversham Press 212, 213
    Community Arts Project (CAP)
        206
    David Krut Workshop 212
    political expression in print
        206–7
    Polly Street Art Centre 204–5
    post-Apartheid 207–8
    screenprints 206
    Sguzu Printmakers' Workshop
        205–6
    ubuntu 207
Soviet Union 168
state **236**
Stein, Aurel 8–10, 11–12
Steinlen, Théophile-Alexandre
    129–30
stone 14, 27
stop-out **236**
sugar-lift **236**

Surrealism 5, 152, 153
Suzuki Harunobu 106, *107*, 122
Symbolism 133

Tempesta, Antonio 55, 66
Thomas, Mickalene 225
Thornhill, James 77
Tiepolo, Giovanni Battista 98
Todd, Ruthven 155–6
Toulouse-Lautrec, Henri de 129,
    130
Toyoharu 109, 110
trial proof **236**
Trinidad Pedroza, José 158
tushe **236**
Tyler, Kenneth 190–2

Ugo da Carpi 38, 39, *40*
ukiyo-e see also Katsushika
    Hokusai
    bijin-ga (images of beautiful
        women) 106, *107*, 111, 121,
        122
    bokashi 108, 111, 120
    colour palette 106, 108, 114,
        122, 123, 131
    culture of 105–6
    eshi (artist-designers) 106–7, 108
    and the French Impressionists
        119–24, 129
    the 'Great Wave' 104, *105*, 113,
        120, 130
    images from Yoshiwara 105,
        108–9
    key block 105, 115, 122
    landscape prints 110–11
    literary source material 109–10,
        118
    nishiki-e (brocade pictures)
        creation process 106–8
    'One Hundred Famous Views
        of Edo' 111–12, *112*, *113*,
        114, 120
    term 105
    Utagawa school 109–12
United States of America *see also*
    Pop Art
    American activists artists in
        Mexico 171–4

